1833

The Armenian Quarter of Jerusalem

The Armenian Quarter of Jerusalem

Urban Life Behind Monastery Walls

Victor Azarya

UNIVERSITY OF CALIFORNIA PRESS

BERKELEY • LOS ANGELES • LONDON

University of California Press
Berkeley and Los Angeles, California

University of California Press, Ltd.
London, England

Copyright © 1984 by
The Regents of the University of California

Library of Congress Cataloging in Publication Data
Azarya, Victor
Urban life behind monastery walls
Includes bibliographical references and index.
1. Armenian Quarter (Jerusalem)   2. Armenians—Jerusalem.
3. Jerusalem—Ethnic relations.   I. Title.
DS109.8.A75A9 1983   306'.08991992056944   83-47847
ISBN 0-520-04749-4
Printed in the United States of America

1 2 3 4 5 6 7 8 9

To Mireille

Contents

Preface

My interest in the Armenian quarter of Jerusalem long preceded the writing of this book. Like scores of other visitors to the Old City since 1967, I did not fail to notice the Armenian names on many of the souvenir and jewelry shops at the Jaffa Gate entrance to the bazaar. Born and raised in Turkey, I knew more about these people than other visitors and was intrigued by rediscovering them here and hearing them occasionally speak Turkish. This special interest in fellow "ex-Turks" took a more professional form in the mid-1970s when I tried to diversify my fields of research, which until then had concentrated on Africa. A study of the Armenian community of Jerusalem seemed to be a good idea because of my special attraction to these people and also because it lent itself to my particular methodological inclinations as a sociologist trained in observation and not well versed in quantitative survey techniques. I first thought of studying their socioeconomic role as entrepreneurial middlemen minorities. A quick look, however, at their patterns of residence convinced me that this would be the focus of my research.

Fieldwork for the research was conducted between 1975 and 1978, although bits of information have flowed in ever since. The data have been updated several times, but undoubtedly changes will have occurred before the book appears in print. During the academic year of 1975-76 I visited the

Armenian quarter several times a week, most often in the afternoons. My visits to the quarter became less frequent in the summer and fall of 1976 and then picked up again in 1977, this time with the help of a resident Armenian priest who worked for me as research assistant. Another period of absence followed in 1978-79 when I spent a sabbatical year abroad. Intermittent fact-finding (or gap-closing) visits have continued since my return in 1979, and the Armenian quarter has been on the standard itinerary of my students of the various seminars on urban communities of Jerusalem. I would like to extend special thanks to my good friend Kevork Hintlian who has always graciously played host and companion to those study tours.

Early in my work I made the crucial discovery, which of course was known to those familiar with the area, that the otherwise modern and secular-looking Armenian shopkeepers and artisans lived for the most part within a large monastery compound surrounded by walls with gates that were closed at night. The thought of a modern lay community living within a monastic institution captivated my imagination, and I could see its potential sociological implications. Monasteries and lay communities were theoretically opposing categories, and it would have been interesting to explain the reasons, the mechanisms, and the effects of their spatial coexistence in this case. From the outset this has been the principal focus of my investigation. Later, it became clear that one could not understand the nature of this coexistence without studying the general economic life, culture, education, and leisure time of the community, as well as its history. However, these issues and other facts of community life were touched upon only insofar as they contributed to understanding how and why the lay and monastic communities lived together. This is not, therefore, a comprehensive ethnographic study, in the sense that it does not attempt to give a general picture of community life but concentrates on points of encounter between the clergy and the laity.

I should stress an important difference between my data collection and the data revealed in most urban community studies, such as those of Suttles, Gans, Whyte, Kornblum, Liebow, Stack, and others which will be referred to in later chapters.[1] I did *not* live in the community during the period of study, nor did I "hang out" with local residents on street corners or "carry out" stores. I did not use the local public facilities for everyday life, and I never pretended to be more than a visitor. I developed familiarity but not intimacy with the people studied. For one thing I did not speak their language; our communication was held in English, Hebrew, and occasionally Turkish. Data were collected mostly by means of extensive interviews (or rather conversations) with informants. These data were supplemented by documentary material on the quarter and its inhabitants (some of it translated from Armenian) and by observations on the community's gatherings and public events, such as church services, weddings, baptisms and funerals, school graduation ceremonies, parties, bazaars, sporting events. The richness of the community's public life made for many of these public events at which I could be an unobtrusive and legitimate bystander. I also spent some time in my informants' stores, exchanging views with them and with their friends who used to drop by for chats or coffee while the shopkeeper was busy serving clients. Eventually I had access to the families and was invited to homes, but admittedly my view of things was mainly from the angle of public territory.

My method of data collection, compared with the more "participant observation" type of urban community studies, is also indicative of the type of community studied. An outsider could not just move in, rent a flat, and take up residence in the monastery, hoping to look at life from within. Nor could one hang out in a corner of the monastery and talk to passersby. There are no sidewalk coffee shops within the compound. An outsider spotted in the courtyard has to be "going somewhere." He has to show at all times that he is there for a specific purpose. This fact in itself is symptomatic of the special closure and self-containment of the Armenian community and is related to the central issues discussed in the book. The salience of the resident-outsider difference is perhaps more similar to the black ghettos of the modern American urban scene than to white ethnic neighborhoods. It is interesting to note that white researchers who study black neighborhoods usually do not take up residence within the neighborhood, unlike their counterparts who study predominantly white neighborhoods. They carry out participant observation by meeting people in shops and coffeehouses during the day. Such semipublic places are not available when a neighborhood is located in the courtyard of a religious institution.

Two "public territories" within the monastery compound in which I spent considerable time were the church during services, and the Gulbenkian library. With regard to church services, I soon found out that this was a convenient place to study the behavior of priests and seminarians but not that of the lay community, because except for special holidays very few of the laity attended services. That the church was no place to meet the local community in its everyday life is an observation of great significance in the context of lay life within a monastery. As for the library, it was not any better attended by the local community than was the church, but it offered an unexpectedly rich source of documentation on Armenians in general and on the Jerusalem community in particular. Of more importance, there I met my other good friend, the librarian Sahak Kalaydjian, the community's true sociometric star. Sahak was always at the center of things, involved in the community's principal projects and activities. Being a librarian was one of his less important occupations. He also worked in the patriarchate administration and in the theological seminary, he was a leading member of one of the clubs, and most important, he was the church's chorus master and the community's undisputed music expert. Besides being a precious source of information, he also helped tremendously by putting me in contact with other informants.

The type of access gained to the research material obviously leads the researcher to emphasize certain issues at the expense of others. Carole Stack looked at the black ghetto from the family's, and especially the women's, point of view since her base of operation was the homes of a few women whom she befriended.[2] She did not stress other aspects of the community's survival strategy, such as voluntary associations, churches, and local politics. Kornblum worked in the steel mills of South Chicago and was involved in the election campaign of a local politician.[3] His study, therefore, stresses work life, trade unions, and ward politics. Whyte and Liebow narrowed their focus to the street corner groups, as this was their main channel of contact with the community.[4] My point of entry was at the level of the community's elite and of public events, hence my focus of analysis remained the community's public life and the points of linkage between the clergy and the laity, with more emphasis on the former. My first contact was with high officeholders in the Armenian patriarchate, and I relied on their status in the community to gain entry. In retrospect, I now see that this may have given me an "establishment" taint, but circumventing them could have provoked their opposition and made it almost impossible to obtain the community's cooperation.

Among the early contacts who assisted me were Archbishop Shahe Ajamian, the former chancellor of the patriarchate, and Kevork Hintlian, a high-ranking lay official mentioned above. Another source of invaluable help was Bishop Guregh Kapikian, the principal of the lay school and also a central figure of the community. Not only did he refer me to other informants but he sat with me for long hours of conversation. The number of times he is specifically mentioned in the book best indicates my great debt to him. In the later stages of my fieldwork I was lucky to work with Father Haigazoun Melkonian, a Detroit-born, newly ordained priest who served as my research assistant. Father Melkonian had lived in Jerusalem for only a few years, hence he did not have the same familiarity with local events as did Bishop Kapikian, Kevork Hintlian, or Sahak Kalaydjian. The fact that he was new in the area, however, turned out to be an even greater asset, because it made him sensitive to aspects of community life which others tended to take for granted. Having been a graduate student of sociology and education at Wayne State University, he also understood my sociological jargon and could articulate issues in that conceptual framework. Role-performance, boundary maintenance, mass versus virtuoso religion, total institutions, were all common language to him.

With regard to the disclosure of my identity and research purposes, my problems were not very different from those encountered by other students of communities. To state that one wants to study the life and organization of a community does not impress local inhabitants for whom the regular flow of community life is precisely the kind of taken-for-granted phenomenon that least warrants investigation, unless of course one is a journalist or a government agent hunting for improper deeds. In order to prevent any such misconception, I carefully avoided mentioning economic matters and business practices in my early conversations. Political issues, especially those related to the Arab-Israeli conflict, were avoided altogether and my knowledge of their attitude on this subject is rather thin. I did, however, indulge in long discussions of "safer" subjects, such as Armenian history, culture, and religion. Interest in history is always welcome, especially by Armenians, as it helps reassert national rights and identity, which for them carry a special importance. I also hesitated about whether or not to disclose my Turkish origins. At first I tended to conceal this fact, fearing that their anti-Turkish feelings would be projected onto me. When the subject could no longer be avoided and my origins were revealed, I was surprised to find that our rapport—far from being hurt—was even strengthened. We now had a common cultural background known to both sides.

I never used a tape recorder and rarely took notes during the interviews. The questionnaire that did emerge after the initial interviews was firmly locked in my own mind, and it was easily changed according to the identity of the informant and the situational context of the conversation. Every visit to the Armenian quarter was followed by hours of writing up field notes from memory. I was compelled to organize my thoughts at the end of each visit. This sensitized my conceptual apparatus and crystallized the theoretical focus as I went along. Much data were undoubtedly lost or were reinterpreted in this process, but since, after all, the final result rests on the general sociological questions raised in the study, the trade-off might have been beneficial. I am also aware that I have broken some stylistic canons of community study reporting. Except for the preface, my style is not as personalized as that of other authors of community studies. There are not that many field stories or direct quotes from informants. In part, this is owing to a different style of writing, but it also reveals that a certain conceptual framework, different from the informants' own words, developed early in the research.

The people who helped me in this study are too numerous to mention separately. They include first my informants from the Armenian quarter, only a few of whom are mentioned by name in the book; fewer still have been thanked above. I am grateful to them all. Outside the Armenian quarter, I owe a great intellectual debt to Gerald D. Suttles and George A. Hillery, Jr., whose own work deeply influenced my thinking. They also read earlier drafts of the manuscript and sent me very useful comments. In my sabbatical year at the University of California, Los Angeles, I had the good fortune to meet Jeffrey C. Alexander and his wife Ruth. Not only did they offer my wife and me their warm hospitality but Jeff read different drafts of the manuscript (and most of everything else I wrote) and always amazed me with the perceptiveness of his comments. To him and to Jerry Suttles I am especially indebted for assistance in seeing the book through to its completion. At UCLA I also was privileged to meet two eminent armenologists, Richard G. Hovannisian and Avedis K. Sanjian, who helped me beyond measure with detailed comments and thoughtful suggestions on factual matters.

Many other eminent scholars read earlier drafts of the manuscript and provided valuable criticism. I wish to thank particularly Joseph Ben David, Moshe Lissak, Samuel Heil-

man, Robert Melson, and Melford Spiro. A special note of
gratitude is due my close friends Baruch Kimmerling and
Nachman Ben Yehuda for their continuous encouragement
and their very helpful comments on earlier drafts. Shmuel
Eisenstadt, Erik Cohen, Morris Janowitz, Ralph Turner,
Melvin Seeman, Rodolfo Alvarez, Jeffrey Prager, and Gideon
Aran probably do not realize how much their casual remarks
in various conversations helped crystallize the ideas formu-
lated here. Orit Ziv, my research assistant in 1975, should be
happy to see that our early, hesitant steps were not all in
vain. I also would like to thank the students of my seminars
on urban communities of Jerusalem for serving as my principal sounding board for raw ideas. Thanks also to Victor Low
and Norma Schneider for editorial help and to Florence Da-
Costa, Betty Gorden, Helga Low, Felicity Krowitz, and Berta
Edwards for typing several drafts of the manuscript over the
past few years. Research for this study was made possible by
the generous financial support of the Israeli National Academy
of Sciences, the Jerusalem Institute for Israel Studies, and the
Harry S. Truman Research Institute of the Hebrew University of Jerusalem. I would like also to thank the Rand Foundation Inc. for a grant made in memory of Leon Miller.

To my wife Mireille, to whom the book is dedicated, go
my deepest love and thanks for her continued comfort and
encouragement. Without full reliance on her support this
work could not have been completed. Finally, I wish to thank
all the inhabitants of the Armenian quarter. Their hospitality
and understanding not only enabled the research to proceed
but also made it a thoroughly enjoyable experience.

1
Introduction

The Old City of Jerusalem, which has attracted the attention of much of humanity for millennia, has naturally been a
favorite subject of scholarship by historians, geographers,
archeologists, students of religion, political scientists, and
others. Students of ethnic and residential communities have
also found in the Old City a most interesting living labora-
tory. The same factors that drew world attention to the city
also brought to it settlers from various geographical, cultural, and religious backgrounds, making it a true "urban mosaic." These settlers created a great variety of communities,
congregating around some holy place or other religious edi-
fice and living in close proximity to one another.[1] Indeed,
rarely could one find people belonging to so many different
cultures living in such proximity, yet leading separate exis-
tences for many centuries. The religious importance of the
city led most of these communities to develop around religious organizations, and many of their members engaged in
religious occupations, as priests, monks, rabbis, or Muslim
clerics.[2] These communities, however, also had a lay component made up of former pilgrims and of converts or followers
who for various reasons settled in the Old City and offered
services to the clergymen, to fellow members of the community, and to the many travelers who visited there. Thus
lay communities took root around different religious nuclei.
These ethnic and religious communities have had very little

1

sense of integration into an overall urban identity. Despite their intensive intercourse in matters of business, they have been very competitive and hostile to each other as a result of long years of struggle for the control of religious shrines. Each had a sense of being an outpost of a wider society located elsewhere, the representative of that society on the holy site, its link to or mediator with the sacred realm. Conflicts over the control of holy shrines thus had an importance that transcended the local scene.

Among the many groups of people who live in the Old City of Jerusalem, the Armenians warrant special attention. Theirs is a very cohesive community that has preserved its language and cultural heritage with remarkable tenacity. Fewer than 2,000 Armenians live in the Old City, whose total population is estimated at 25,000 people.[3] Despite its small number the Armenian presence in the Old City is strongly felt. One could trace back to the fourth or fifth century A.D. the continuous existence of an Armenian presence in Jerusalem, and for most of that history in its present location at the southwestern quarter of the Old City. The Armenian quarter covers roughly thirty acres, about one-sixth the area inside the Old City walls.[4] The prominence of the Armenians is manifested by the fact that their quarter is one of the four principal sections (although the smallest one) into which the Old City is now divided (the others are the Christian, Muslim, and Jewish quarters). It is centrally located and found on the itinerary of many visitors (map 1). Not all of what is customarily called the Armenian quarter is inhabited or controlled by the Armenians,[5] but their institutions and living quarters, nevertheless, occupy a disproportionately large area compared to the size of their community in the Old City, in Israel and the West Bank of Jordan, or in Christendom as a whole.[6]

The Armenian church also owns much property beyond the Armenian quarter, both inside and outside the Old City. This property is rented to businesses and government agencies, and most of the tenants are non-Armenians. The Armenian church is also prominent in its control over Christian

Holy Places in the Jerusalem area. It has sole jurisdiction over the St. James Cathedral and the houses of Annas and Caiaphas and shares with some other Christian churches control of the Holy Sepulchre, Mary's Tomb in Gethsemane, the Church of the Ascension on the Mount of Olives, and the Church of the Nativity in Bethlehem.[7] In terms of overall control of Christian Holy Places the Armenian church is ranked third, after the Greek Orthodox and the Roman Catholic churches, and ahead of many larger Christian churches, such as the Russian Orthodox and the various Protestant churches.

Map 1. The Old City of Jerusalem

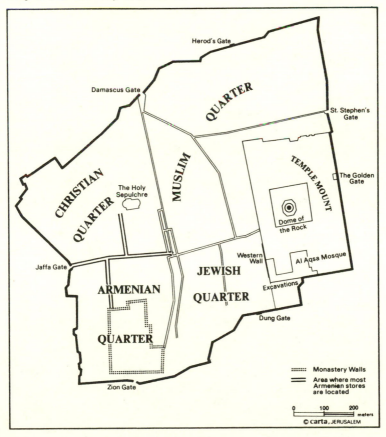

Despite their long-standing roots and impressive presence in the Old City, the Armenians are not a "local" group at
all. Their region of origin and their religious and cultural
center are far away, around Mt. Ararat in today's Turkish
Eastern Anatolia and in Soviet Armenia. The Armenian community of Jerusalem has always been and felt itself to be a
diaspora, that is, a distant outpost away from the largest
concentrations of its people and/or the place that shaped the
specific history and culture that created the collective identity of its people. The lack of deep local roots has always
accompanied Armenians in Jerusalem as well as in other diasporas.[8] The Armenian community of Jerusalem is thus different from other Middle Eastern Christian communities whose
ethnocultural nucleus is located in Arab lands much closer to
Jerusalem. In this sense the Armenians are distinguished
from the Copts, Jacobites, Maronites, and others.[9] The Armenian church is also differentiated from the European
Christian churches (i.e., the Roman Catholic, Protestant,
Greek, and Russian Orthodox) in its opposition to proselytism. All the European denominations proselytize actively
and have gained many converts among the local population,
to the extent that today the great majority of their lay followers and even some of their priests are of local Arabic
origin and retain their Arabic national identity while adher-
ing to the church. For this reason, all the European congrega-
tions have undergone a certain degree of arabization, this
being true even of the more "national" churches such as the
Greek Orthodox, Russian Orthodox, and Anglican.[10] The
Armenian Apostolic church,[11] in contrast, has not engaged in
proselytism and has made no efforts at converting the local
people. On the contrary, by making conversions very difficult, it has tried to limit its followers to those who are ethnically and nationally considered part of the Armenian
people.[12]

The Armenians are, therefore, special in their maintenance of a strict separation between themselves and other
ethnic or national groups. Unlike all other Christian churches

and communities in Jerusalem (with the possible exception of
the Ethiopians) there has been no mixing of local Arab or
other populations in the Armenian Apostolic church. While
some Armenians did convert to Catholic and Protestant
churches and still retained their Armenian national identity,
the opposite has not been possible: no one could become a
member of the Armenian Apostolic church without also
being a member of the Armenian nation. The few non-Armenians who were converted to the church (almost always as a
result of marriage to an Armenian) also were expected to
undergo a national-cultural armenization, speaking the Armenian language, adopting Armenian customs, and identi-
fying with Armenian history and the fate of Armenian
people throughout the world.[13] In that sense the Armenian
church has been a truly national church: religious and
national identity have been indistinguishable, as is the case
with the Jews,[14] and in some contrast to the universalistic
tendencies of Christianity.

In addition to these features that distinguish the Armenians from other ethnic and religious communities in Jerusalem, there is another feature that warrants special attention
and prompted the present study. The great majority of Armenians who inhabit the Old City actually live *within a monastery*. The many visitors who every day pass along the
Armenian quarter on their way from Jaffa Gate to the Western Wall or Mt. Zion are hardly aware that the neighborhood
they are passing is almost entirely composed of one very
large monastery surrounded by walls (map 2). The gates of
the monastery (three minor ones and a major one near St.
James Cathedral) are constantly guarded and closed at night.
Strangers venturing through these gates are asked to identify themselves and state the purposes of their visits. Only by
special permission can anyone enter or leave the area after
the gates are closed. Except for a few houses found on the
road surrounding the monastery walls, the residential areas
of the Armenian quarter are located *within* the monastery in a
maze of narrow alleys and backyards sprawling throughout

Map 2. The Armenian Quarter of Jerusalem

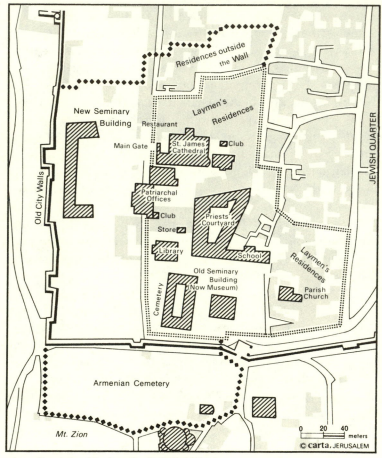

◆◆◆◆   Boundaries of the Armenian Controlled Area
::::::::   Monastery Walls

the monastery compound, at certain places forming two or three stories. In this place not only the clergymen live but also a lay community of about 1,500 people with families and children of all ages.

Most of the laymen who live within the monastery are secular in their outlook, lifestyle, and occupations. While some work for the church as clerks or as teachers in church-run schools, most are independent shopkeepers and businessmen whose workplaces are outside the monastery. Many are highly educated. In fact the Armenians pride themselves on being the most highly educated of all the Old City inhabitants. They are in close contact with fellow Armenians in other countries and many have traveled abroad. In other words, these laymen are not a remnant from a past premodern situation still clinging to traditional ways. On the contrary, modern circumstances determine this peculiar habitat. Nor is the laity a mere supplement to the ecclesiastical community. They form the great majority of the monastery's inhabitants. Compared to nearly 1,500 laymen living within the monastery compound, there are only about twenty clergymen and about fifty seminarians being trained for priesthood. This study will explore the reasons why laymen live in the monastery and are accepted by the clergy even though they necessarily disrupt the monastic way of life. It will also examine the mechanisms of adaptation that enable the lay and religious groups to live together, the strains this causes, the role-modifications each side undergoes, and how mutual adaptation is reflected in patterns of interaction and use of common space.

Monasteries and lay communities are customarily thought to be at different poles of localized collectivities. Usually monasteries strive to separate themselves from conventional lay community life to perform better their monastic mission. They are considered significantly different from regular residential communities in their goals, internal structure, and interactions within the in-group and between the in-group and the outside. The Armenian quarter thus presents an interesting coexistence of two collectivities which theoretically are expected to be in tension with and keep distant from each other. The analysis of the symbiotic relationship between these two collectivities is the principal objective of the book. Before the symbiosis is discussed, however, the difference between its component prototypes

should be explained. Why indeed are monastery and residential community very different analytical types? For this purpose, the next few pages will discuss the inherent differences
between the types of collectivities and situations that happen
to be found together in our Armenian case. This will also
raise certain theoretical issues and a conceptual framework
that will accompany us in the subsequent parts of the book.

MONASTERIES AND RESIDENTIAL COMMUNITIES

A discussion of prototypes should start with a declaration
of intentions regarding the concept of community that has
been plagued by such diverse and contradictory approaches
and definitions that it has become almost impossible to use.
(Hillery at one time counted ninety-four different definitions
of community.)[15] To avoid yet another controversy over the
definition of the term, I have deliberately used the somewhat
awkward term *residential community*, thus limiting the discussion to *localized* collectivities, that is, to groups of people who
live in a specific location. This eliminates all nonterritorial
communities such as *professional community*. It also ensures that
we do not employ the term in the sense of psychological
community or "community feeling," denoting a kind of fel-
lowship or shared feeling that its Latin root *communis*
implies.[16] It will be seen that most residential communities
indeed display some commonly shared feelings, but this is not
a necessary condition nor part of our definition of residential
community.

Monasteries and Total Institutions

In his pioneering study Goffman included monasteries
together with prisons, mental hospitals, and army barracks in
the category of "total institution," which displays some basic
contrasts with regular communities.[17] Starting the discussion with total institutions enables us to spotlight these contrasts. A more careful examination of the monasteries
reveals, however, that while they do share some of these
basic contrasts, they also display marked differences from

total institutions. Unlike the prototype of total institutions modeled on prisons and mental hospitals, monasteries do not have a rigid staff-inmate split with no possibility of passage from one to the other and in which the former monopolizes the instruments of power and has absolute authority over the latter. Monasteries come closest to the staff-inmate division when they operate theological schools (or priests' seminaries) or have initiation rites for new recruits who are put on a probation period before they are accepted as full members of the monastic brotherhood. But the sharp differentiation of power and the humiliation to which students and new recruits are subjected are temporary devices that precede full membership. Among the full members, a much more egalitarian structure prevails.[18]

Even when a hierarchical structure does exist in monasteries there is still a basic unity and integration that derives from belief in common values and that is so lacking in total institutions. The monastery is a united body and not an antagonistic dual world. Monastic brothers are strongly attached to their monastery; they identify with it and are loyal to it. Monasteries are voluntary organizations even when they are hierarchical. Relations between monastery members are primarily based on normative compliance, that is, compliance deriving from members' mutual attraction to one another and their internalization of common norms and values, as opposed to coercive compliance that predominates in total institutions.[19] Unlike a village or a friendship clique, however, the normative compliance in the monastery is not left at the level of diffuse understandings and latent codes of conduct assumed to be known and shared by fellow members of the group. Rules are specified, formalized, and codified, and they govern all aspects of life.[20] There is more regimentation in monasteries: all phases of daily activity are highly scheduled and the whole sequence is imposed from above by formal rules.

In some characteristics, such as closure, lack of privacy, standardized rules, and uniform life-styles, monasteries do display striking similarities to total institutions, but these traits could also be found in varying degrees in some residential communities, such as isolated villages or crowded urban ghettos.[21] Hence, on these points it might be preferable to refer to *degrees of totality* found in different types of organizations and communities, rather than regard total institutions as a separate type.

Despite the above-mentioned differences between monasteries and total institutions, there is little doubt that monasteries share the inherent tension of total institutions with regular residential communities. Monasteries, like total institutions, are special organizational devices meant to keep certain people outside of regular community life for the performance of certain special tasks (whether punishment, cure, training, or ties with the supernatural realm). The need for separation and differentiation from the regular community is the very reason for their existence. Together with other aspects of totality, such as dense congregation, uniform lifestyle, standardized rules, and strict daily routine under centralized authority, it enables the organization to fulfill better the goal for which it was established. For the same reason total institutions are incompatible with family life and this is one of the sharpest qualitative differences between such organizations and regular residential communities whose basic units are family households. From the viewpoint of the total institution families are part of the external environment with which contact should be closely regulated, if not limited, in order to fulfill the organization's goal.[22] Thus monasteries, like total institutions, have a closed space whose boundaries are well delineated and cause a rupture or discontinuity with the environment. Maintaining this rupture is an essential requirement of the collectivity's very existence.

The Sacred and the Profane

The importance of discontinuity and indeed the more general tension between monastery and residential community could also be regarded in terms of the difference between the *sacred* and the *profane*, which seem to be in constant touch

in our Armenian case. As Eliade rightly points out, the sacred
sphere inherently requires a break in the continuity of space
and time to distinguish it from the profane.[23] The discrimination of space and time, by giving special significance to some
portions over others, is a condition of their very sacredness.
For profane experience, on the contrary, space and time are
homogeneous and neutral. No break qualitatively differentiates the various parts of their mass. Therefore, lack of differentiation would spread the profane at the expense of the
sacred. To maintain sacredness, passage from one sphere to
the other should be limited and the very act of passage, that
is, the acknowledgment of the difference between the two
spheres, should be emphasized. In Eliade's words, "The
threshold that separates the two spaces also indicates the
distance between two modes of being, the profane and the
religious. The threshold is the limit, the boundary, the frontier that distinguishes and opposes two worlds—and at the
same time the paradoxical place where those worlds com-
municate, where passage from the profane to the sacred
worlds becomes possible."[24] Monasteries, as places where
sacred activities take prominence, thus should keep clear
boundaries between themselves and the profanity of ordinary community life.

The need to separate the sacred and the profane also
creates some tension in the monks' daily life, between the
more sacred activities, such as prayers and religious activities, and the more mundane ones, such as eating, cleaning,
maintenance, purchasing material goods, and the like. The
latter have to be clearly separated in time and space or else be
given special religious meaning, that is, be elevated to the
sacred realm, perhaps by ceremonial ritualistic performance.
This tension is inherent to monastic life, since as Geertz
stated:

> But no one, not even a saint, lives in the world religious
> symbols formulate all the time and the majority of men
> live in it only at moments. The everyday world of

common-sense objects and practical acts is, as Schutz
says, the paramount reality in human experience—
paramount in the sense that it is the world in which we
are most solidly rooted . . . and from whose pressures
and requirements we can least escape.[25]

The presence of laymen in monasteries could, paradoxically, reduce this tension if the laymen perform special tasks
that relieve the monks from some of the profane activities of
everyday life. The monastery could also be inhabited for a
while by lay visitors, such as pilgrims or students who seek a
temporary immersion in sacredness. In this case, not only is
the threshold preserved between the two worlds, but by
becoming mediators and gatekeepers of the sacred sphere the
resident monks enhance their own ties to sanctity. If, however, as in the Armenian quarter of Jerusalem, laymen are
not simply visitors in the monastery but permanent inhabitants with families and children, and if they do not fulfill
specialized functions that would free the clergy for more
religious activities, then the sacred and the profane tend to
merge and have to be kept separate by special means.

Inward and Outward-Oriented Goals

There is another very crucial difference between monasteries and residential communities which was alluded to in
the comparison with total institutions but should be stated
more explicitly. The various activities of members of monasteries, as of total institutions, "are brought together as parts
of a single overall rational plan, purportedly designed to fulfill the official aims of the institution."[26] These goals,
whether educational, therapeutic, punitive, or protective as
in most total institutions, or more religious as in monasteries
(protecting holy shrines, conducting Divine Office, entering
into contact with deities, or discovering religious truths), are
all external to the collectivity itself. Patterns of organization
and interaction among members of the collectivity are only
the means to achieve these external goals. In residential communities, by contrast, the principal goals are related to the

maintenance of desired interactions within the collectivity. Their goals are primarily inward-oriented.

On the basis of their collective goals, one can think of localized collectivities as stretching between the poles of formal organization and residential community. In formal organizations the collectivity is a mere instrument created to coordinate the efforts necessary to attain preexisting specific goals.[27] Residential communities, by contrast, have primacy of diffuse and inward-oriented goals. Monasteries, like schools, churches and prisons, armies and political movements, are closer to the formal organization pole than to that of the residential community.[28] Collectivities of varying extents of totality can be found at either end of the spectrum. The presence or absence of families, however, is more clearly related to the types of goals. Whenever families appear they tend to become ends in themselves. Therefore, the more specific and outward-oriented a collectivity's goals, the more it would tend to exclude families as its components.[29]

This distinction is similar to the one proposed by Hillery (and further developed by Gottschalk)[30] between communal and formal organizations, but their classification stresses the specificity versus diffuseness of goals more than their inward or outward orientation. Comparing residential communities with formal organizations Hillery wrote:

> We are thus distinguishing between groups which come into existence because they are purposely created to do certain things and groups which are seldom if ever specifically created but which evolve because other groups bring them into being.[31]

The goals of formal organizations are sharp and recognizable. They are specific in the sense that they can be clearly identified as output and be used as input into another system.[32] Examples include making an economic profit, producing a commodity, or obtaining an educational degree. By contrast, such generalized goals as happiness, love, and freedom are excluded. Indeed Hillery takes pains to distinguish specific goals from general purposes:

Purposes are not easily defined but they refer generally
to values, standards, or conditions, the attainment of
which is believed to be desirable by the members of a
group.[33]

Communal organizations might have purposes but they are
not oriented toward the attainment of such narrowly defined
specific goals. Corporations, associations, governments are
examples of formal organizations compared with families,
friendships, ethnic groups, and communities, which are communal organizations. Communal and formal organizations,
when viewed as inclusive units, could also include subunits of
the opposite kind, as, for example, informal communitylike
friendship groups among workers of an industrial organization or voluntary associations within a residential community.[34]

Despite its careful formulation, Hillery's classification
does not account for the fact that collectivities may be organizational instruments with external goals even though their
goals are rather diffuse, as in the case of political movements
or, closer to us, in the case of monasteries. Praying, serving
God, entering into contact with the supernatural realm, or
discovering religious truth are not more specific than having
safe streets, better education, or ethnic purity, goals that
might determine the composition, structure, and boundaries
of residential communities. What differentiates them is that
the former are oriented beyond the collectivity, while the
latter seek the achievement of desired interactions and
behavior within the collectivity. Thus it is perhaps not so
much specificity or diffuseness of goals but whether they are
primarily internal or external to the collectivity that differentiates between the goals of monasteries and residential communities.[35] The importance of this point will be seen in a
comparison of the collective goals of the lay and ecclesiastical
sectors in the Armenian quarter.

There are, of course, cases of residential communities
with primacy of specific and/or outward-oriented goals.

Planned communities formed as a result of urban development schemes are created with specific objectives (such as
reducing overcrowding or preventing crime), but these objectives generally relate to the patterning of desirable community life and are not external to it. The same is true of
retirement communities. In contrast, "company towns"
might be considered to have an external goal in that they
exist mainly to provide manpower to some large industrial
enterprise and indeed are often built by the industrial enterprise itself. In the latter case, the residential area is simply an
appendage to the formal organization, not very different
from other benefits, such as free parking or recreational
facilities, that the organization offers to its workers. But
with time, residents of company towns tend to develop goals
related to their common life.[36] Frontier stockade communities or politically motivated settlements in newly conquered
territories (such as Jewish settlements on the West Bank of
Jordan) are other examples of residential communities with
primarily outward-oriented goals. These and many others
are composite types which include traits of both formal
organizations and residential communities.[37] One might try
(as Gottschalk did with relative success) to account for the
composite types by building more complex, two- or three-
dimensional classificatory schemes,[38] but this is beyond the
scope of this study. It would be easier to avoid the pitfalls of
absolutism by turning the distinction between inward- and
outward-oriented goals (or between specific and diffuse goals
for that matter) into a continuum along which various residential communities are ranged. We should bear in mind,
though, that most communities are situated nearer the
inward-oriented pole, while most formal organizations, total
institutions, social movements, and monasteries are situated
nearer the outward-oriented pole.

Monasteries and Communes

Traits that characterize residential communities and
social movements are found together in communes whose

members also display special bonds of communion similar to those found in monasteries and different from those of most residential communities. Monasteries and communes have much in common. Both are voluntary groups that base their interactions on normative compliance, though they both stress discipline and obedience to the collectivity's rules and norms. They attribute great importance to commonly held values and moral concerns; they stress group solidarity and exemplary life and separate themselves from the larger conventional society to achieve these values and beliefs; they are easily identified as entities with clear territorial boundaries and a limited membership; and they also display similar uniformity, regimentation, and lack of privacy. Members of communes and monasteries live a collectivistic life, dwelling under one roof and sharing resources. They abolish sectorial loyalties and interests that could endanger their unity. In communes, unlike monasteries, this rarely goes to the extent of abolishing families, though it might lead to taking away child-rearing functions from families.[39]

Monasteries and communes are also similar in the diffuse and primary relationships that members display to one another. Members interact with each other as wholes, relating to all aspects of one another's lives and not in terms of specific roles that characterize formal organizations. Such diffuse ties are common also to villages and small communities and differentiate them from more complex residential communities such as cities. However, in contrast to the *gemeinschaft*-like features of villages and other small residential communities, communes and monasteries display ties that could better fit Schmalenbach's *communion* type.[40] Like gemeinschaft they are close, intimate, diffuse, nonrational ties, which create great solidarity within the in-group and sharply distinguish it from the out-group, but they also are less spontaneous, less primordial, more emotionally laden than gemeinschaft, and most important, they are not taken for granted by members as gemeinschaft ties are. Quoting from Schmalenbach:

Community i.e. gemeinschaft implies the recognition of something taken for granted and the assertion of the self-evident. Generally speaking one will not expressly sanction or condemn those communities to which one belongs. One is usually not fully aware of them. They are given. They simply exist. As a rule we are not likely to take much notice of our membership in them.[41]

Communion, in contrast, requires fairly intense involvement of members with one another and in the collectivity and keen awareness of those ties as we indeed encounter in religious sects, monasteries, and communes. Great importance is laid on the meaningfulness of social ties, which is not always apparent in the gemeinschaft-like residential communities. As a matter of fact, many communes are formed by people in search of meaningful ties which they cannot find in their original community.[42]

At this point an important difference appears between monasteries and communes. Monasteries do not negate the communities from which they separate themselves; they do not see themselves *replacing* those communities but simply performing specialized functions that cannot be performed within the community. Communes, however, see themselves as *the* community, the alternative to the larger society.[43] For this reason, while monasteries recruit their members only from the outside, communes have an important function of self-generation and perpetuation to perform and this explains why most of them are bisexual and allow the existence of families. In other words, the primary goals of the communes are oriented to the collectivity itself, even if they are inspired by forces or values coming from outside the given collectivity. In Kanter's words:

Unlike monastic orders which may serve the interests of a wider Church community . . . the commune operates to serve first and foremost its own members; any benefits it provides for the outside are generally secondary and based on the need to support its own.[44]

Admittedly, we are treading here on a very thin line, especially when we compare monasteries with religious communes. Some religious or ideological communes do have external goals or "missions," especially if they belong to larger social or religious movements that see in the establishment of communal settlements a means of achieving their goals.[45] I still think, however, that the distinction is valuable and has crucial analytical implications. Communes do vary in the extent to which they have outward versus inward-oriented goals, but compared to monasteries they are more concentrated near the inward-goal pole. They are closer to residential communities than to formal organizations, while monasteries and social movements are closer to the formal organization pole.

THE ARMENIAN QUARTER: THE MEETING OF OPPOSITES?

The preceding discussion has shown that important qualitative differences exist between formal organizations and residential communities, and that monasteries occupy an intermediate position between them. The monastery's rather diffuse goals and interactions and its normative bases for compliance create some similarity to residential communities. Such similarity is even more marked when residential communities take the form of communes, or at least base their interactions on communion-type ties. Nevertheless there exists an inherent tension between monasteries and residential communities as analytical constructs. Not only are monasteries, unlike residential communities, oriented primarily toward goals beyond the collectivity, but achievement of these goals also requires a separation from the regular flow of community life.

The Armenian quarter thus presents an encounter of opposite collectivities and situations. Lay families cohabit with a monastic brotherhood, the sacred is intermixed with the profane. Groups sharply different in outlook, life-style, social organization, goals, and role obligations are found together. This is a rare phenomenon, but it is not in itself so surprising or unique. Contradictory ideal types of collectivities may be found to coexist in practice. Examples range from civilian populations inhabiting medieval castles to company towns and family quarters on military bases. Such composite or hybrid types usually result from special circumstances and lead to certain role-modifications and goal displacements in the collectivities in question. They obviously create some role-tension and require special measures of adjustment, but they do not necessarily weaken the ideal types. On the contrary, explaining the special features of the hybrid types might further our understanding of the inherent differences between the prototypes as analytical constructs against which reality is measured.

It should be pointed out, however, that the compatibility of the Armenian quarter to other hybrid types has its limits. Diplomatic enclaves and family quarters on military bases, for example, have a very high population turnover and do not create a local second generation, in contrast with the Armenian quarter. In this sense the historical examples of civilian populations living in castles, forts, or strategic hamlets show greater resemblance to the Armenian case and so does the company town in which the new generation replaces the old as labor force. The Armenian quarter also differs from the above-mentioned hybrid types in the clearer separation of the two collectivities sharing the same space. In most other hybrid types, at least one member of the families residing in the community is also part of the organization, as soldier, worker, or the like. This is the very reason for, and condition of, the existence of the residential community within the organization's territory. In the Armenian quarter, by contrast, laymen may or may not work for the church but are never part of the monastic brotherhood. Their service to the church is not a condition of their residence within the monastery. Regarding other historical examples of lay inhabitants living within monasteries, we shall see that in most cases laymen lived around the walls of the monastery rather than inside; and in those cases in which they lived within the monastery, they generally did not form the overwhelming majority of the monastery population (compared to the clergy), as occurs in the Armenian quarter.

The Armenian quarter of Jerusalem should also be examined with reference to other collectivities that are not necessarily hybrid types. First and foremost, as chapter 7 will show, the Armenian quarter presents striking similarities to traditional urban neighborhoods in terms of closure, self-containment, and territorial layout (internal walls and gates, narrow alleys, courtyards). However, the special patterns of habitation of the Armenians in the Old City are not a traditional legacy but are the result of rather modern circumstances which will be discussed in chapters 2 and 3. The Armenian quarter will also be seen to present important similarities to *modern* urban defended communities, as well as traditional ones. Such communities, inhabited by populations who stress their difference from the outside, usually on an ethnic or cultural basis, have been studied extensively and have formed a dominant topic in modern urban community studies.[46] The Armenian quarter will be compared with other modern defended neighborhoods in terms of in-group interactions, boundary-maintenance, internal organization and, most important, the meaning attributed to the preservation of communal ties. Suttles noted that many urban neighborhoods have a tendency to develop communion-type ties, especially when they try to defend their distinct identity and lifestyle against potential encroachers.[47] The importance of this observation to the Armenian case will be discussed. The ties linking the inhabitants of the Armenian quarter will be seen to have much in common with those of the inhabitants of modern ethnic neighborhoods, even though the ecological form of habitation is quite different. We shall also see why bonds of communion are stronger among Armenians than among most other ethnic communities and how the special features of Jerusalem and of life within a monastery further strengthen those ties.

The coexistence and symbiotic relationship between a monastery and a lay residential community in the Armenian quarter thus created the opportunity to give a more comparative and theoretical focus to this study. By detecting the emerging patterns of coexistence, conflict, and interdependence between different types of collectivities that share the same territory, we hope to learn more about the structures, goals, and roles performed in each. Discussion of the reasons why these two groups share the same space will enable us to explore issues related to the nature of solidarity and the relative importance of territorial proximity as a basis for ethnic or cultural affiliations in both traditional and modern urban settings. The intermixing of the sacred and the profane and the role-modifications necessitated by this coexistence will lead to a more general discussion of the essence of monastic role, compared with pastoral and apostolic ones. This may also indicate ways in which the religious excellence of the few (or borrowing a Weberian term, *virtuoso* religion) manifests itself and is distinguished from mass religion.

The order of the following chapters moves gradually from the Armenian case to more general sociological issues. The first two chapters are historical: chapter 2 acquaints the reader with the Armenian people through their history, culture, and collective consciousness; chapter 3 surveys the history of Armenian presence in Jerusalem and explains the emergence of a lay community within a monastic institution. Chapters 4 and 5 examine the various aspects of contemporary community life among the lay and ecclesiastical sectors of the Jerusalem Armenians. They indicate the extent of the laity's dependence on community services offered by the clergy and the pervasive nature of these services. The discussion also underlines the extent of "totality" in each sector's daily life and the entire community's relative self-containment and closure to the outside. Chapter 6 examines the patterns of coexistence and conflict between the clergy and the laity. It stresses the challenge of role-modification faced by clergymen from a monastic virtuoso role to a more communal pastoral one. It also analyzes the boundary-maintaining mechanisms between the two groups that keep segmentation in territorial proximity. With chapters 7 and 8 the analysis moves beyond the Armenian case. In chapter 7 the Armenian case is compared with other similar examples. After brief mention of some modern hybrid types, such as diplomatic enclaves and family quarters on military bases, the discussion focuses on: (a) other cases of lay inhabitation in monasteries, (b) preindustrial city wards, and (c) modern "defended" neighborhoods. The last example leads to chapter 8 in which the principal findings are summarized and concluding remarks offered on the relative importance of territory as an associational principle and on the significance of preserving ethnic solidarity in modern urban settings.

2

The Armenians in History

ARMENIAN IDENTITY AND EARLY HISTORY

The Armenians were among the earliest inhabitants of today's Eastern Anatolian plateau, a mountainous region extending from the Pontus mountains in the north to the Taurus in the south and from the Euphrates river in the west to the lakes of Sevan and Urmiya in the east (map 3). Many peaks of volcanic origin rise above this high plateau, the principal one Mt. Ararat, the national symbol of the Armenians. The Armenian traditions trace their origin to an archer named Hayk who saved his people from the tyranny of a giant named Bel and brought them out of Mesopotamia to the mountains of Eastern Anatolia. Other accounts trace them to the Armens coming from Thrace (in today's Balkans). Whatever their origin, it is known with greater certainty that the Armenian ethnic identity started to crystallize in about the sixth century B.C. around the various people who lived in or migrated to the ancient kingdom of Urartu. With the decline of Urartu, the Armenians became the dominant people in the area, also assimilating the original Urartians and the other local groups.[1]

Ever since their first development as a separate people, the Armenians have had to withstand the pressure of politically stronger neighbors. Their territory's strategic position exposed them to repeated invasions.[2] Their history is one of

Map 3. Armenia Past and Present

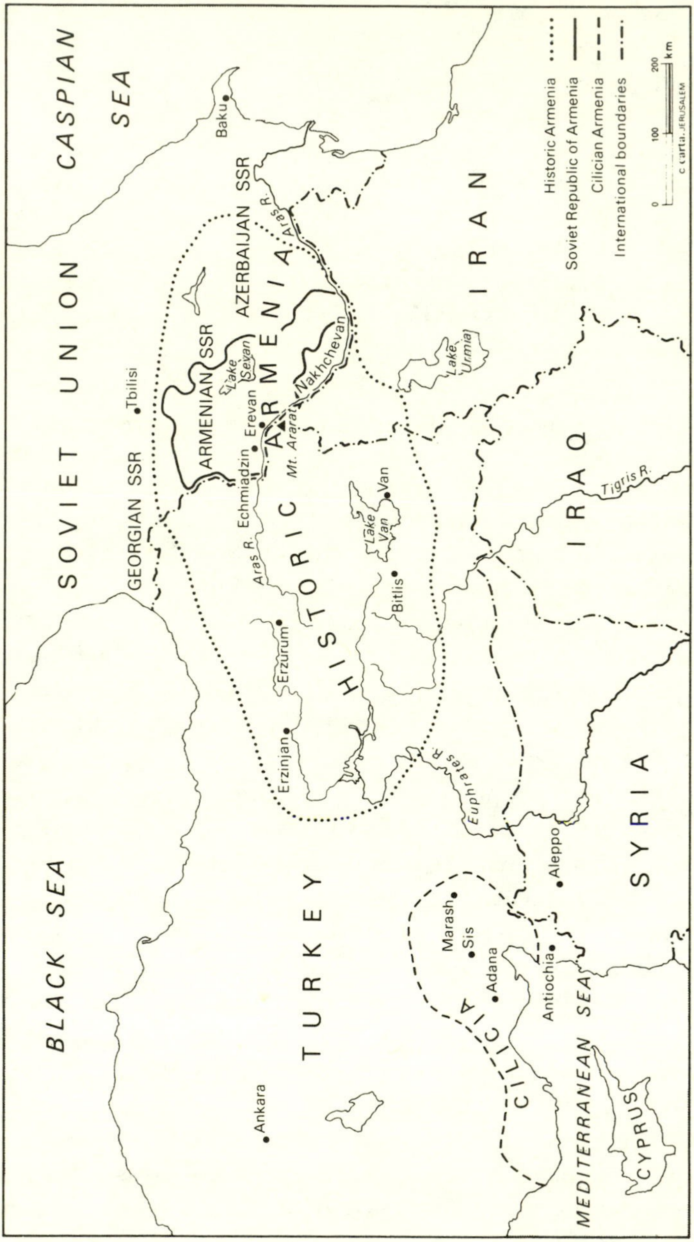

constant effort to keep their separate identity and resist assimilation with other people who ruled them, whether Persians, Byzantines, Arabs, Turks, or Russians. Surveying Armenian history we find short periods of political independence, separated by longer ones of subjection to foreign rule with varying degrees of internal autonomy. Armenian history is also characterized by great political fragmentation. Most of the Armenian kingdoms that emerged at different periods ruled over portions of the Armenian land and people and each often fought for the control of the other's part. The basic structure of the Armenian society persisted under foreign power, with the people ruled by local princes or feudal lords who depended on foreign kings.[3] The Armenian struggle with neighbors was oriented not only to preserve political sovereignty and unity, which in most cases they failed to secure, but also to preserve their *cultural* and *ethnic* identity and to resist assimilation by the conqueror's civilization.

A further point of extreme importance to Armenian history is the tendency of the Armenians to migrate from their country and establish large settlements in foreign lands where they engaged mostly in trade and other entrepreneurial occupations.[4] During Persian rule, Armenian settlers and traders were found in Pontus, Cilicia, Cappadocia, and Syria. During the Hellenistic period, they formed important trade colonies in Antioch and northern Syria. Under the Byzantines, the number of Armenians in Cilicia reached such proportions that they were able to set up vassal kingdoms outside Armenia proper. Similar trends of migration toward Palestine occurred under Arabic and Crusader rule. In the Ottoman period, many Armenians settled in Istanbul and Western Anatolia. It should be pointed out that not all migrations were voluntary. Sometimes foreign conquerors forced Armenian populations to leave their homeland. Under Safavi rule, for example, they were forced into the interior of Persia, from which some later moved on to India and Southeast Asia. Similar forced migrations occurred under Byzantine rule. Even when the migrations were involuntary, Armenians adjusted rather easily to their new environment. They engaged mainly in commerce and craftsmanship and moved farther on in pursuit of economic profits. However, they did not lose their cultural distinctiveness and they kept close contact with each other. Migrations rose as conditions of life deteriorated in Armenia, following new waves of conquests and more repressive foreign rule. As a result, large Armenian colonies were established far from home, while at the same time the Armenian population dwindled within the country. This territorial dispersion made it impossible to unite all Armenians under one political rule. It also had a very adverse effect on their territorial claim to Eastern Anatolia in the nineteenth and twentieth centuries, because by that time they no longer formed the majority of the population in most of their historic homeland.

The emergence of the Armenians as a separate people corresponded roughly with the extension of Persian rule to their country, and it was followed by the Hellenistic empire and its Seleucid heir. Autonomous Armenian kings ruled the country but paid tribute to their Persian or Hellenistic overlords.[5] One of the few truly independent periods of Armenia came with the decline of the Hellenistic era at the beginning of the second century B.C. Following the defeat of the Seleucids at the hands of the Romans in 190 B.C., the Armenian king Artashes proclaimed his independence. Under one of his successors, Tigran the Great, Armenia reached its apogee, uniting other Armenian kingdoms under one rule and expanding to northern Mesopotamia, northern Syria, Phoenicia, and parts of Cappadocia. By 70 B.C. Tigran's empire extended from the Caspian Sea to the Mediterranean and from the Caucasus to Palestine. However these successes resulted from the temporary political vacuum created by the breakup of the Hellenistic kingdoms. The Romans who came to replace them not only took back most of the territories conquered by Tigran but also captured Armenia itself and transformed Tigran into a Roman vassal (66 B.C.).[6] Henceforth, Armenia became a buffer zone and battleground between rival empires, each using the Eastern Anatolian high plateau as a base for military operations against enemies in the surrounding lowlands. The Romans and the Parthians fought for the control of Armenia and were followed by their respective successors, the Byzantines and the Sassanids, until the latter partitioned it between them in A.D. 387.[7]

THE ADOPTION OF CHRISTIANITY

At the beginning of the fourth century, an extremely important development took place in Armenia with the adoption of Christianity as state religion. According to Armenian traditions, Christianity was brought to Armenia in the first century by two apostles, Saint Bartholomew and Saint Thaddaeus. Christians were persecuted by pagan rulers in the second and third centuries, but they finally triumphed in A.D. 301 when Saint Gregory the Illuminator converted the Armenian King Trdat (at that time a vassal of Rome) and Christianity was proclaimed the state religion. This made the Armenians the first nation to adopt Christianity, a fact they pride themselves on to this day. Following the proclamation of Christianity as the state religion, Saint Gregory became head of the Armenian church and was given the title of Catholicos. With the help of King Trdat he organized religious institutions, trained clergymen, and opened churches all over the country; rapidly and at times coercively, he converted the rest of the population.[8]

The Armenians were thus not only the first nation to adopt Christianity but they adopted it collectively, upon the urging of the state. From its beginning the church was closely associated with the secular political center and Christianity became a basic tenet of Armenian culture and identity. Lay delegates participated in the election of the Catholicos and each congregation participated in the selection of its own bishop.[9] The seat of the Catholicos was always located in the capital of the strongest Armenian political authority of that period. As the capitals changed, the seat of the Catholicos moved with them, from Echmiadzin where it was first established to a long list of towns including Dvin, Aghtamar, Ani, Zamindia, Sev-Ler, Rhomkla, Sis, and finally back to Echmiadzin.[10] The ties between the nation and the church were further strengthened at the beginning of the fifth century, when a priest named Mesrob invented an alphabet for the Armenian language in order to translate the Bible into Armenian. The invention of the alphabet led to a great upsurge in Armenian literary and cultural activities. Henceforth the preservation of the written language became as cherished as the preservation of the church and of the national identity. The inventor of the alphabet was canonized as a saint in the Armenian church.[11]

For most of its history the Armenian church was part of the landed nobility, owning large tracts of land on which subject peasants worked. The traditional Armenian society was divided basically into a land-owning ruling class and a subject class of cultivators, craftsmen, and traders who worked for the ruling class, provided them with goods and services, paid them taxes, and served in their armies.[12] The church's holdings were even more stable than those of the political rulers because they were not as easily confiscated by rival feudal lords or foreign conquerors. The church was also a constant guardian of the distinctive Armenian culture and traditions; as such it occasionally clashed with kings or princes who were too receptive to foreign cultural influences. The church also assumed the sole national leadership role when no dominant Armenian political authority existed. In fact, this coalescence of religious and national identity to a large extent was caused by the very political weakness of the Armenians. Without a strong, united, independent state to protect their cultural and ethnic identity, and becoming territorially more and more dispersed, the Armenians relied on their kind of Christianity as the focus of their collective identity and distinction from other populations.[13] In the words of Dekmejian:

It was significant that during the centuries of foreign rule the Church served as the repository of almost all creative activity—artistic, religious, social, political, and even scientific. Heavily laden with tradition, the Armenian Church remains even today, much more than a religious organization. It represents the keystone of Armenian existence even in its communist and secular manifestations.[14]

Many of the struggles waged by Armenians for their ethnic and cultural survival took the form of resistance to attempts made by their neighbors to force them to relinquish their religious beliefs and institutions. Such attempts were either made by non-Christians, such as the Sassanid Persians who tried to enforce Zoroastrianism upon them, or by other Christians, such as the Byzantines who wanted to assimilate them into the Greek Orthodox church. Sassanid religious pressures on the Armenians led to military revolt, which culminated in the battle of Awarair in A.D. 451. The Armenians were defeated in the battle, but the fierceness of their resistance induced the Persians not to force their own religion on the Armenians. Politically the Armenians were subjugated to the Persians; after a time they even lost their own kings and were ruled by centrally appointed Persian officials. But the cultural battle against the Persians was won and any threat to the assimilation of the Armenians within Persian identity was averted. For this reason, despite their military defeat, the battle of Awarair is considered a great victory and its date is celebrated as a national and religious holiday.[15] The fifth century is considered a golden age in Armenian history, despite its political failures, because of the religious, literary, and artistic achievements of the time.[16]

While no similar battles were fought against Byzantium for the preservation of Christianity, the Armenians had to withstand continuous attempts of assimilation by the Byzantine (Greek Orthodox) church. Throughout history Armeno-Byzantine relations were marred by the religious rivalry of their respective churches.[17] The relations between the two churches deteriorated sharply following the Monophysite controversy that rocked Christianity in the fifth and sixth centuries and in which the two churches took opposing stands. A great theological debate developed at that time on the divine versus the human nature of Christ. The Nestorians, who were strong at the time, professed a certain separation between the two natures and stressed his humanity. The church of Alexandria (which later developed into the Coptic church), in contrast, affirmed a close union between the two natures and stressed his divinity. In the third Ecumenical Council held at Ephesus in A.D. 431 the Alexandrine doctrine triumphed and the Nestorian teachings were condemned. In the years following the council, however, the sees of Constantinople and Rome rose against certain interpretations of the Alexandrine doctrine (set later by a priest named Eutyches) that overemphasized the divinity of Christ and endangered the perception of dual nature fundamental to Christian trinity. To stress their view and quell all further heresies in this matter they induced the Byzantine emperor to convene a fourth council at Chalcedon in A.D. 451. The Armenian church did not participate in the council and refused to recognize its acts. Together with the churches of Alexandria and Antioch, which also rejected the acts of the Council of Chalcedon, it has been known ever since as Monophysist (i.e., stressing one nature of Christ).[18]

The Armenian church and the churches of Alexandria and Antioch were not technically Monophysist. They refused to emphasize the separate natures of Christ but they accepted both. It should be noted that the Armenians were at that time in a deadly struggle with another dualistic religion, Zoroastrianism. They also had special reasons to fear Nestorianism, because its influence was strongest in areas neighboring Armenia (eastern Syria, upper Mesopotamia, and Persia). Beyond the dogmatic theological debate, the Monophysite controversy involved a struggle for power between the predominant Christian centers of the time. The Council of Ephesus had ushered in a period of Alexandrine dominance not well regarded by either Rome or Constantinople. This was no doubt part of their reason for convening the Council of Chalcedon. The reaction to the council reflected the resistance of Alexandria, Antioch, and Armenia to the growing power of Constantinople. Opposition to the Council of Chalcedon was also opposition from the non-Greek Christian populations of Egypt, Syria, and Armenia, to the dominant Greek cultural element in Byzantium.[19]

The Monophysite controversy put the Armenian church on a dogmatic collision course with the Greek Orthodox, but also provided it with the doctrinal legitimation for creating its own branch of Christianity, complete with liturgical, musical, literary, and architectural manifestations.[20] It created a strong impediment to assimilation in the Byzantine culture and hence helped preserve a separate Armenian identity.[21] The Byzantine empire sought to bring the Armenians into the Greek Orthodox fold by every means of persuasion, intimidation, and persecution. Some Armenians did adopt Greek Orthodoxy and a few of them even became Byzantine emperors (such as Basil I and Leo the Armenian). Efforts to win the Armenians into Greek Orthodoxy continued unabated during their rule but had little success.[22] Byzantium also encouraged (sometimes even forced) the emigration of Armenians to Western and Central Anatolia, hoping that their territorial dispersion would facilitate their political and cultural assimilation. While these results were not obtained, Byzantine policies did reinforce the Armenian emigration from their homeland.[23]

The advent of the Arabs who replaced the Persians on the political scene did very little to alter Armenia's situation as a buffer zone. As the Arabs and Byzantines waged wars on each other between the seventh and ninth centuries, Armenian towns and provinces passed time and again from one side to the other. At the end of the ninth century, however, relations between the Arabs and Byzantium for once favored the Armenians. Taking advantage of the interest of both sides in Armenian neutrality, the Bagratid family formed a virtually independent kingdom. Both the Arabs and the Byzantines claimed suzerainty over the Bagratid kingdom, as symbolized by the fact that the Arab caliph and the Byzantine emperor sent respective crowns to the enthronement of the first Bagratid king.[24] Bagratid allegiance belonged primarily to the Arab caliphate, but in practice the kingdom followed an independent policy and tried to keep its neutrality toward the two powers. This was one of the few periods of Armenian political strength and independence in its long history. The political unity of this kingdom was very short-lived; rivalries among members of the royal family and among feudal lords soon led to a division of the country into various small kingdoms and principalities, tendencies that were encouraged by Armenia's powerful neighbors.[25] In the eleventh century all semblance of independence was lost when the Bagratid dynasty was abolished and the country fell prey to conquests, first by the Byzantine and then by the Seljuk Turks who spread to Eastern and Central Anatolia.[26]

ARMENIANS IN CILICIA

The Seljuk invasion of Eastern Anatolia began a long period of extreme hardship for the Armenians. Their country was subject to recurrent invasions, raids, and plundering by various nomadic tribes often waging war against one another, and the insecurity of life prompted large numbers of Armenians to flee their homeland.[27] Countless others were killed by the invaders or were eventually assimilated into their culture and religion. The nomadic invasions changed the demographic composition of eastern Anatolia considerably. Over the next several hundred years, many Muslim peoples, mostly of Turkish origin, replaced the Armenians and other Christians and laid claim to the most fertile soils. The Armenian feudal lords gradually disappeared and were replaced by Turkish-Muslim landowners. By the fifteenth century the traditional landed military class was decimated and the warrior image of the Armenians was lost. Large tracts of agricultural land were transformed into pasture for the use of the pastoralist Turkish tribes.[28]

Armenian emigration from the homeland was directed mainly toward Cilicia (in today's Southern Anatolia), which had already been a center of attraction for some time. In the early eleventh century, even before the final Turkish assaults on Eastern Anatolia, so many Armenians had settled in Cilicia that they had become the dominant element in the region and had formed principalities dependent on the Byzantine empire. In the twelfth and thirteenth centuries the Armenian dominance in Cilicia grew even further. One of the Armenian principalities, formed by the Rubenid family, rose at the expense of the others and conquered most of Cilicia.[29] The Byzantine emperors tried to assert nominal suzerainty over the Rubenids but their kingdom was in effect independent and even waged war against the Byzantines. Thus, just as the Armenian presence declined in Eastern Anatolia, a new Armenian center emerged hundreds of miles away. Following the principle that the central religious institutions be seated at the strongest political center, the Catholicosate was moved to Cilicia and in 1293 was established at Sis, the capital of the Cilician kingdom.[30] The Rubenid king was confirmed by the Catholicos as "King of the Armenians," giving religious and national legitimacy to his rule. Between the eleventh and fourteenth centuries Cilicia became the cultural and religious as well as political center of the Armenians.

The rise of Armenian power in Cilicia corresponded to the period of the Crusaders. The Cilician Armenians were the only Eastern Christian group who welcomed the Crusaders and cooperated with the Frankish principalities they established in the Middle East. Strong bonds existed between the Armenian upper classes and the Crusaders. Armenian kings and noblemen intermarried with Crusaders. Latin and French were widely spoken in the Armenian court and French customs became widespread. Some Armenian kings took French names. When one of the Armenian kings died without an apparent male heir, the kingdom even passed for a time to a Frankish nobleman, Guy de Lusignan, the deceased king's nearest relative through marriage.[31] The French and Latin influence exerted on the Armenians of Cilicia also had its religious manifestations. Catholicism made some inroads among the Armenians but stopped short of massive conversion because of the strenuous resistance of the Armenian National church. Resistance to Catholicism at times created serious friction between the Armenians and the Franks; at other times it pitted the church against Frankish-leaning Armenian kings.[32] At the beginning of the fourteenth century, opposition to pro-Catholic kings even led to appeals for Mongol help against them, thereby showing a willingness to jeopardize political independence when the survival of the separate church was at stake (later in the century this did not prevent the advent of Catholic kings of the Lusignan family at the last stages of the Cilician Armenian kingdom).[33] The ties with the Crusaders had, however, very favorable economic consequences for the Armenians. The brief hegemony of the Crusaders in the Levant stimulated international trade and maritime activity to a degree not attained since Roman times. The Armenians knew how to exploit this development and took an important part in the commerce of the area.[34]

The decline of the Armenian Cilician kingdom accompanied that of the Crusaders. The kingdom was considerably weakened in the fourteenth century and finally ceased to exist in 1375, when its capital Sis fell to the Mamlukes and the last king, Leo V, was taken captive to Egypt. With the decline of the Cilician kingdom, the center of Armenian national life moved back to the Eastern Anatolian highlands and pressures mounted for the transfer of the Catholicosate back to the Armenian homeland. As the Catholicos of Sis demurred, a new Catholicos was established in 1441 in Echmiadzin. Although the church was founded there originally, Echmiadzin had not been the seat of the Catholicosate for approximately one millennium (since A.D. 485).[35] Now that the Armenian power in Cilicia was no stronger than in the original homeland, there was no real reason for locating the

Catholicosate so far from the Armenian heartland. The establishment of the church headquarters in Echmiadzin also could help reinforce the Armenian presence there and stem the tide of population change in the area. In any event, the reestablishment of the Catholicosate of Echmiadzin was not recognized by the existing Catholicos of Cilicia and created a basic split in the Armenian church which has persisted to the present.[36] Two Catholicosates came to exist within the Armenian church, each with a distinct geographical area of jurisdiction. With time the Catholicosate of Echmiadzin asserted its supremacy over that of Cilicia, which eventually acknowledged the spiritual superiority of Echmiadzin but still maintained total parity in matters related to the administration of the church and control over the respective dioceses.[37] This split developed into open rivalry and antagonism in the twentieth century, the two churches fighting for control of various dioceses in the diaspora. This split, with its profound impact on Armenian history, will be discussed later in more detail.

ARMENIANS UNDER OTTOMAN RULE

Between the sixteenth and seventeenth centuries, most of the Armenian communities came under the rule of the newly expanding Ottoman empire. The Armenians of Cilicia fell under Ottoman rule following the latter's victories over the Mamlukes. In Eastern Anatolia the Ottoman victories over the Safavi dynasty of Persia brought most of the Armenian territories under Ottoman rule. However, the supreme religious center, Echmiadzin, located in the province of Erevan, remained outside the Ottoman borders.[38]

At first Ottoman rule brought a degree of stability and security to Armenian-inhabited areas. It also created new economic opportunities. The Armenians played an important role in Ottoman trade and finance, specializing in money-changing, banking, goldsmithing, jewelry, and foreign

trade.[39] In contrast, the Turks shunned economic entrepreneurial activities and concentrated on administrative and military tasks. The Armenians continued to move out of Eastern
Anatolia at an accelerated pace in pursuit of economic opportunities. Many Armenians settled in Western Anatolian
towns, especially in the capital, Istanbul, where their
numbers reached 150,000 to 200,000 by the mid-nineteenth
century, making this the largest Armenian community in the
world.[40] In Istanbul and the provincial urban centers, Armenian financiers bankrolled high Ottoman officials and gained
considerable influence in the highest government circles. In
contrast, in the rural areas where most Armenians continued
to live and were engaged mainly in agriculture, the people
were subject to heavy taxation and extortion by local rulers.
Certain areas were also raided occasionally by Kurdish or
Turkoman tribal chiefs who served as intermediaries for
Ottoman rule.[41]

As Christians, the Armenians were subjected to the discrimination common to all the non-Muslim populations of
the empire. They were forbidden to bear arms or serve in the
army and instead had to pay a heavy redemption tax. They
were not admitted to civil service. They were subject to a
score of petty humiliations, such as the obligation to wear
distinctive clothes, the prohibition of riding on horses (they
could ride on donkeys instead), and the building of houses
taller than those owned by Muslims. The reforms of the
nineteenth century abolished all these discriminatory clauses
and also brought a significant surge of Armenian representa-
tion in Ottoman public service.[42]

The Armenian position in the Ottoman empire until the
nineteenth century thus presents a mixed picture. While they
suffered discrimination, they also profited from relative stability and thrived economically. The Armenians also seem to
have gone through a more extensive acculturation to Turkish customs than either the Greeks or the Jews, perhaps
because they were spread more widely in small communities
among Turkish populations. Among Cilician Armenians

(who had always been more open to foreign influences), one-third of the population spoke Turkish as their first language in the nineteenth century.[43] Still, their Christian identity and the strength of their national church prevented full assimilation into the Turkish people.

The Armenians, like other non-Muslim groups living in the Ottoman empire, were organized for administrative purposes in autonomous religious communities called *millets*. The millet system officially recognized the existence of autonomous religious communities and invested the religious leadership with civic authority over the population. A few years after the conquest of Constantinople, Sultan Mehmed II, keeping an old promise, appointed the Armenian bishop of Bursa as patriarch of Constantinople and recognized him as "community head" *(millet bashi)* of all Armenians (and other Monophysite Christians) living under Ottoman rule.[44] As head of the community, the patriarch and the church officials appointed by him were responsible for keeping law and order within their own community and for collecting taxes for the government. The community was governed by its own religious laws in matters concerning civil status (marriage, divorce, and inheritance). It also maintained its own schools, as well as its cultural and charitable institutions. To perform his functions as head of the community, the patriarch disposed of considerable means of power. He had his own court, local police, and even prisons. Clergymen could be imprisoned or exiled at will by the patriarchal court, and while the consent of the Ottoman government was needed to impose such sanctions on laymen, consent was almost automatically granted because the patriarchate was considered the Ottoman government's representative in the community. The community also needed the patriarchate for such services as marriages and funerals, and for issuing birth certificates and vouchers of honesty without which one could not legally travel within the country. Thus, in its local administrative functions the patriarchate had political as well as religious authority over the members of its community.[45]

The communal autonomy granted to the Armenians by the millet system helped them keep the separate national and cultural identity for which they had fought during most of their history. It also strengthened the church by officially investing it as spokesman for the community. The church's leadership position was not shared by princes or feudal lords as in the past but, informally, it came under the sway of a few wealthy laymen called *amira*. Through their influence on high-ranking Turkish officials, the amira indirectly controlled the selection process of the patriarchal officeholders and hence the administration of the community.[46] In 1863 some degree of democratization was introduced when the Ottoman government promulgated the "National Constitution," whereby the administration of the community and the selection of the patriarch were vested in a popularly elected General Assembly and its executive organ, the National Council.[47] The National Constitution was hailed as the first step toward real national autonomy. It also accelerated the development of political emancipation movements among the Armenians.

The millet system, by equating ethnic and religious identities, also discouraged the conversion of Armenians to other Christian faiths. All Armenians, whether they believed in the Apostolic creed or not, were, insofar as they were identified as Armenians, under the jurisdiction of the National Apostolic church. This enabled the church to persecute those Armenians who, under Western missionary influence, adopted Catholicism or Protestantism. Conversion to Catholicism dated from the time of the Cilician kingdoms but was revived during the seventeenth and eighteenth centuries as a result of intensive missionary activity, especially of Jesuit fathers. Protestantism started to spread in the nineteenth century, largely because of the work of American missionaries. The spread of Catholicism and Protestantism never reached mass proportions and the Apostolic church used all the means that the millet system provided to discourage such tendencies.

Catholic or Protestant Armenians could not legally get married, baptize their children, or hold religious funerals. Their leaders were put in the patriarchate jail or were turned over to Ottoman authorities who imprisoned or exiled them. Only in the mid-nineteenth century did the Ottoman government recognize Armenian Catholics and Protestants as separate millets and discrimination against them ceased.[48]

While the millet system thus strengthened the position of the Apostolic church within the Armenian community, it also caused an internal shift of power that had some unsettling effects on the church. Supreme authority passed from the religious centers of Echmiadzin and Sis to the patriarchate of Istanbul (Constantinople), which was merely a creation of the Ottoman state. The Ottoman government forced all sees under its rule to obey the patriarchate of Istanbul, even if they had higher standing in the ecclesiastical hierarchy, such as those of Sis, Aghtamar, and Jerusalem.[49] Only Echmiadzin was unaffected because it remained beyond Ottoman rule, but for this very reason it was also cut off from the bulk of the Armenian people. This created uneasy relations between the different branches of a church already suffering from the split between Echmiadzin and Sis.

THE WORLD WAR I MASSACRES

The life of the Armenians under Ottoman rule deteriorated sharply with the decline of the empire. By the nineteenth century, while the Tanzimat reforms brought certain advantages to Armenians living in the cities, those living in rural areas fared much worse. Insecurity due to periodic Kurdish raids and looting of Christian communities rose considerably in the countryside, as did taxes and extortions paid to an increasingly corrupt officialdom.[50] Furthermore, hostility against Christians grew as the Ottomans started to lose their wars against European Christian forces and many Christian-inhabited provinces broke away from the empire.

The Armenians were unfortunate to be the last Christian people to ask for reforms and emancipation. By the time the Armenian emancipation movement had started, most other Christian populations were on the verge of achieving independence.[51] The Armenians also had the disadvantage of being geographically isolated from the other Christian minorities of the empire. Late in coming, the hostility against Armenians tragically developed into large-scale massacres between the 1890s and the 1920s.

So much has been written about the Armenian massacres that the subject will be treated very briefly here.[52] The first thing to be noted about them is, ironically, that they did indeed take place, a fact that has yet to find a place in Turkish history books. It is generally accepted that between one and two million Armenians, or about one-fourth to one-third of the total Armenian population, were killed in Anatolia between the 1890s and 1920s.[53] To what extent those killings were coordinated and ordered by high Ottoman government circles is a subject of hot dispute among historians, though most scholars concur that at least between 1894 and 1896 and 1914 and 1915 they were encouraged by high policymaking circles and aggravated by the eruption of additional local violence. The 1894 through 1896 massacres were conducted under the rule of Sultan Abdulhamid II. As part of a pan-Islamic policy, he encouraged the persecution of Armenians by Kurdish irregulars who were incorporated into a local army called Hamidiye. Attempts by Armenians to resist those attacks led to larger massacres in which about 300,000 Armenians perished in different parts of Eastern Anatolia.[54] The overthrow of Abdulhamid by the Young Turks temporarily stopped the persecution, but it soon started anew and reached genocidal proportions during World War I. Probably by order of top government officials, a systematic extermination of Armenian populations took place throughout Central and Eastern Anatolia. Thousands were killed by local mobs or police forces, while a greater number were "deported" to the Syrian and Iraqi deserts where most of them were killed by

Ottoman forces and local irregulars or died of the hardships of the journey.[55] Some killing also occurred during the Kemalist war of independence between 1918 and 1923 as the Turks fought against the carving up of Anatolia among the Greeks, Armenians, and Allied forces after World War I. At that time it also spread to the Western Anatolian town of Izmir, many of whose Christian inhabitants were killed when the town was reconquered from the Greeks in 1922.[56]

The Armenian genocide resulted from an extreme reaction by an intensely nationalistic faction of the Turkish elite, deeply frustrated at the rapid dismantling of the Ottoman empire by European powers that used the empire's treatment of its Christian subjects as the principal issue upon which to force on it territorial concessions. After enduring the rage and humiliation of being unable to stop the loss of the empire's European possessions, except for a narrow strip to protect Istanbul itself, the ruling Turkish elite felt that a similar danger was imminent in the East, in an area much closer to the Anatolian heartland and where Christian Armenians lived at almost numerical parity with Muslim (mostly Turkish) populations. Armenian demands for reforms and autonomy were perceived by the Turks, on the basis of past experience, as the precursor of the territory's detachment from the empire. This they were determined to prevent, if necessary by extreme measures.[57]

The question of which group formed the majority in the area has been hotly disputed by reference to contradictory statistical data, which derive from biased Turkish or Armenian sources. As Richard Hovannisian pointed out, however, even if the high figures of the Armenian patriarchate of Istanbul are accepted as accurate, there was still conclusive evidence that the Armenians did not represent a majority. There were at least as many Muslims as Christians.[58] The intertwined nature of Turkish and Armenian settlements did not make partition a realistic prospect, while the fragmentation of Armenian settlements facilitated attacks against them. The religious animosities between Muslims and Christians and the resentment felt by the Kurds and Turks, who were more often warriors and peasants, against the economic superiority of the more entrepreneurial Armenians exacerbated but did not generate the conflict.[59] What gave the killing genocidal proportions, especially in 1915, was its organization and coordination by the state apparatus. It was also facilitated by World War I, which created an "emergency" situation and allowed the victims to be portrayed as a dangerous fifth column. In addition to the killing of Armenians, their churches, books, art objects, and other property were destroyed. Even place-names were changed, as if to erase all symbolic and cultural traces of Armenian presence in the area. The holocaust thus received a cultural dimension beyond physical annihilation.[60] By contrast, the Armenian community of Istanbul numbering 150,000 people remained virtually untouched by the massacres that befell their kinsmen in other areas, with the exception of the arrestation (and subsequent killing) of a few hundred of their national leaders on April 24, 1915. This date came to be the symbolic day of commemoration for the entire genocide.[61] Armenians who lived in Arab lands (Syria, Lebanon, Iraq, and Palestine) were, for the most part, spared the deportations and massacres,[62] probably because those areas were not inhabited by Turks and the presence or absence of a large Armenian population could not have affected Turkish assertion of political rights over those territories. It should be noted, finally, that European intervention on behalf of the Armenians hurt more than helped. European meddling only rekindled anti-Christian feelings among the Turks and increased in their eyes the urgency of eliminating the Armenian population in Eastern Anatolia to prevent the area from following the example of the Balkans. In fact, the first wide-scale massacres of Armenians from 1894 to 1896 occurred soon after Muslim refugees from the Balkans, who were resettled in Anatolia, spread terror stories of how their land was lost to the Christians.[63] Military occupation of the Armenian-inhabited areas by a European power could have changed the situation but that was averted, first by intra-European conflicts—the British and the Germans opposed Russian expansion toward the Mediterranean—and then by the Bolshevik revolution that took Russia out of World War I.

ARMENIANS OUTSIDE OTTOMAN RULE

Before analyzing the effects of the genocide on Armenian consciousness and community life, mention should be made of the Armenian provinces that remained outside the Ottoman empire. Until the nineteenth century these areas experienced a rather lenient Persian rule; the Armenian church performed communal leadership functions and had jurisdiction over civil status. Armenians cultivated crown land and paid taxes to the state; they were active in commerce and established Armenian trading colonies as far away as India and Southeast Asia.[64] One notable exception to the lenient Persian rule was the forced relocation of about 50,000 Armenians by the Persian Shah Abbas in 1604. In his retreat from Ottoman forces, the shah adopted a "scorched earth" policy, burning all the towns and villages in his path. Some of the Armenian inhabitants of these locations were forced to move along with the Persian army and were reestablished in a separate quarter of Isfahan called New Julfa, after the important town of Julfa destroyed by the retreating Persians.[65]

In the nineteenth century, Persian-ruled Armenia and some parts of Ottoman-ruled Armenia passed into Russian hands. Russian rule was welcomed by Armenians as that of a Christian and more Westernized people. Russia had championed the cause of Christian peoples against Muslim rule everywhere in the Balkans and the Middle East and the Armenians expected that Russian rule would bring them closer to Westernization and national emancipation.[66] Russian rule proved to be a mixed blessing. On the one hand, it undoubtedly brought many Western innovations, led to more economic development, and encouraged the emergence of a Westernized elite and nationalist movement among the Armenians. On the other hand, Russian rule was accompanied by a Russification campaign which ran counter to Armenian nationalist aspirations. In 1881 Russian language and curriculum were enforced on Armenian schools, Armenians were encouraged to russify their names, and the church was brought under close government control. In 1903 the church lost its control over education and community matters, and all church property not directly related to religious functions was expropriated. This led to mass demonstrations against Russians and violence against government officials. The order was rescinded two years later; the Armenian church regained its confiscated property and was allowed to reopen parochial schools.[67] These events showed again the pivotal role played by the church in Armenian national consciousness. They also showed that the Armenian nationalist elite was torn between its wish to use Russian support against Ottoman rule and its opposition to Russian assimilationist policies. The dilemma of how to exploit Russian help against the Turks without being assimilated by Russia itself deeply preoccupied the newly emerging nationalist leaders and often split them into opposing positions. The attitude toward Russia was to create a very deep split in the Armenian communities which has persisted up to the present.

THE ARMENIAN NATIONALIST STRUGGLE

Armenian nationalist aspirations started to receive political expression in the late nineteenth century. The Armenakan party, formed in Van in 1885, generally is considered to be the first Armenian nationalist party.[68] It was closed down by the government after a few years and its leaders went to France. In 1887, the Hunchak party was formed in Geneva by Armenian students strongly influenced by Marxist and other Socialist Russian intellectual circles. Hunchak branches later were opened in the Ottoman empire and trained people for armed resistance to Turkish and Kurdish attacks. In 1896 some nationalist elements left the Hunchak party over disagreements on the doctrinaire internationalist Marxist orientation of its leadership and formed a separate group called

"Reformed Hunchaks." In 1921 they merged with some other liberal groups who had formed the Ramgavar party in 1908. The Ramgavar was basically an "establishment party," favoring ideological pragmatism, rejecting revolutionary solutions, and opting for incremental changes. It represented the views of economically well-to-do sectors in the Armenian communities. The party played a minor role in the events preceding World War I but developed rapidly after the war, mainly because of support received from the leading Armenian charitable association, the Armenian General Benevolent Union (AGBU). The Ramgavar became one of the two major Armenian parties, while the Hunchak steadily declined and now has minor importance in Armenian life.

The main rival to the Hunchak at the turn of the century was the Hay Heghapokhakan Dashnaktsuthiun party (henceforth Dashnak), formed in 1890 in Russian Transcaucasia and later established in the Ottoman empire. The Dashnak party stressed more nationalistic causes than did the more international-socialistic Hunchak. It also took a less favorable attitude toward Russia and stressed that Armenian emancipation had to be obtained from the Russians as well as from the Turks. Unlike Hunchakists, Dashnakist leaders cooperated closely with the Young Turks for several years after the 1908 revolution. With the outbreak of World War I the Dashnakists officially proclaimed neutrality in the struggle that pitted Turks against Russians and in which Armenian soldiers had to fight on opposing sides. The official neutrality obviously disappeared with the massacres of 1915, but while turning resolutely anti-Turkish, the Dashnakists also turned strongly anti-Russian after World War I. The Dashnak party represented the predominant Armenian nationalist movement at the turn of the century. After the war, following the decline of the Hunchak, the Dashnak party remained the major rival of the rising Ramgavar.[69]

Russia's withdrawal from World War I following the Bolshevik revolution created a power vacuum in the Armenian homeland. After the failure of a short-lived Transcaucasian Federation, the Armenians declared an independent republic

on May 28, 1918, the first independent state in their homeland for more than a thousand years. The Republic of Armenia was dominated by the Dashnak party, the leading
nationalist movement at that time. At the end of World War
I, the Republic found itself in a favorable situation. The
defeat of the Ottoman empire and the support that the Armenians received from the Allies opened the possibility of
strengthening the Armenian state and extending its rule
over a large part of Eastern Anatolia. In contrast to its Transcaucasian neighbors, Georgia and Azerbaijan, which in Allied
eyes were tainted as collaborators of the defeated enemy
powers, Armenia stood a loyal and martyred nation. The
holocaust elicited expressions of outrage and promises of res-
titution in every Allied country.[70] Again, however, European
wishes and policies were not accompanied by military means
to enforce their plans. The Allies failed to secure demobiliza-
tion of the remnants of the Ottoman army and the British
evacuated Transcaucasia after a brief occupation. The Turkish forces, reorganized under Mustafa Kemal, not only
regained control of Eastern Anatolia but, defeating Armenians, moved into the former Russian Armenia and threatened the capital city of Erevan. Meanwhile, a Bolshevik force
from Azerbaijan had also closed in on Erevan, allegedly to
save Armenia from Turkish occupation. The government of
the Republic of Armenia, on the verge of total defeat by the
Turks, agreed on December 2, 1920 to relinquish power to
the Bolsheviks who seemed to be the only force capable of
stopping the Turks. As Walker and Lang put it, they decided
to be "better Red than dead."[71] Thus the Soviet Republic of
Armenia was born and joined the Soviet Union.[72]

Whether the Soviet occupation of Erevan and the establishment of the Soviet Republic was indeed a rescue mission
aimed at stopping the Turkish offensive or was tacitly coordinated with the Turks in order to partition Armenian territories, the result was the termination of the short experience
of Armenian independence. The Soviet Republic of Armenia
was formed on a territory even smaller than the area ruled by

the Russians before World War I and covered about one-tenth of what Armenians considered their historic homeland (see map 3). It included the political capital Erevan and the religious center of Echmiadzin, but it left the Armenian national symbol, Mt. Ararat, just beyond the border, rising above Erevan but still cruelly beyond reach, a constant source of frustration for Armenians.

The events of the late nineteenth and early twentieth century had traumatic effects on Armenian consciousness and community life. Armenian cultural and population centers under Turkish rule were utterly destroyed and survivors of the massacres either fled or were driven from their homeland. Of more than two million Armenians who lived under Ottoman rule, fewer than one million survived and only about 100,000 remained in Turkey,[73] most of them in Istanbul. The rest scattered all over the world. Some took refuge in what later became Soviet Armenia, but many more went to the Americas, France, Iran, and the Arab Middle East. Of a total of five to six million Armenians, 2.5 million now live in the Soviet Republic of Armenia and close to a half million live in other parts of the Soviet Union. Virtually no Armenians remained in present-day Turkish Eastern Anatolia. Other large concentrations of Armenians are found in the United States (500,000), France (200,000), Lebanon (180,000), Syria (150,000) and Iran (200,000).[74] The massacres also brought a great loss of cultural treasures and institutions. Numerous churches and monasteries were ruined; thousands of manuscripts, religious, historical, literary, and artistic works were completely lost. The patriarchate of Aghtamar was destroyed and the Catholicosate of Cilicia had to move to Lebanon together with the remaining Armenians of Cilicia when the French withdrew from the area and handed it to the Kemalist forces in 1922.[75]

Unlike the Jewish genocide of World War II, the massacres committed against Armenians were never acknowledged by the perpetrators. Nor was the holocaust followed by the establishment of a lasting independent national homeland.

The Armenian Republic founded in 1918 could not survive more than two years because of Soviet and Turkish enmity and what Armenians perceive as Allied duplicity. The loss of the independent republic was a further shock to Armenians around the world who already were traumatized by the massacres. National redemption, which could have given some collective meaning to the apocalyptic events that preceded it, remained unaccomplished. Hopes were shattered again, the rebirth did not take place. The holocaust was followed by still another defeat. One can imagine the traumatic effects of such developments on the Armenian collective consciousness. Armenians experienced a deep-seated feeling that a terrible injustice had been committed against their people. They felt that the world neglected them and was uninterested in their plight. Their deep frustration and state of unfulfilled aspirations have persisted to the present and have kept the "Armenian cause" alive in diaspora communities. It is deemed extremely important to maintain the collective memory, to preserve the ethnic identity and culture and to articulate collective grievances and aspirations.[76] This, indirectly, has enabled Armenian political parties to keep a strong hold on community life. Political issues and cleavages related to the events of the early twentieth century have continued to preoccupy future generations and have divided them into rival camps.

The events of the turn of the century also had a strong impact on migration patterns. Armenian migration not only rose in magnitude but also created a completely new type of emigrant. For centuries Armenians had migrated voluntarily in search of better economic opportunities. This entrepreneurial type of emigrant was now replaced by the entirely destitute refugee type, forced out of his country against his will after losing all his belongings and probably most of his family. Unlike the earlier emigrants who usually had means to care for themselves, the new emigrants were in desperate need of emergency welfare and comfort. This situation gave impetus to a great development of welfare work in the Armenian communities. Each community became highly conscious of the need to organize its efforts to help and absorb refugees. International Armenian welfare associations played a major role in financing and coordinating the welfare activities in different communities.

Prominent among the Armenian charitable organizations is the Armenian General Benevolent Union (AGBU) founded in Egypt in 1906 by Boghos Nubar, whose father Nubar Pasha had served as Egyptian Prime Minister.[77] The AGBU opened local chapters in Armenian communities around the world, while its center moved from Egypt successively to France, Switzerland, and after World War II, to the United States where its richest local chapters were located. Through its local chapters, the AGBU provided considerable financial support to charitable and cultural services in Armenian communities. It also sponsored a repatriation drive in which thousands of Armenians emigrated to Soviet Armenia in the interwar years and again after World War II. The close ties that the AGBU maintained with Soviet Armenia came under criticism in certain sectors of the Armenian diaspora. The AGBU has been informally affiliated with the Ramgavar party.

The main rival of the AGBU, the Armenian Relief Society, was formed before World War I by Dashnak supporters, but it did not match the AGBU's financial strength and prominence as a charitable organization.[78] A third important dispenser of welfare to Armenian communities has been the Gulbenkian Fund, created upon the will of the Armenian oil magnate Calouste Gulbenkian. The Gulbenkian Fund, unlike the other two organizations, is an international philanthropic enterprise, run partly by non-Armenians, that finances non-Armenian as well as Armenian projects, though the latter receive a disproportionately large share of the funds.[79] In addition to these three major organizations there are many smaller local welfare associations in Armenian communities. Indeed, welfare and cultural associations have acquired an unprecedented influence in community affairs as a legacy of the upheavals these communities have experienced since the turn of the century. Non-Apostolic Armenians, mainly Protestant Armenians from the United States, have been very active in Armenian welfare associations. Because the Armenian Apostolic church is so pivotal in community affairs, however, and so closely identified with Armenian culture and history, the welfare associations always have worked in close cooperation with the church rather than as an alternative to its leadership in the community.[80]

THE BIG RIFT IN THE ARMENIAN COMMUNITIES

While the Armenian communities in the diaspora were adjusting to the influx of refugees, the events related to the creation of the independent Armenian Republic and its replacement by the Soviet Armenian Republic caused a deep rift within them. With the establishment of the Soviet Armenian Republic, Armenians had lost the brief total independence gained between 1918 and 1920. Nonetheless an autonomous Armenian homeland was created, and could be considered as a national nucleus and center of attraction for all Armenians around the world. However, that would have also legitimized the Communist regime and Russian control over Armenia, and a sector of the Armenian population was unwilling to grant such legitimacy to Soviet Armenia. This opposition found expression in Dashnak party policies. As ardent nationalists, the Dashnakists could not tolerate the fact that Armenia was not truly independent. They were the ruling element in the short-lived independent republic and fell from power when it was replaced by Soviet Armenia. In 1921 they led an uprising against the Soviet government that temporarily succeeded in toppling it, until Red Army units reconquered Armenia and reestablished the Soviet regime later that year. Thousands of Dashnak supporters were killed or fled across the border to Persia.[81] Henceforth the Dashnak party remained in strong opposition to the Soviet Armenian regime.

While the Dashnakists were inconsolable at the loss of the independent republic and could not bring themselves to recognize the Soviet regime, other political groups less emotionally attached to the independent republic favored the strengthening of Soviet Armenia as the only existing representative of Armenian national aspirations and culture. These groups had not participated in the government of the independent republic and hence saw that brief episode basically as a Dashnak affair. Small groups with leftist sympathies, such as the Hunchakists and Communists, obviously favored the legitimizing of the Soviet Armenian regime for ideological reasons. But even the much more influential liberal Ramgavar party adopted a pro-Soviet Armenia approach, out of practical reality. The Ramgavar was not involved in the events that led to the formation and demise of the independent republic. Although it disliked the Soviet regime, the Ramgavar supported it as the only existing territorial nucleus of Armenian national identity. While the fight to regain lost territories in Eastern Anatolia was not renounced, emphasis was put on strengthening the single area where some Armenian self-rule existed. The ideologically lax Ramgavar was less bothered by the ideological tendencies of the Soviet Armenian regime. The Ramgavar moved from a neutral attitude to increasingly closer ties with the Soviet Republic. The AGBU which was affiliated with it invested large sums in Soviet Armenia, first in temporary relief efforts and later in long-range economic and educational development.[82]

There has been considerable fluctuation in the policies of the Soviet government in Armenia. At first the government conducted a strong antichurch policy that was considered by Armenians in the diaspora to be an antinational policy. In the 1920s all religious institutions were taken over by the government, the theological seminary was closed, church publications and the study of religion were banned.[83] The government also encouraged the formation of reformist splinter groups within the church in order to weaken the religious establishment.[84] A thawing of relations between the church and government occurred in the late 1920s and early 1930s, as the Soviet Union gained more respectability on the international scene. The Soviet government realized the economic and political advantages of promoting Soviet Armenia as a cultural nucleus and showcase for Armenians living in Western countries. This policy was interrupted in the late 1930s by the Stalinist purges, which hit the Armenian clergy hard, but it resumed after World War II. In 1945 a new Catholicos of Echmiadzin was elected with the participation of delegates from Western countries and the church gained back some of its lost power: the theological seminary was reopened, the church's official publications reappeared, and many churches including the Cathedral of Echmiadzin were restored. The rapprochement between the church and the Soviet Armenian government has increased since the election of the present Catholicos, Vasken I, in 1955. There has been a revival of religious life in Armenia and the church cooperated closely with the Soviet government in the attempt to make Soviet Armenia a showpiece for Armenians throughout the world.[85]

As part of this "showcase policy," the Soviet leadership also encouraged immigration of Armenians from other parts of the world to Soviet Armenia. This move was enthusiastically supported and financially backed by the AGBU, which saw in it both a partial solution to the problem of homeless refugees and a means of strengthening Soviet Armenia as the territorial nucleus of Armenian national culture and identity. Ten thousand Armenians emigrated to Soviet Armenia between 1930 and 1936, most of them from the refugee camps of the Middle East; 88,000 emigrated between 1945 and 1948, again most were from the Middle East and the Balkans.[86] The repatriation drive ended in 1950 when the Soviet government lost interest in it, but some immigration has continued up to the present, mainly from northern Iran.[87] Immigrants from the diaspora, generally, were not well integrated in Soviet Armenia.[88] They remained strangers, regarded with suspicion by the local population. Linguistic differences between immigrants, most of whom came from western (Ottoman) provinces, and local (eastern) Armenians added to this feeling. The immigrants also suffered economic hardships (even though some help was offered to them in matters of housing and employment) and did not adjust easily to the communist political system.

The split among diaspora Armenians on the attitude toward Soviet Armenia had very deep repercussions on their community life. The opposing factions mobilized support in each community through services in nonpolitical fields. The welfare organizations associated with the Ramgavar and the Dashnak have been mentioned already. Each group also had its own youth movement, cultural club, sports organization, and newspapers and publishing houses for propagating its views. While these organizations predated the split among diaspora Armenians, when it occurred they gained additional importance and were put to use by each side. All aspects of Armenian community life in the diaspora, from welfare and social gatherings to cultural and artistic work, came to be dominated by the two antagonistic political groups. Political differences drew the lines of social allegiances, making the split much more pervasive. The two factions competed in providing community services, and members of one group rarely attended social affairs of the other. The split also was transmitted to members of the next generation who followed one or the other group as a "family tradition," because their closest friends and relatives all belonged there.[89] In Atamian's words:

> Each political orientation developed around it a following in the community. The charities, musical and literary activities, the social picnics and outings, the very important political rallies and meetings, the educational lectures—all took place in a segmented community in which the adherents of one party, as a rule, did not attend any affairs or participate in the activities of another party.[90]

Very few people could remain uncommitted to one of the groups; participation became a virtual necessity if one wanted to be involved in community affairs. As such, certain symbols gained increased value, not because of their political importance but as collective identity symbols binding the followers to the group. The Dashnak supporters, for example, revered the flag of the independent Armenian Republic and celebrated May 28, the day of the Republic's formation, as "independence day." The Ramgavar and other anti-Dashnak groups, in contrast, recognized the Soviet Armenian flag and celebrated independence day on the day of the Soviet takeover of Armenia. Opposing celebrations, complete with songs and processions, often turned into bitter confrontations between the two groups and further deepened the split.[91] The parties, however, were not involved in the politics of the host country; they dealt only with matters internal to the Armenian community.

The church could not remain unaffected by this rift within the Armenian community. The clergy was deeply divided along the same political lines as were the laymen. Because the supreme religious authority, the Catholicosate of Echmiadzin, was now under Soviet rule, its survival depended on some accommodation with the Soviet government. This drew sharp criticism from the pro-Dashnak circles, which decried the church's loss of independence and accused the Echmiadzin hierarchy of being a Soviet tool.[92] The conflict between the Dashnakists and Echmiadzin turned violent in 1933, when the Armenian primate of the United States was killed, allegedly by a Dashnak follower, as a result of controversies that arose from the primate's refusal to officiate under the flag of the former republic. In the aftermath of this incident, a formal split occurred between Echmiadzin and the pro-Dashnak elements in the United States. The pro-Dashnak clergymen formed their own church and refused to recognize Echmiadzin's authority. Two rival Armenian Apostolic churches thus came into existence in North America and started long and protracted fights for the control of followers and church property.[93] For a time, the pro-Dashnak church was effectively boycotted by the pro-Echmiadzin church hierarchy, but in 1956 when pro-

Dashnak clergymen gained a dominant position in the Catholicosate of Cilicia (over the strong opposition and active intervention of the Catholicos of Echmiadzin)[94] the pro-Dashnak Church of North America became affiliated with the Catholicosate of Cilicia, thus solving its problems of religious legitimacy and recruitment of clergymen. However this further exacerbated the conflict by creating a parallel between the attitude to adopt toward Soviet Armenia and the centuries-old dispute on religious authority between Cilicia and Echmiadzin.[95] Echmiadzin and Cilicia fought for the control of churches and parishes not only in North America but also in Syria, Iran, and Greece. In Syria the Baath government's closeness to the Soviet Union and its conflict with Lebanon, where the pro-Dashnak faction was dominant, created an unfavorable situation for the pro-Dashnak Catholicosate of Cilicia. A number of Syrian Dashnakist leaders were arrested and accused of political subversion and the Catholicos of Cilicia lost a degree of control over its Syrian dioceses.[96] In Iran and Greece, by contrast, the pro-Western tendencies of the regimes then existing enabled the Dashnakists and the Catholicos of Cilicia to challenge Echmiadzin's control over the local dioceses. In these areas not even religious services were insulated from the basic split that divided the community. Lately, the rift has attenuated somewhat. Younger leaders of the two camps feel closer to each other and are more united in their anti-Turkish feelings, while their attitude toward the Soviet Union has taken a back seat. The basic division, however, still exists and profoundly affects the Armenian community life in the diaspora.[97]

Paradoxically, just when the death of more than a million Armenians between the 1890s and the 1920s reinforced Armenian national consciousness and coalesced them into tightly knit communities around the world, the aftermath of those tragic events created a basic division within each community. Just as Armenians gained a new sensitivity to their ethnicity as a result of their traumatic experience and realized the common fate that separates them from non-Armenians, a deep schism occurred among them. Perhaps the schism itself was the result of the new sensitivity to the nation's plight. The choice of an attitude toward Soviet Armenia was a central focus of collective attention but one on which no consensus existed. Deep interest in the subject, without a common approach, was bound to engender deep disagreements. It also strengthened a core of high ethnicity by providing both sides with a political-ideological rationale for maintaining great interest and involvement in Armenian affairs.[98]

3

Armenians in Jerusalem:
Historical Background

CONTROL OVER HOLY PLACES

The Armenian presence in Jerusalem can be traced back in history to the first centuries of the Christian era. Armenian mosaics, probably dating from the fifth century, are the oldest relics of the Armenian presence in the city, and it is widely believed that there has been an uninterrupted Armenian community living in Jerusalem since that time.[1] The early conversion of Armenians to Christianity made them very prominent among the early Christian inhabitants of Jerusalem. They were among the first pilgrims and monks to arrive in the Holy Land. At first they shared hostels and monasteries with other monks and pilgrims and only later did each nationality build its own institutions. Vardapet Anastas, who made a pilgrimage from Armenia to Palestine in the seventh century, has left a list of seventy Armenian monasteries then in existence in Jerusalem and its surroundings.[2] The Armenian propensity to migrate for commercial purposes might have given further impetus to their presence in Jerusalem, as traders accompanying the many visitors who arrived for religious purposes. In those days Armenian trade colonies were found in a string of cities linking Armenia to Palestine.[3]

The Armenians were active participants in the great efforts to construct religious edifices in the Holy Land following Byzantine Queen Helena's allegedly "miraculous" rediscovery of sites sacred to Christianity in A.D. 324. At first, the Armenians cooperated closely with the Greeks; the effects of the Monophysite controversy were rather late in coming to Jerusalem. Heterogeneous Christian communities remained united under the authority of the Bishop of Jerusalem for about a century after the Council of Chalcedon. When the split occurred in the late sixth century, the Armenians were subjected to some discrimination by Byzantine rulers and lost some of their religious institutions to the Greeks, but Byzantine pressure over Armenians in Jerusalem was cut short by the Arab conquest of the city in A.D. 638.[4] In any case, the Armenians' early prominence among Christians enabled them to gain control of places sacred to Christianity. The history of their presence in Jerusalem is one of constant struggle with other Christian churches for control of the Holy Places, the outcome of the struggle determined mainly by which side gained the favor of ruling authorities. For most of its history since Roman times, the fate of Jerusalem and its inhabitants was most often controlled by states that originated and were centered far from the city. As a religious center of utmost importance it attracted the attention of various populations and cultures, yet it also was very dependent on external political centers and was used as an instrument of political struggle between them.

Greek Orthodox and Armenian churches have contradictory claims on the rights conferred on them by the Arabs. Armenian sources allege that, predicting the Arab invasion, the head of the Armenian church traveled to Mecca and received from the Prophet Muhammad an edict that safeguarded the life and property of Armenians living in Jerusalem and recognized their church's rights over all religious sanctuaries under its control. These promises were confirmed, according to Armenian sources, by another edict issued by the Caliph Umar upon his conquest of Jerusalem.[5]

The Greeks, however, also have their own edicts showing that Caliph Umar entrusted to them custody of the Holy Places. Scholars doubt the authenticity of these documents, which could have been fabricated to support rival claims to Christian sanctuaries.[6] Authentic or not, the documents indeed were used by other Muslim rulers in following centuries as bases for conferring rights on holy places to the rival Christian churches. They also reflected the general Muslim policy toward Christian subjects, allowing them to pursue their religious beliefs and control their religious institutions. Under Arab rule the Armenian church's stature in Jerusalem nominally equaled that of the Greek Orthodox; the association of the latter with the Byzantine empire rendered it suspect in the eyes of the rulers. Sanjian reports, however, that Armenians lost a substantial number of their holdings during this period, partly as a result of continued Greek efforts to obtain control over them and partly because the Armenians could not pay the excessive taxes imposed on those holdings by the Arab rulers.[7]

The position of Armenians in Jerusalem improved considerably under the rule of the Crusaders because of close cooperation between Latin kingdoms of the Levant and the Armenian kingdom of Cilicia.[8] Armenians profited from their prominence to enlarge their possessions and the most important addition has been their present center, the Church of Saint James near Mount Zion, at the site where James the Minor, first bishop of Jerusalem, lived and was buried. It was also believed that the head of James the Major, brother of John Evangelist, was buried at the same place after he had been beheaded by Herod Agrippa in A.D. 44.[9] A Georgian Greek Orthodox church that existed in this place was ceded to the Armenians in the eleventh or twelfth century; over this structure the Armenians built a cathedral and a large monastery that became headquarters for the Armenian presence in the Holy Land.[10] The clergymen were organized into a monastic order called the Brotherhood of Saint James.[11] Living accommodations were built within the monastery, not only for the benefit of the priests but also for the numerous Armenian pilgrims who arrived annually, most of them from Cilicia. At the time of the Crusaders the secular Armenian colony also grew considerably. As elsewhere, the Armenians of Jerusalem were prominent in trades and it seems that they had a market of their own.[12]

It is not clear when the head of the Armenian church in Jerusalem was elevated to the rank of patriarch. The Armenian sources consider Bishop Abraham, who lived in the mid-seventh century, to have been the first patriarch. The edict of Caliph Umar indeed refers to him as patriarch, but that might be a general term used by Muslims for all heads of Christian churches. There is no mention of the title patriarch for the followers of Abraham who headed the church for the next several centuries. Most foreign and some Armenian sources claim that the patriarchate was established much later, perhaps in the eleventh century, or more likely in the fourteenth century (1311) when the Saint James Brotherhood refused to accept the latinophile policies of the Catholicosate of Cilicia and proclaimed its head, Sarkis, patriarch in order to assert its independence from that Catholicosate.[13] In any event, whether formally called patriarchate or not, the separate identity of the Armenian church in Jerusalem was crystallized in the seventh century as a result of the Monophysite controversy, and it was greatly strengthened in the eleventh or twelfth centuries when it acquired its present headquarters, built the Saint James monastery, and organized the monastic brotherhood that became the guardian of the Armenian-controlled Holy Places.

The favorable situation of the Armenians changed little when Jerusalem was conquered by Salahaddin Ayubi. Perhaps Salahaddin showed special favor toward Armenians because, in his enmity toward both the Latins and the Greeks, he found it expedient to favor a rival church at their expense. Salahaddin recognized the charters given to the Armenians by previous Muslim rulers. The Armenian residents of Jerusalem, numbering about 1,500 at the time, were exempted from the ransom money and head tax demanded from Christians who had come to the city with the Crusaders.[14] Following the Ayubi rule, the city as a whole suffered from a period of political instability. In 1300, Hethum II, Armenian king of Cilicia, conquered Jerusalem and held it for three years. Shortly thereafter Palestine, and later Cilicia itself, fell under Mamluke rule, which like its Muslim predecessors safeguarded the religious rights of the Christian communities. Under Mamluke rule Armenians successfully withstood Georgian attempts to retake the Church of Saint James, but they had to relinquish to them (and eventually to the Greek Orthodox church) parts of the Holy Sepulchre.[15]

The Ottoman rule that replaced the Mamlukes at first brought little change to Christian churches in Jerusalem. The Ottomans guaranteed each group its respective possessions of the holy sites and the security of their community. The charter given to the Armenians also put the other Monophysite churches (the Jacobite, Coptic, and Ethiopian) under their dependence. This dependence existed under previous Muslim rulers but was more institutionalized by the Ottoman millet system. Today the dependence is maintained at a symbolic level, as I witnessed in the traditional visit paid to the Armenian patriarch by the heads of the Coptic, Ethiopian and Jacobite churches during Easter celebrations in which they offer him their respective bundles of Holy Fire candles.[16]

Even though Ottoman rule at first did little more than sanction the status quo, the four centuries of their rule in Jerusalem were to witness major struggles between rival churches for control of the Holy Places. The Greek Orthodox and Latin churches made great efforts to extend their holdings at the expense of other churches. The Greek Orthodox was favored by the Ottomans because most of its followers were Ottoman subjects, while the Latins were subjects of foreign governments often at war with the Ottomans. By favoring the Greek Orthodox the Ottomans were in effect protecting their own citizens' interest against foreigners. Often such considerations were set aside by the heavy presents and bribes conferred by all sides on the Turkish officials.[17] Decisions often were made and reversed by changing sums of bribes. In the eighteenth and nineteenth centuries, with the decline of Ottoman power, support of foreign powers became an asset rather than a liability. European powers became increasingly involved in the struggle among the churches, France and Austria usually siding with the Latins, while Russia protected the interests of the Greek Orthodox. During this period the struggle for the control of Christian holy places, like Christian rights elsewhere in the Ottoman empire, became an important issue on the European diplomatic scene. International crises were caused by it (such as those leading to the Crimean War) and international treaties included clauses on it (such as the Treaty of Paris in 1855 and of Berlin in 1878).[18] After centuries of relative neglect, the city of Jerusalem thus gained a political importance more reminiscent of contemporary times. In this regard Armenians were severely handicapped without a foreign power to patronize their cause. Heavy bribes to local Ottoman officials and influence of Armenian bankers in Istanbul were often used to offset adverse influences. As a nineteenth-century traveler put it:

> The Greeks and Latins both enjoy the countenance of powerful European monarchs whence they derive an importance at Constantinople which, independent of this, they would not possess: the Armenians make up by their wealth what they lack in this respect and are thus able to sway the decisions of the Porte.[19]

On the whole, the Armenians waged a long and sometimes losing battle against encroachments by the Greek Orthodox and the Latins. They lost some privileges in the Holy Sepulchre as well as control of some other sites, though less than other Eastern churches.[20] In three separate instances (from 1616 to 1659, 1734 to 1739, and 1808 to 1813) the Armenians came close to losing their own center, the Saint James Monastery, to the Greeks.[21] (Indeed, they did lose control of the monastery to the Greeks for eighteen months during 1658 and 1659.) The last threat, in the nineteenth century, was averted by Sultan Mahmud II's edict of 1813. Shortly afterward, in 1852, Sultan Abdulmejid issued the famous *firman of status quo*, which rejected any further demands for changes in the different churches' control over Holy Places.[22] The firman of status quo was observed scrupulously in the remaining years of Ottoman rule and in succeeding British, Jordanian, and Israeli rules. It became the centerpiece regulating relations between different churches and communities in Jerusalem. What privileges and possessions each community had acquired by the 1850s remained theirs to this day.[23] Nevertheless, great tension persisted between rival Christian churches, especially in the sites under joint control. Disputes often erupted on the use of lamps, decorations, pictures, on cleaning and repairing parts of the sanctuaries, and on prompt and unfailing performance of religious services, since all of these were used as symbols of control and laxity in these matters could lead to a weakening of rights by default.[24] For example:

> In 1924 there was a dispute over the right to dust the door leading to the Coptic courtyard between Columns 10 and 11. The Armenians claimed full ownership of the section and of the courtyard and, therefore, contended that dusting their doors was their right. The Copts demanded the right to dust the doors. The Mandatory Government ultimately accepted the Armenian contention.[25]

Such tension has continued up to the present and is most apparent on those occasions, such as Easter festivities, when the largest number of pilgrims arrive at Jerusalem and several denominations hold services simultaneously in the Holy Sepulchre. Each church tries to surpass the other in pomp and is very sensitive to the rights conferred on it by the status quo agreement as to its territory and the precise order and procedure of the services. I personally witnessed fist-fights between rival groups, including respective clergymen, during Easter festivities in 1977. It is, therefore, not surprising that my Armenian informants unanimously declared their dislike of the Easter services in the Holy Sepulchre, much preferring the one in their own Saint James Cathedral where their dominance is not questioned.[26]

THE RELIGIOUS AND LAY COMMUNITIES

The Armenian community of Jerusalem was basically a religious community. Its very existence and activities were motivated by religious considerations and had religious legitimation. The core of the community was the monastic brotherhood of Saint James. Members of the brotherhood retained their membership and were considered part of the community even when, fulfilling religious duties in other places, they did not actually reside in Jerusalem. They came for frequent visits and were received with great honor. Even now, when nonresident members of the Saint James brotherhood come to visit Jerusalem, they are subject to ceremonial reception depending on their rank.[27] The monastery was also an important place of religious learning and spiritual communication, though the constant flow of pilgrims and the continuous political battles that had to be fought with rival churches did not enable the development of a secluded monastic life as it existed in other monasteries in the Middle East and in Armenia.[28]

Notwithstanding its special religious features, the Armenian community of Jerusalem was also a lay community. There have always been laymen permanently settled in Jerusalem, their numbers ranging from a few dozen at one time to a few thousand at another. Among the Armenian laymen now living in Jerusalem are a few families who can trace back their residence in the city 300 to 500 years; and there is one family that claims to have been in the city since the establishment of the present monastery in the eleventh or twelfth century.[29] Many of the lay settlers were pilgrims who decided to remain permanently in the city, either from religious motivations or because they could not afford the journey back home. Others might have come in the course of their pursuits of better economic opportunities, though Jerusalem, despite its steady flow of visitors, never distinguished itself as an economic or commercial center. The church was very interested in having a large community in the city, because that buttressed its claims for control of the Holy Places. For this reason, the church encouraged the pilgrims to stay permanently. When the number of laymen fell to dangerously low levels, the church asked Armenian princes and feudal lords to send scores of subjects and dependents to settle in Jerusalem and regenerate the secular community.

Some of the laymen were employed by the church, mostly in menial jobs, such as guards, cleaners, and cooks, but a few also held high-ranking administrative positions in the patriarchate. Others had independent occupations but also served the church as traders, craftsmen, and in services offered to pilgrims. Lay families were customarily offered certain ceremonial functions in religious services such as carrying flags and banners or the holy fire during Easter celebrations. Such ceremonial functions were considered great honors and were scrupulously preserved by families who passed them on to their descendants. Lay families still can be seen performing these functions in major holiday religious services.[30] In the nineteenth century Armenians occupied top economic positions in Jerusalem due to their Western education and business acumen. As such, many Armenians became representatives of foreign companies and a few even served as consuls for Western powers such as Austro-Hungary and Prussia. The Austrian post office, the first post and telegraphic office to operate in Palestine in 1869, was located in the Armenian quarter and staffed by Armenians.[31]

Laymen lived clustered around the monastery, but it is not clear whether some also lived inside the monastery or whether the monastery compound was reserved only for clergymen and pilgrims. We do know that, following great construction activities in the seventeenth century, enough space was created within the monastery to accommodate about 2,000 pilgrims.[32] Some of the pilgrims lived for a long time in those quarters within the monastery compound, but it seems that they moved out to buildings located on the street surrounding the monastery walls when they finally decided to settle permanently in the city.[33] As visitors they did not disturb the sacredness of the place, but as permanent residents it was apparently preferable that they move outside the walls.

FUNCTIONS PERFORMED BY THE MONASTERY

The Armenian monastery of Saint James performed myriad functions, some more properly religious than others. Above all it was the guardian of the Holy Places, preventing them from falling into non-Christian or, almost as bad, other Christian hands. The control exerted over holy places had great symbolic significance and went far beyond the provision of services to pilgrims or to monks, clergymen, or followers established in the area. Performing religious services in the holy sites and maintaining religious edifices linked the church and its followers to the "core" from which truth and order emanated. They made the church more genuinely Christian, they legitimized it in the eyes of its followers and other Christians living in distant lands. As Wardi wrote about the Latin patriarchate:

> The Patriarch of Jerusalem is in charge not only of the interests of the Catholic community of Palestine, but also of the Catholic World's interest in Palestine. His Diocese is the Holy Land to which the thoughts of millions of Catholics all over the world turn in love and reverence.[34]

Holy sites constituted the preeminent link between the sacred and the profane, between meaning and randomness. Representing the transcendental realm, they continually resanctified the world.[35] As in many other examples of religious or historical sites, we see here the symbolic significance attributed to a territorial link, which in this case gained added importance because it was carried out in a competitive framework. Different churches competed with each other for prominence in the eyes of all believers. Physical presence or link with the holy site enhanced the stature of the church throughout Christendom. For most churches this stature was also instrumental in propagating their creed at the expense of their rivals. The Armenians, in contrast, had no such goal. Yet, the separate identity of their church was so closely related to their national identity that custody of the Holy Places linked them indirectly to the legitimizing core of their national existence as well. Even though they were located far away from the Armenian homeland and cultural zone, the Holy Places of Jerusalem were of primary importance as symbols of national identity.

Closely related to its function as custodian of the Holy Places, the monastery facilitated pilgrimages to the holy sites by guiding and protecting pilgrims, as well as by supplying living accommodations and religious services. Every year about 2,000 pilgrims arrived in Jerusalem, most of them from nearby Cilicia. It was customary for those pilgrims who could afford it to bring lavish presents to the monastery, which in turn mobilized its resources to supply the pilgrims with the best possible facilities. The contributions received from pilgrims constituted the patriarchate's most important revenue despite the fact that some pilgrims had no financial means and had to be taken care of by the monastery. In addition to financial donations, many pilgrims brought to Jerusalem precious ecclesiastical vestments and ornaments that make up part of the patriarchate's present treasury.[36]

The wealth of the churches, the sumptuousness of their religious services, the beauty of their decorations or sacred vestments had an important bearing on the church's socio-religious standing in the Holy Land and, through impressed pilgrims returning to their home, in the Christian world as a whole. Each church tried its best to create an impressive public face. Making up for its other disadvantages, the Armenian church hardly ever let itself be surpassed by its rivals in this repect. As a nineteenth-century traveler noted:

> But the decorations of the Armenian Church of Saint James are nowhere equalled in richness and their sacred vestments are peculiarly splendid: the great wealth of the community and the universal interest felt concerning Jerusalem allowing them to provide for the public service of God more sumptuously than any other communion.[37]

The pilgrims were taken under the care of the patriarchate as they entered Palestine. Monasteries and hospices were built in the port of Jaffa where most pilgrims coming by sea route landed and in the town of Ramla, the principal way-station between the coast and Jerusalem. There, pilgrims were given accommodations and their transportation to Jerusalem was arranged by the patriarchate. While they were asked to pay for all these services, the amount varied according to their economic means.[38]

The monastery of St. James was also an educational and cultural center. Sanjian claims that Jerusalem did not distinguish itself as a center of learning and scholarship compared to other Armenian monasteries.[39] Nonetheless, pilgrimage to the Holy Land offered special opportunities for the meeting of prominent scholars, writers, and religious thinkers. Often the patriarchate took advantage of an eminent scholar's visit to Jerusalem and prevailed upon him to remain in the city for a number of years and offer religious instruction. Until the mid-nineteenth century education was conducted informally, with pupils gathered around a scholar of renown to study, so to speak, at his feet.[40] These educational functions were institutionalized in 1843 with the establishment of a seminary for priests. After functioning for two years in the Saint

George monastery in Ramla, the seminary was moved to Jerusalem and established within the monastery compound. Seminary students, from Egypt, Syria, and Lebanon, were given living quarters in rooms originally intended for pilgrims, and they formed an important new component of the monastery population. Until World War I the seminary failed to achieve high academic standards, but after its reopening in 1920 (following closure during the war) it was completely reorganized, better teachers were brought in (some fleeing the massacres in Anatolia), and it emerged as one of the most important centers of religious learning. It is now a major center, training priests for all the Armenian communities in the world.[41] The patriarchate also set up parochial schools for the children of the lay community in areas under its jurisdiction. A school for boys was founded in 1846 in Jerusalem, followed by a school for girls in 1862. In 1929 the Saint Tarkmanchatz (Holy Translators) School for boys and girls replaced the other parochial schools. Schools also were opened in other urban centers that depended on the patriarchate.[42]

In addition to its educational functions, the monastery also emerged as a general cultural center for the Armenian people. Many literary and art works were created by the residents of the monastery or brought as presents by pilgrims. The monastery's collection of Armenian manuscripts and other art and cultural works is second only to that of Echmiadzin.[43] Not only was it spared the destruction that befell similar works located in churches and monasteries in Eastern Anatolia but the Jerusalem collection was enriched when some of those works that could be salvaged were brought to Jerusalem by Armenians fleeing from Anatolia.

The monastery also set the pace in modern cultural developments. A printing press was established in the monastery in 1833 (the first in Jerusalem) and in 1866 a monthly publication called *Sion* began to appear; it became a powerful transmitter of Armenian religious and literary work. As with the seminary, the pre-World War I years of the printing press and of *Sion* were inconspicuous, but their importance rose significantly afterward. Closed during the war, *Sion* reappeared in 1927 and immediatley became the leading Armenian publication on religious, philosophical, literary, and historical topics. The press published the most important Armenian literary works and supplied most of the liturgical books used in Armenian churches around the world.[44] The 1920s and 1930s thus were the years in which the Saint James monastery, relatively unscathed from the destruction that befell other Armenian institutions and communities, emerged as the leading cultural and learning center of the Armenian people.

In addition to the functions mentioned above, the Saint James monastery also performed important communal-administrative tasks. It was the seat of the patriarchate of Jerusalem, which until 1930 had jurisdiction over dioceses in Syria, Lebanon, Cyprus, and Egypt, as well as in Palestine and Transjordan. (In 1929 dioceses in Syria, Lebanon, and Cyprus were handed over to the jurisdiction of the Catholicosate of Cilicia, which had moved to its new location in Antelias near Beirut. Earlier, the Egyptian dioceses passed to the jurisdiction of Echmiadzin.)[45] Moreover, according to the Ottoman millet system, the patriarchate's authority over Armenians under its jurisdiction extended to civil administrative as well as religious matters. The patriarchate was invested with great power by the Ottoman government in the local admnistration of the community (including collection of community taxes in the name of the Ottoman government). In order to exercise its authority, the patriarchate was provided with means of coercion of its own in the form of local guards, police, penitentiaries, and religious courts whose jurisdiction extended to all civil affairs of the community. The religious courts could inflict prison and exile sentences on any member of the community. Police functions, prisons, and far-reaching secular powers of the court were abolished under British rule. The present guards, called *kavas,* who serve now more as doorkeepers, still symbolize those police functions of the past. In ceremonial dress the kavas still carry swords, emblematic of their once coercive power.[46]

Under Ottoman rule the patriarchate of Jerusalem was subordinate to that of Istanbul in administrative functions even though it did not recognize the latter's supremacy in religious affairs or in the formal church hierarchy. Throughout Ottoman rule, relations between the two patriarchates were marred by controversies over the extent of control of the patriarch of Istanbul over Jerusalem's financial affairs, internal administration, and election of new patriarchs.[47] In addition to its administrative subordination to the patriarchate of Istanbul, as forced by the Ottoman government, the patriarchate of Jerusalem also depended on its Istanbul counterpart for financial support, because the principal backers of the Jerusalem community in times of need were wealthy Armenians living in Istanbul. With the end of Ottoman rule after World War I, the patriarchate of Jerusalem gained complete independence from Istanbul. A new constitution gave the monastic brotherhood of Saint James absolute authority to govern its own affairs.[48]

The controversy over the degree of control exerted over Jerusalem by Istanbul was often intermixed with controversies over the degree of democratization of government *within* the patriarchate of Jerusalem and the extent of lay participation in it. Until 1725 the authority of the patriarch of Jerusalem was uncontested within the community. After 1725 a series of reforms granted a share of power to other members of the monastic brotherhood but not to the laymen of the community. The reforms in fact reduced the participation of laymen in the community's governing position as the patriarch's appointees or as supervisors sent from Istanbul.[49] The same trend continued when, under British rule, the patriarchate gained total independence from Istanbul. A large measure of democratization was introduced into the government of the monastic brotherhood, but again laymen were excluded from its administration because the Jerusalem community was considered to be simply a monastic brotherhood governing itself and not a regular lay community. In contrast to all other Armenian communities in the world, democratization in Jerusalem had the paradoxical result of reducing rather than increasing the control of laymen over their own community affairs. A peculiar situation thus emerged in which laymen, as part of the millet, were under the jurisdiction of religious authorities in civil as well as religious matters; but not being part of the religious brotherhood, they could not participate in the administration of the community.

Brief mention should be made of the existence of small numbers of Armenian Catholics and Protestants in Jerusalem. There has been a distinct Armenian Catholic community in Jerusalem for at least two centuries. Even though their numbers never exceeded a few hundred, they succeeded in gaining control of the fourth station on the Via Dolorosa where they established their own religious and communal organization (in the past they also controlled the third station but had to relinquish it to the Poles). Not recognized as a separate millet until 1831, they were persecuted by the Armenian Apostolic church and sought protection of the Latins. In 1831 they were recognized as a separate community and built their own church in 1881. Since 1855 priests have been sent to them from the patriarchate of Catholic Armenians at Bzommar (in Lebanon) on which all Armenian Catholics in the world depend.[50] According to the Catholic Armenian church's registration figures, 693 Catholic Armenians lived in Jerusalem before 1948; their number fell to 171 just before the 1967 war but remained stable (166 people) after 1973.[51]

Catholic Armenians are very similar to their Apostolic kinsmen in stressing their separate identity. They form their own community and religious institutions, being careful to keep their separation from Latin Catholics except for acceptance of the supreme authority of the Pope. Their religious rites and liturgy stress Armenian language and culture and, unlike other Catholics, they engage in no proselytism among non-Armenians, with the result that no arabization has occurred among them.[52] In all these respects Armenian Protestants are in marked contrast to Catholics. Armenian Protestants are a smaller and late-coming group in Jerusalem and hold no control over holy places. Unlike the Catholics, the Protestants do not have a separate religious organization or communal identity of their own. They belong to various Protestant denominations that are open to non-Armenians as well. The Church of the Nazarene, where the greatest concentration of Protestant Armenians is found, is now very strongly arabized. A few Armenian Protestant families are known to live now in the Old City, but they cannot be considered a separate community.[53]

The Armenian Catholic church performs necessary administrative duties incumbent upon it as head of the millet, registering births, deaths, and marriages. At present, however, it cannot hold a religious court for lack of enough priests (there are just two in the community). Therefore, religious litigation (such as in divorce) that occurs within the community is handled by the Latin patriarchate's court. In contrast to the Apostolic church, the Armenian Catholic church does not supply many community services to its followers. The hospice and kindergarten run by the church are open to anybody willing to pay for them and not especially to fellow-Catholic Armenians. Not able to provide community services to its followers, the Armenian Catholic church (or at least its present head) does not seem to mind that they turn to the Apostolic church for them, as "the most important thing is to remain among Armenians."[54] Unlike their Apostolic kinsmen, Catholic Armenians do not live clustered together in or near their church compound. They do maintain their own social club, Arax, which is a principal meeting place and organizes community activity; it is located, free of charge, on the premises of the church's hospice.[55]

RADICAL CHANGES IN THE TWENTIETH CENTURY

The lay Armenian population of Jerusalem underwent very important changes at the turn of the twentieth century with the arrival of refugees from the persecutions in Anatolia. Their influx reached its climax during and immediately after World War I. It seems that the period that preceded those events was one of rather low Armenian population. Ben Arieh reports about 500 Armenians living in Jerusalem in 1800, the number rising to 550 in 1850 and 640 in 1870.[56] Following the actions against Armenians in the 1890s and in 1908, the number of Armenians in Jerusalem started to rise and reached about 1,300 in 1910.[57] These numbers were insignificant compared to the flood of refugees in the next ten years. By 1920 about 10,000 Armenian refugees had arrived in Palestine.[58] Almost all the newcomers were completely destitute; having lost their families and all their belongings, they were sent to Jerusalem from the refugee camps of Syria, Lebanon, and Iraq where they had received temporary relief. As the patriarchate of Jerusalem was situated nearby, with accommodation facilities usually reserved for pilgrims or visiting clergymen, it became a major recipient of the overflow of refugees. All those coming to Palestine were cared for by the monastery and about 4,000 were given shelter within its compound which was transformed, in effect, into a large refugee camp.[59]

This new population showed striking differences from other laymen who had settled in Jerusalem in earlier times. The refugees did not come to Jerusalem out of religious motivation nor were they in pursuit of better economic opportunities. They had fled their country for sheer physical survival. All were traumatized by the massacres, but they were also very sensitive to their collective, as well as personal, plight. While less religious than their predecessors, they generally felt a stronger national consciousness. Some had participated in the Armenian nationalist movements and had even fought against the Turks. Unlike the local laymen who, through long years of living in Jerusalem, had been acculturated to their Arabic environment, this group had few cultural or other ties with the new environment. Their cultural ties were with their country of origin and, despite their virulent anti-

Turkish feelings, many of them in fact spoke Turkish as their first language.[60] They also arrived in much larger numbers and under far more difficult conditions than their predecessors. They were completely uprooted, having lost their closest friends and relatives. Their movement was sudden, without any of the careful planning and preparations that characterize most pilgrimages and voluntary migrations, and because of the sheer numbers and suddenness of their arrival, the patriarchate was less ready to receive them. Unlike the other laymen who lived around the monastery, the World War I refugees were settled inside, under much more crowded conditions and in complete dependence on welfare from the monastery.

Most of the World War I refugees remained within the monastery for only a short time. The great majority was sent on to, or left for, other countries.[61] Of those who remained in Palestine, some moved to other towns or to the new neighborhoods in Jerusalem. In the thirty years of British mandate, these refugees displayed a great ability to recover from their plight and to improve their economic positions through aggressive entrepreneurship, business flair, and Western educational and professional skills. They served in the mandatory administration. They prospered as representatives of foreign firms or as local shopkeepers. Some wealthy families left the monastery compound and settled in newly built higher-status western neighborhoods outside the Old City.[62] Many more settled in the monastery, however, the temporary relief measures taking on a more permanent nature. The patriarchate continued to dispense help even to those who had improved their economic position.

The monastery was greatly transformed by the existence of a large secular population within its compound. Monks found themselves living in an overcrowded lay community. All territorial distance between clergymen and laymen disappeared, as many of the rooms used by the clergy, as well as gardens and open spaces within the monastery, were converted into housing for refugees. The functions performed by the monastic community also changed considerably. Its communal, administrative extrareligious work expanded greatly. Not only did the monastery respond to the special problems of refugees in desperate need of economic and spiritual help, it also had to provide for the regular needs that any lay residential community would have had. Because the Ottoman millet system was maintained by the British, local administrative matters concerning the new lay population were still the patriarchate's responsibility. The patriarchate also had to supply such services as schools, playgrounds, and cultural and entertainment activities to the new population. A bigger lay school (the Saint Tarkmanchatz School) was opened in 1929 on the site of the old girls' school. From the start it instituted coeducation, quite a novelty for a school run by priests and located within a monastery. Earlier an orphanage was set up inside the monastery for the 100 or so orphan refugees with the financial support of the AGBU. In 1929, again, the Gulbenkian library was opened, with donations from the oil magnate whose name it carried.[63]

The interwar years also saw the establishment of the first secular social clubs among the Armenians of Jerusalem. While the initiative for the formation of these clubs came from laymen, the buildings used for their activities belonged to the monastery. The first club, the Benevolent Union, was opened in 1925 by laymen who had lived in Jerusalem before the refugee influx. Its formation no doubt responded to their need to assert a separate identity vis-à-vis the refugees. Later, two other social clubs were formed by refugees within the monastery compound: Hoyetchmen was formed in 1929 in Haifa and moved to Jerusalem a few years later and Homenetmen was founded in Jaffa in 1935 and moved to Jerusalem the next year. Unlike the apolitical Benevolent Union, these clubs were informally affiliated with Armenian nationalist movements. This also showed the greater politicization of the refugees compared to the pre-World War I local population.[64]

The Armenian community of Palestine was shattered again by the Arab-Israeli war in 1948. With the outbreak of the war nearly all Armenians who lived in the coastal towns and new neighborhoods of Jerusalem took shelter within the monastery in response to the patriarch's call.[65] During the war the monastery suffered from its location near the fire zone between Israeli and Arab lines. Stray shells and bullets fell on the monastery, killing about thirty people. After the war those refugees who fled from areas that remained on the Israeli side could not return to their homes. Their property, like that of Arab refugees, was confiscated by the Israeli government and put under the charge of the Custodian of Abandoned Property.[66] The monastery was faced with a new wave of homeless refugees, some of whom had left it recently only to become refugees again. This time the patriarchate had more limited resources to help them. Most housing within the monastery already was occupied by the previous (World War I) wave of refugees, and the bulk of the monastery's assets remained across the border, frozen by the Israeli government. In 1949 the latter agreed that assets of religious institutions be released from the Custodian of Abandoned Property and part of their income be transferred to Jordan while the balance remain in Israeli banks.[67] This decision brought a partial improvement in the Armenian patriarchate's financial situation, though it obviously was insufficient to cover the additional expenses incurred by the new flow of refugees. Further support was obtained from wealthy Armenian communities in the diaspora and especially from international Armenian welfare organizations, such as the AGBU, the Armenian Relief Society, and the Gulbenkian Fund.[68]

The 800 or so Armenians who continued to live in Jaffa, Haifa, and the Israeli sector of Jerusalem were cut off from the center of Armenian community life between 1948 and 1967.[69] They were allowed to visit the patriarchate and their relatives living under Jordanian rule only once a year, on

Christmas. The patriarchate kept a resident priest on the Israeli side and leading clergymen frequently crossed from Jordan to visit their kinsmen living in Israel.[70] With the unification of Jerusalem under Israeli rule in 1967, unrestricted contact was resumed between all Armenians and the monastery.

As a result of the 1948 Arab-Israeli War, the members of the Saint James monastic brotherhood found themselves involved in still more extrareligious functions. Their welfare and communal tasks expanded. Clergymen were sent on fundraising tours for the refugees among the diaspora communities. Such tours were not uncommon in the past but were conducted for narrower religious purposes, that is, to secure funds to embellish churches or to bribe officials in order to ensure custody of holy sites. Now the funds were raised mainly for the lay sector of the community.[71] Clergymen also found themselves in the midst of delicate diplomatic relations, having to engage in negotiations across closed borders and to deal with two governments (Israel and Jordan) at war with each other. The unification of Jerusalem under Israeli rule made little change in this diplomatic balancing act, because the future of the city was uncertain and the patriarchate represented an important community living in Amman. On the financial front, however, the unification facilitated the patriarchate's control over its assets in the Israeli sector.

The situation gradually stabilized after 1948. Within a few years most new refugees emigrated to other countries, mainly to Lebanon, Soviet Armenia, and Western countries. Those who remained in Jerusalem were found homes and jobs. Again, as in the 1920s and 1930s, they recovered quickly from their misfortune, improved their economic situation, and became less dependent on direct financial help from the patriarchate, which was discontinued in 1956. Emigration declined with the passing of the emergency, though it has continued up to the present. The refugees from 1948, like their predecessors from World War I, were incorporated into the economy of the Old City and adjusted to life in the Armenian quarter. No significant change seems to have occurred in this respect after Jerusalem was unified under Israeli rule in 1967.[72]

4

The Life of the Lay Community
in Jerusalem

This chapter will examine more closely various aspects of the laymen's life with a view to detecting the special effects of life within the monastery and under its authority. Rather than offer a full descriptive account of the laymen's daily life, my purpose is to analyze those aspects of lay life in which the impact of life within the monastery is most clearly felt and patterns of dependence on the monastery most clearly emerge. As we shall soon find out, however, the monastery offers such a wide-ranging set of services to the lay sector that virtually every aspect of lay community life is affected by them. The pervasiveness of lay dependence on the monastery will indeed be the main theme emerging from this discussion.

HOUSING AND FAMILY

The special residential arrangements that have created a lay community within the monastery also have made housing the scarcest resource and single most important commodity among the Armenians of Jerusalem. The size and place of one's apartment is a major determinant of status differentiation among lay families. It is also a good indicator of closeness to the church hierarchy, because the patriarchate[1] owns all the apartments and is the exclusive decision-maker on their allocation to laymen. Allocation of housing is the issue through which the clergy can exert most power over laymen, but the clergy's rights have not gone uncontested and occasionally bitter conflicts have erupted over occupancy rights of lay tenants on monastery property.[2]

The great majority of Armenian laymen living in Jerusalem resides inside the monastery compound. Less than one-fourth, including all the "locals" (i.e., those whose families were in Jerusalem prior to World War I), live in the structures surrounding the monastery walls, and a few of the wealthiest families live entirely outside the Armenian quarter, in the high-status northern suburbs of Shuafat and Beit Hanina and in the town of Ramallah, about fifteen miles from Jerusalem.[3]

Living inside the monastery has many inconveniences. The housing is substandard and overcrowded. Originally, the dwellings were designed for priests and pilgrims and thus were unfit for family living. They were of the "dormitory room" type, that is, a juxtaposition of rooms with no separation between them and with common kitchen and toilet facilities. When families moved in, some alterations and improvisations were introduced to make the dwellings more suitable for family use. Some internal walls were torn down, doors were installed between rooms, backyards were closed and transformed into living rooms or verandas. Some small rooms were turned into kitchens, but bathrooms for the most part remained outside the building and/or were shared by a number of households. Virtually no apartments had running water, gas, or electricity when they were first inhabited. Electricity was installed in the Jordanian period and running water began to be introduced mainly during Israeli rule.[4] Wells still exist in the courtyards, but they are almost never used today. The structures are centuries old, without proper plumbing and sewage facilities and in need of frequent repairs. The overcrowding eased somewhat as many families emigrated from the country and some moved outside

the monastery. Yet, young married couples still have difficulty obtaining a place of their own and some must live with
parents after their marriages.[5] With families living in close
proximity to each other, in a mazelike setting lined by narrow
alleys, there obviously is not much possibility for privacy.

This mazelike territorial layout with internal courtyards
and narrow lanes gives the residential area a very attractive
visual appearance for visitors, in marked contrast to the dull
or deteriorating appearance of most urban slums or lower-
class neighborhoods on which urban community studies have
concentrated. The residential area within the monastery
creates a feeling that space never ends, that something different, perhaps another courtyard with trees, gardens, and
wells, remains to be explored beyond every corner. The same
components of this visual attractiveness also inhibit the visitor from exploring "beyond the corner," because every
crossing of a narrow passage is felt as an intrusion and the
visitor is left with very little public space in which he can feel
at ease.

Laymen living inside the monastery are also in the immediate presence of clergymen and have to respect certain rules
of monastery life. By far the most important of these is the
closing of monastery gates at night. The main gate is shut
at about nine to ten P.M. The three side entrances to the
monastery are closed even earlier and lately one of them has
remained shut throughout the day. After the gates are closed
it is virtually impossible to get in and out of the monastery,
except with special permission from the responsible priest.
This is not easily granted, if only because it necessitates keeping the doorman awake until the designated hour. By closing
the gates at night the patriarchate wants to stress that the
area is above all a monastery and not a regular living quarter
or neighborhood.[6] The closing of the gates is also an important security device to prevent thefts and entrance of unde-
sirable elements into the residential area after dark. It did
not, however, prevent a recent burglary (carried out in
December 1980) in which money and precious religious

objects were stolen at gunpoint from a leading clergyman. Perhaps the monastery walls are more porous than they look; nevertheless, the closing of the gates effectively shuts off the community from cultural events and entertainment facilities that the city offers in the evening. This is replaced by more intensive ties with neighbors and relatives and greater reliance on entertainment supplied within the community, largely by clubs that stay open late into the night. Outside entertainment is transmitted mainly by television sets, which are found in every home.[7]

Like the closing of monastery gates at night, the architectural layout of residential buildings inside the monastery is conductive to intensive contacts. The inner courtyards created by the arrangement of buildings around an open square offer excellent gathering places. Religious and other public buildings, churches, school, library, printing press, health clinic, and social clubs are located in the two largest inner courtyards; the residential area proper has its own smaller courtyards. In Kendall's words:

> One is struck most by the intimate character of the smaller courtyards with their cluster of buildings entirely given over to domestic purposes. In such cases the courtyard is literally used as a room being surrounded by buildings, direct sunlight reaches the yard for only a few hours a day, sufficient to ventilate but not too long to make it unbearable in the summer.[8]

Better housing conditions are obtained in the area surrounding the monastery walls. There, too, houses are old, lack adequate facilities, and need frequent repairs, but the area is less crowded, the apartments more spacious and designed from the outset for family living and not as dormitory rooms. People who live in these houses are also freer from restrictions imposed by monastery life. They are not in the immediate presence of clergymen and are not confined to their neighborhood at night. However, while they have freer access to city life they cannot enter the monastery at night and because most social and cultural activities are conducted there, they are the ones who feel relatively shut off from the rest of the community. Nor do they participate much in the entertainment opportunities offered by the city; hence they make little more use of this advantage than do their kinsmen who live inside the monastery.

Nevertheless, living outside the monastery walls generally is preferred to living inside. At first the area surrounding the walls was inhabited only by locals while refugees lived inside the monastery, but gradually some refugees have moved to buildings outside the walls as these were vacated by outgoing locals. In 1964 the patriarchate built a modern apartment complex for refugees adjacent to the monastery walls, as a partial solution to the housing shortage. This building, called "the Gulbenkian Building," because it was financed by the Gulbenkian Foundation, had the double advantage of a modern residence and a location outside the monastery walls. It was, therefore, in great demand but only those willing to pay a relatively high rent live there and thus form a privileged group among the inhabitants of the Armenian quarter.[9]

The closure and lack of privacy that characterize the Armenian quarter strengthen the overall social control and conformity in the lay community. This is true especially within the monastery compound but applies also to those who live in the surrounding streets. Physical proximity, the sanctity of the place, and the close encounters with clergymen force upon laymen a rather discreet and conservative lifestyle. Because everything is done in the public domain, one has to be careful about appearances. One of my clerical sources noted,[10] for example, that young people would not date each other openly, partly out of respect for priests, but even more out of fear of being seen by neighbors who would no doubt notify parents. Being continuously on stage in full view of other community members has a sobering effect on personal idiosyncracies and restrains deviance. When acts of deviance occur they usually involve or are directed toward non-Armenians. (There has been, for instance, a famous Armenian drug connection, linking a well-known personality from the community to a country-wide ring of drug dealers. Not surprisingly my informants have been very tight-lipped about this subject.) This is similar to what Gans reported on the Italians of the West End in Boston but seems to be different from other slum neighborhoods where deviance is oriented inward as well as outward.[11] Violent crime is virtually unheard of within the Armenian quarter but there have been thefts and burglaries, which the residents claim have originated outside. Instances of alcoholism, drug addiction, and sexual promiscuity are very rare, though with regard to the last gossip abounds. I was surprised to find the topic of sex mentioned frequently by lay informants in thinly veiled innuendos about fellow residents' social lives.[12] Such gossip probably exaggerates or distorts events and perhaps prevents them from actually happening, thus serving as a very effective device of social control. It is also of particular interest that many of the innuendos about illicit sexual activities involved clergy-laity ties, perhaps as a reaction against too much proximity between the two sectors (see chapter 6).

The peculiar habitat also affects relations within the family. Armenian families in Jerusalem are usually small and closely knit. As refugee families they lost some of their members (and some came to Jerusalem as orphans) or have relatives in other countries. Larger family units are found among descendants of those who lived in Jerusalem prior to World War I. Lay households within the monastery compound usually are composed of a nuclear family with two or three children and possibly some grandparents or other elder relatives living with them. In some cases young married couples are forced to live with their parents for lack of suitable housing, but these unstable and unsatisfactory solutions do not last long. The Armenian community is also a relatively old community. According to Schmelz's figures its median age in 1972 was 24.4 compared with 16.7 for the entire population of Jerusalem.[13]

While family units are small, they are closely surrounded by friends, neighbors, and relatives. Indeed, the boundaries between family and neighborhood life are blurred. People not belonging to the household frequently go in and out of the house. During the day housewives visit each other and in the evenings husbands join in or else gather by themselves in a separate part of the house.[14] The intensity of peer group socializing is similar to that observed in most studies of ethnic neighborhoods; but here most of the socializing takes place at home or in the courtyard and not so much in coffeehouses, taverns, pubs, or other patronized public places, beyond the reach of the community in the evenings because they remain outside monastery walls. Clubhouses take their place to some extent, but clubs are places for more organized activities and they serve mainly the youth. In any event, a family rarely spends its leisure time alone. This has a cushioning effect on tension among family members, because it reduces the exclusivity of their relations. Family members have to be poised in their interactions, which occur under the close scrutiny of neighbors.

By and large this congestion of domestic life works to preserve the family unit (divorces are very rare) but reduces the need for great intimacy among family members. Also, Armenian women, unlike other non-Jewish women in Jerusalem, are almost equal to men in education and modern outlook. While few women have independent occupations, many are prominent in community affairs. This leads to an attenuation of male authority in family and community though a basic inequality still exists. Finally, the closing of monastery gates at night obviously helps parents keep control over their children. My teenage informants complained, of course, about their inability to take part in the city's night entertainment, to which their parents responded that the gates should remain closed for this very reason—if for no other—because they are the best device for keeping children from money-spending, alcohol, and mixed marriages.[15]

PROPERTY OWNERSHIP

All the buildings inhabited by Armenians in the quarter are owned by the patriarchate, whether located inside or outside the monastery. Laymen are tenants of the patriarchate, though very little rent is paid. The patriarchate legally can evict most people from their homes. This is almost never done,[16] because it might lead the evicted to cut all their ties with the community, but it could be used as a threat in the case of serious conflicts between the church and certain laymen or in order to prevent some serious deviation from community norms and morals (such as severe drunkenness, prostitution, or marrying outside the church).[17] Tenants cannot sell or rent their apartments, but in some apartments located outside the monastery they can, with the patriarchate's approval, "sell the keys" to other tenants (i.e., sell occupancy rights but not ownership). Homes can be passed to one's children, but special patriarchate permission is needed to add rooms or make any building alterations within the apartments. Public utilities are usually paid by the tenants but are supplied only at the patriarchate's request. Necessary repairs, painting, and other maintenance work are done by the patriarchate at its expense. The patriarchate's view is that because these buildings are monastery property they should be kept in good condition whether laymen live in them or not. The tenants not only do not participate in the maintenance of their homes but also frequently complain that the patriarchate does not do enough for cleaning and repairs.

No one in the community disputes the patriarchate's ownership of the entire residential area, but conflicts often erupt on rent to be paid and on occupancy rights of tenants. Prior to the influx of World War I refugees, the few laymen who lived in Jerusalem enjoyed free housing on the patriarchate property, because many of them served the church and because the patriarchate was interested in having a large lay population in Jerusalem that could bolster its rights to the Holy Places. With only a few hundred laymen living in the Old City, there was no housing shortage; and because they occupied only a small fraction of the patriarchate's large holdings, they did not cause a significant loss of income to the patriarchate. With the coming of World War I refugees an acute housing shortage developed, but in their destitute state it was unthinkable to demand rent. Thus, like the locals before them, the refugees lived virtually rent-free on the patriarchate property. This situation remained unchanged when what seemed to be a temporary relief measure took on a more permanent form.

Lately, the patriarchate has tried to assert its proprietor's rights over tenants. In the 1960s it started asking laymen to sign leases that would clarify their tenant status and spell out their rights and obligations. As the leases were clearly designed to limit the tenants' rights, they aroused great opposition among the laymen. The locals were the most adamant in their refusal to sign them. Traditionally they had enjoyed greater rights on their residences than did the newly arrived refugees. No property registration or deeds existed to prove ownership on the buildings, which some of them had occupied for a century or more. They could not be evicted easily from their homes,[18] they paid hardly any rent, and they had more freedom in the use of the property though no legal sale could be executed. The signing of the leases would have taken away the locals' special rights and would have reduced them to a regular tenant status. Most of them thus refused to sign the leases, but a few gave in to the patriarchate's pressure and signed them together with many of the refugees.[19] It should be pointed out that even in its relations with the locals the patriarchate had important means of pressure. Not only was it the nominal owner of the residences, but it could exert pressure in unrelated spheres, such as education, employment, recreational and cultural activities, civil status registration, and life cycle ceremonies.

The patriarchate also faced stiff opposition from the laymen when it tried to raise the rent above the symbolic rates. Even the wealthiest refused to pay higher rent. According to some informants an absurd situation emerged in which some people owned private apartments outside the Old City that they rented to others at market prices, while they lived or had their businesses on patriarchate property for which they paid hardly any rent.[20] In this case too, rather than opt for coercive measures, which could cause serious quarrels within the community, the patriarchate prefers to induce laymen into compliance by manipulating their general dependence on monastery services. One of the most important trump cards of the patriarchate is its control over vacant housing units. Whenever a new room or apartment is built or is vacated (such opportunities often present themselves because of the steady flow of emigration) the patriarchate offers it to those who are ready to pay a higher rent and agree to more restrictive occupancy rights. Laymen thus have to choose between remaining in the small and very crowded residences first allocated to them or moving to better places by paying higher rents (still much lower than market price) and signing more restrictive leases. The same pattern also exists with regard to Armenian businesses established on the patriarchate's property. Those who acquired them in the past pay virtually no rent and are not evicted. But if a tenant wants to enlarge his shop or move to a better location, he must pay higher rents and sign leases that restrict tenant rights.

While laymen cannot own apartments in the Armenian quarter, they can obtain better housing and enhance their tenant rights by "buying the key" to certain apartments. Buying the key by payment of a substantial sum gives the purchaser important advantages over other tenants. While the property still belongs to the patriarchate, the tenant cannot be evicted and is freer in using it. Buying the key is possible only for apartments located outside the monastery compound, and it was indeed a principal way in which well-to-do refugees obtained better housing and moved out of the monastery. The case of one of my informants is typical. His father was a successful jeweler who lived until 1948 outside the Old City in an area that remained on the Israeli side. Unable to return to the home from which he fled during the war, he lived for a few years as a refugee inside the monastery. He then bought from a local the keys to an apartment outside the monastery walls, a transaction approved by the patriarchate with the signing of a document in which his father acknowledged that the property belonged to the patriarchate. Occupancy rights passed to my informant when his father died, and he now pays a rather low rent to the patriarchate. He can do repairs and alterations on the apartment, but all the additions remain patriarchal property. He can sell his "rights to the key" only to another Armenian, and he has to pay the patriarchate one-third of the sales revenue. The new buyer would then have to pay a much higher rent to the patriarchate than that paid by my informant.[21]

A small group of Armenians have moved completely out of the Armenian quarter. During the British mandate the trend was to move to the western suburbs of the New City, which remained on the Israeli side after 1948. Now a few affluent Armenians have moved to the northern suburbs of Jerusalem and to Ramallah. Leaving the Armenian quarter increases one's independence from church control and enables living in much better housing, but the market price has to be paid for it (either buying or renting), a price that is especially high in Jerusalem because of the general housing shortage and high construction costs.[22] The cost of housing outside the Armenian quarter is beyond the reach of all but a few of the wealthiest Armenian families. Those who leave the quarter also place themselves far from the center of Armenian community life. They live far from their children's school, from their friends and relatives, and most probably from their shops or other places of employment. Experience from the not-so-distant past has shown, furthermore, that in the event of political disturbances Armenians might need to take refuge in the monastery and that proximity to it would be less disruptive to their lives. For all these reasons, relatively few people have moved out of the Armenian quarter, even though living outside the Old City not only raises the level of material comfort but is also a symbol of higher status. Most of the lay population, including quite a number who could afford to live elsewhere, have continued to live in the Armenian quarter and even within the monastery compound under the shadow of the church.

OCCUPATIONS

The traditional Armenian tendency to take up economic entrepreneurial jobs is reflected in the occupational structure of the Armenians in Jerusalem. The great majority engages in a trade of some sort. Many are shopkeepers in the central business streets (the bazaar streets) of the Old City, specializing in jewelry, souvenir shops, and photography. Certain trades and crafts have come to be considered Armenian specialties, such as ceramics, goldsmithing, photography, and pharmacy. Two of the most prominent ceramic manufacturers are Armenians, as are many of the pharmacists, photographers, and goldsmiths in the Arab sector of the city. Shoemaking also used to be an Armenian specialty, but it has now disappeared under the competition of the shoe industry.[23] These occupations are typical of Armenians not only in Jerusalem but throughout the world. They are probably passed from one generation to another and kept within the family or ethnic community. The first ceramic industry was established in Jerusalem during the British mandate by expert Armenian potters brought from Kütahya in Anatolia, a traditional center for that craft.[24] Most Armenians run truly family businesses, with sons, brothers, and other relatives helping out in the work. Very few non-Armenians are employed in Armenian crafts and businesses. Most of the Armenian shops are located close to homes though not in the Armenian quarter proper, which is outside the principal business axes. Very few shops are located in the quarter and all of

these are run by fellow Armenians. In this regard the Armenian quarter is very different from slum districts where
shops are owned and run by nonresidents who do not belong
to the local ethnic group.[25] Proximity of the shop to home,
just beyond the residential area, is greatly appreciated by
Armenian shopkeepers. Many of them state the advantage of
being able to walk home for lunch every day. Shops are also
important meeting places. Friends and relatives drop by to
chat and drink coffee during the day and many family and
community affairs are discussed there. Occupational life,
thus, is not separated in any way from family and community
life.[26] This points to another difference from some ethnic
communities discussed in the literature (and from many
middle-class communities) in which male residents work far
from their neighborhoods, leaving them to women and children during the day.[27] No such abrupt change of outward
appearance occurs in the Armenian quarter between morning and evening hours.

     In contrast to their strong propensity toward commerce
and selected specialized crafts, very few Armenians have
entered the liberal professions (with the exception of pharmacists). My notes show just one Armenian Catholic dentist,
one doctor, and one lawyer who lived in the Jewish sector of
the city. There were, to my knowledge, no practicing engi-
neers or architects, though some shopkeepers claimed to
have engineering degrees.[28] Except for hiring the lawyer,
who has a substantial Armenian clientele, the community
relies on the services of non-Armenians in these fields. Armenians claim that there were many more professionals in
Jerusalem in the past but that they were among the first to
emigrate, because they had less difficulty in finding jobs
abroad and had fewer business investments in the city. These
professionals, also, require university education, which is
obtained mostly abroad and is a major channel of emigration.

     Like most other businessmen in the Old City, Armenians
do not own the property on which their businesses are estab-

lished. Most property belongs to religious institutions: exempt from property taxes, they have found it a profitable investment and have become the largest property owners in the city.[29] Under Jordanian rule some attempts were made to restrict the property controlled by Christian institutions in Jerusalem. A law promulgated in 1953 prohibited Christian charitable and religious institutions from buying new property near holy sites without special government approval. In 1965, responding to Muslim pressure, the law was made more stringent, prohibiting Christians from acquiring property in the entire Old City whether by buying, hiring, accepting gifts, creating endowments, or by any other means. This law was repealed two years later when Israeli law was extended to Jerusalem.[30] According to Gosenfeld, in 1976 land held by religious institutions and exempt from taxation in East Jerusalem amounted to 47.4 percent of the total. The largest property owners were the Greek Orthodox church and the Muslim *Waqf* (an endowment made for religious, educational, or philanthropic reasons), which together owned 46.8 percent of the commercial property used by Christian businesses and 39.2 - 43 percent of the commercial property used by Muslim businesses (the difference depends on the origin of the Muslim businessmen). The Armenian patriarchate's share was incomparably smaller, only 1.3 percent of the *total* commercial property in the Old City. The larger part of the Armenian patriarchate's property is in the western (Jewish) sector of the New City.[31] Nonetheless, most Armenian shops are established on that small fraction of property that the patriarchate owns in the Old City.

The occupancy rights and obligations of Armenians to their shops are similar to those discussed earlier in relation to their residences. Armenians pay little rent for the commercial property of the patriarchate that they occupy, and because most of the patriarchate's property in the Old City is occupied by fellow Armenians, the income generated from it is negligible. Most of the patriarchate's rent income comes from property outside the Old City that is occupied almost entirely by non-Armenians. Thus even in business life conducted outside the monastery, in which laymen show greatest independence from the church, they still depend on preferential use of monastery property.

While most Armenian shopkeepers and businessmen are counted among the wealthier people of Jerusalem, two Armenian businessmen stand far above the others in wealth and are regarded as models of economic success by the rest of the community. They are both engaged in large-scale industrial manufacture, a field into which most Armenians refrain from entering. Both live in Ramallah at the northern outskirts of Jerusalem where their factories are located, like most of East Jerusalem's industry. The scope of their businesses, the number of people they employ (almost all non-Armenians), and their contacts with political authorities put them a cut above the other Armenian businessmen. They are also completely independent of the monastery. One of them, a candy and chocolate factory owner, does not even belong to the Apostolic church; he is Armenian Catholic and hence has tenuous ties with the community.

The other, a tissue paper factory owner, belongs to the Apostolic church and is very influential in the community. His sons and his wife lead social and cultural activities and are active members in one of the clubs. The family contributes heavily to organized lay community activities but somewhat less to the church itself. Armenians are very proud of the two families, even though one of them does not even belong to the national church. They are mentioned by all as prime examples of Armenian business skill. Together with the owners of the two Armenian potteries and a number of wealthy shopkeepers they form the community's economic elite. People turn to them for help and advice in economic matters, for contacts with non-Armenian authorities, and mainly for financial contributions. Their total independence from the monastery would enable them to become alternative foci of power in the community, but they have not used this opportunity and have not challenged the prominence of the church.[32]

Very few Armenians hold public office and even fewer occupy high-ranking positions in them. One of my prominent informants is a highranking official in the UNRWA (United Nations Relief and Works Agency), which dispenses help to Palestine refugees. He is also one of the Armenians who feels most closely integrated in the local non-Armenian population and at the same time occupies a leadership position in the community. He lives in the Armenian quarter but outside the monastery walls. During the British mandate a few Armenians occupied civil service positions and two Armenians reached top positions in European banks. As a whole, however, Armenians shun public office or salaried jobs and much prefer self-employed entrepreneurial occupations. Some young people recently have worked as bank or hotel reception clerks, but these are usually temporary jobs, left when the first opportunity for independent employment arises. Another fairly recent development is the employment of educated women before they marry. Married women rarely work outside their houses and hardly ever outside the community. Some are teachers in the school or kindergarten. Others help in their husbands' businesses but most are housewives.[33]

A large group of laymen work for the monastery. About fifty are full-time employees of the patriarchate. They include workers in the printing press and library, clerks in the patriarchate administration, guards, janitors, cleaners, and cooks. Some laymen hold high-ranking positions such as the secretary of the patriarch, the director of the printing press (before he emigrated), and the vice-director of the lay school. There are also about thirty laymen employed, usually on a part-time basis, as teachers in the seminary and the school. In all about eighty people, or roughly one-fourth of the heads of households, are employed by the monastery (based on an estimate of a population of 1,600 and 5 people per household). Unemployment is not a problem in the Armenian community, but for a few who have difficulty finding work the monastery is always there to help, either absorbing them in a church-related job or finding them some other kind of employment. Laymen working for the patriarchate receive higher salaries than clergymen in comparable positions. The monastery also covers their medical expenses. In the past the monastery also fed its workers, together with the seminarians and clergymen, but this has been discontinued. In short, job security is taken for granted by laymen and is inseparable from the more general feeling that the patriarchate will always help in times of need. This is another illustration of the basic dependence built into the relationship of laymen with the religious organization.[34]

Employment by the patriarchate enhances a layman's status in the community only if he occupies a top administrative position; otherwise it has a downgrading effect on status. The independents are not only richer but also more prestigious, and their influence on community affairs does not fall below that of the patriarchate's employees, except for the highest officials. The leading lay officials of the patriarchate and successful businessmen form the two main types of elite within the lay community (this does not necessarily imply a confrontation between them). Lay officials are usually the more educated, intellectual elements but lack business acumen. They have inside knowledge of the affairs of the patriarchate, which they can use to their advantage, but they are under direct rule of clergymen and depend on them for their livelihood. Businessmen are less educated and farther from inner circles of the patriarchate, but they are admired for their economic success and relative independence from the monastery hierarchy. The ideal combination is to be financially independent of the patriarchate and still take an active part in community affairs, sponsoring or directing club activities or educational programs, performing symbolic functions in national and religious festivities, giving speeches at the commemoration of the genocide or similar national occasions. The last task is considered a special honor because it recognizes the intellectual capabilities of the speaker and positions him as a spokesman for the entire lay community.

CONSUMPTION

The Armenians of Jerusalem display very Westernized patterns of consumption. They are the most Western-looking Old City inhabitants after the Jews. They are well-dressed, in the latest European fashions, and attuned to the slightest changes that occur in Western life-style. The women make generous use of hairdressers, cosmetics, and jewelry. Inside their homes one is impressed by the well-furnished rooms and the abundance of modern household appliances,[35] in striking contrast to the outside view of the buildings. However, two items which figure among the basic Western commodities, cars and telephones, are conspicuously absent.

Relatively few laymen own cars. Many who could afford to buy them do not because they have little use for them in their daily lives. They work at walking distance from home and leisure time is spent within the neighborhood, its small alleys and narrow streets (whether inside or outside the monastery) inaccessible to motor vehicles. Weekends are spent visiting, going to the clubs, or shopping in the bazaar or the new business district, all at walking distance. The fact that in Jerusalem, Muslims, Jews and Christians close their businesses on different days (Friday, Saturday, and Sunday respectively) enables shopping on one's own weekend holiday. While the Old City's bazaar is filled with Jewish shoppers on Saturday, Sundays are appropriate for Christians to shop in the Israeli sector. On Sunday afternoons many Armenians stroll in the New City's business district where stores are most attractive and most expensive. Picnics or trips outside Jerusalem are usually collective affairs organized by a number of families or by the clubs (sometimes by the patriarchate itself), and for these outings a pickup or bus generally is hired.

As with cars, very few lay families have telephones in their homes, though more have them in their stores. There is little need for a telephone within the community, because people can easily walk to each other's houses or even talk across yards. For communications with the outside, the patriarchate telephone may be used free of charge. Most outside communication is for official business and consequently laymen prefer to involve the patriarchate and allow it to intercede on their behalf. The use of its telephone (which includes incoming calls and taking messages) indirectly puts the patriarchate in a mediating position in the laymen's dealings with the outside world (including this author). This is also a principal reason why the patriarchate allows its telephone to be used. Not only does it wish to maintain a customary privilege that laymen take for granted but the patriarchate retains crucial control over the flow of information regarding all members of the community. The patriarchate also receives and distributes the incoming mail to all inhabitants within the monastery, as the latter have no separate "home address." These functions of mediation and "gate keeping" performed by the monastery on behalf of the lay community enhance its leadership position and power.[36]

The relative lack of private cars and telephones is symptomatic of two characteristics of the lay community emphasized here: its great enclosure and its dependence on the monastery. In this respect, there is a striking difference between the use of telephones and of radio and television. Almost every household has radio and television through which Armenian laymen are in touch with the outside world; they learn and are entertained by what happens outside their community. But the message is an impersonal one that does not force upon them an immediate personal involvement and responsibility. The telephone is a more personal link with the outside world. It demands an immediate response and creates direct involvement, obligations, and responsibility. Armenians of Jerusalem would rather avoid this kind of link with the outside or at least have the patriarchate act on their behalf.

The lack of a separate home address underlines another particular aspect of closure that differentiates the Armenian quarter from other urban communities discussed in the literature. The winding alleys and courtyards in which most Armenian community life takes place are, from the municipality's point of view, internal areas of a residence. They are like backyards, lobbies, and stairways of a building rather than a neighborhood street. The cleaning, lights, repairs of this area are not the municipality's direct responsibility. For the same reason, no mailman would pass beyond the central gate. Internal lanes do not have street names nor do the houses have numbers. As far as the city is concerned, this is just one institution with a single address rather than a neighborhood and relations are held with the official representative of the institution, that is, the patriarchate.

The close ties binding the Armenian community led me to expect that its residents would collectively patronize a few shops and funnel most of their consumption to them. I was surprised to find that this is not the case. Armenians diversify their shopping and hunt for bargains. Most groceries and other items of daily necessity are bought in the bazaar section of the Old City. Clothing and electrical appliances are purchased more often in the Israeli sector where higher quality goods are found. Armenians do not even patronize shops owned by fellow Armenians unless they obtain some preferential treatment, such as lower prices or free home delivery. Preferential treatment is expected as a natural consequence of ethnic solidarity. At the same time there seems to be a tacit understanding that one should not hurt a fellow Armenian's business by asking for such preferential treatment, if the same goods can be sold at a higher profit to a non-Armenian. The Armenian shopkeeper, reciprocally, does not expect kinsmen to buy at his store if they can find better bargains elsewhere.[37] The Armenian restaurant (now reverted to a grocery store) located outside the main entrance to the monastery used to do more business with tourists than with local kinsmen, and so do all the Armenian shopkeepers of the bazaar. Some of my clerical sources, however—perhaps because they were not businessmen—were furious that fellow Armenians prefer to buy cheaper church candles outside than those sold in the church. Armenian businesses thus are oriented mainly toward non-Armenians, because as both sellers and buyers they find it more profitable to deal with people outside their own ethnic group.[38]

EDUCATION, CULTURE, HEALTH

Armenians pride themselves on being among the most highly educated groups in the Old City. Schmelz's figures show that only 22.8 percent of the entire Armenian population and 19.1 percent of the male population have no formal education.[39] Almost all the children of the community, including some who live outside the Old City, go to the Armenian school (Saint Tarkmanchatz) located within the monastery and run by the patriarchate. Even some Armenian Catholics and Protestants and a few non-Armenians (five in 1975) attend the school. Education is divided into two years of kindergarten, six of primary school and five of secondary school. The school's principal is one of the high-ranking priests in the monastery; but only three of the twenty-six teachers were clergymen in 1975, and they taught only armenological studies. The staff also includes a number of non-Armenians who teach Hebrew, Arabic, and a few other courses for which Armenian teachers could not be found. In 1974-75 enrollment figures show sixty-five pupils enrolled in the kindergarten, one hundred twenty-five in the elementary school and fifty-five in the secondary school.[40] About thirty of the kindergarten and elementary school pupils form a special group. These are boys brought from Turkey, most of them from poor families or orphanages. They live in boarding-school conditions under the care of the monastery and are expected to continue their secondary education in the priests' seminary. Some of them eventually become priests, while for the others education in the monastery is seen as a way to strengthen their national identity and culture.[41]

The Saint Tarkmanchatz school is the principal transmitter of Armenian culture to the local community's children. It also stresses religion. Pupils are expected to follow religious observances and attend church. During religious holidays they are required to attend church services as a group, wearing their school uniforms. The language of instruction in schools is Armenian, ensuring its preservation as the principal spoken and written tongue in the community and preventing any slipping toward local languages. In addition to Armenian, the study of English is emphasized to enable pupils to pass British high school matriculation examinations. Arabic and Hebrew also are taught as secondary foreign languages, though during my field work the school had difficulty obtaining the services of a regular Hebrew teacher.[42] The fact that so many languages are taught in school is a good indication of the basic cosmopolitanism of the Old City and of the diversity of external political centers to which it has had to adapt itself.

The goal of preserving the national language in school faced a serious threat toward the end of Jordanian rule. The government promulgated a law that, if implemented, would have made Arabic the principal language of instruction, allowing Armenian to be taught only as a second language. Furthermore, it would have allowed only one foreign language to be taught, forcing the school to forego the teaching of English if it were to keep Armenian. The law was not implemented until 1966 (although it was passed in 1955) because of the stiff resistance to it by all Christian communities. It finally was abrogated following the establishment of Israeli rule in 1967.[43]

The Turkish language has a special position in the community, even though the use of Turkish is strongly discouraged. In the past there were signs in the clubs urging people not to speak Turkish out of respect to their slain kinsmen. Yet old people continue to speak Turkish at home (and often switch to Turkish radio stations to listen to old country songs), and most children born outside Turkey have learned the language from their parents. While the school makes important efforts to rid the community of such cultural ambivalence, the coming of Armenian students from Turkey since the early 1970s has caused a certain recrudescence in the use of Turkish. One can hear them speaking the language among themselves in the seminary building, in the soccer field, or on their way to and from the church.[44]

In addition to its cultural and educational functions, the Saint Tarkmanchatz school is also an arena for social activities. Unlike the clubs, which compete with each other and perpetuate divisions within the community, the school is a social integrator of different groups and factions. The graduation ceremonies and the school's annual field day are among the most important social events of the year, bringing together clergymen and laymen, locals and refugees, and followers of different political parties, attracting crowds from as far as Jaffa and Haifa. Field day teams are carefully selected to cut across community divisions in terms of family ties, club membership, and political allegiances. Seminary students do not participate in the festivities, but they can be seen watching the events from the top of the old seminary building walls adjacent to the soccer field.[45]

As with all other services of the monastery, the lay community is asked to pay very little for the school. Tuition is proportional to the estimated income of each student's family, but even those who are asked to pay the highest rate still pay less than the service's market value. Thus the lay community is indebted not only culturally but also financially to the religious establishment. In this case, however, the patriarchate insists that the school be self-supporting (it is not quite clear to me why the school was singled out in this respect), and because tuition cannot pay all the expenses, the difference is covered by donations collected mainly from rich Armenians abroad. The principal also was successful in organizing a group of community women (called by another informant "the principal's women's brigade"), who organize bazaars and charity dinners to raise money for the school.

This is one of the rare instances in which local laypersons participate (although indirectly and on a purely voluntary basis) in the financial burden of a service provided them by the monastery.[46]

One educational service that cannot be obtained within the monastery is university education. Rather than use the local non-Armenian facilities, the Armenians of Jerusalem prefer to go abroad for higher education. They refrain from studying in Israeli universities for a number of reasons. They have difficulty with Hebrew, the language of instruction. Their high school diplomas are not accepted by Israeli universities; and a preparatory year is required before admission. Uncertainty about the performance of Israeli rule and the fact that Israeli degrees are not recognized in Arab countries also preclude them from turning to Israeli institutions for higher education. The Palestinian Bir Zeit College in Ramallah and the College in Bethlehem offer very limited college-education programs and are far from satisfying Armenians' educational aspirations.[47]

Until the outbreak of the civil war, Lebanon was the center of attraction for the Jerusalem Armenians seeking higher education. Most of them studied at the American University of Beirut and at the Haigazian College, an Armenian institution of higher education.[48] The Lebanese civil war, which included the partial burning of Haigazian College, put a halt to that tendency. Most Armenians now go to Western European and North American universities. Some also attend the University of Erevan in Soviet Armenia on scholarships offered by the Soviet government.[49]

Only about half of those who study abroad return to Jerusalem. The others settle in the countries where they study, or having acquired a profession, emigrate more easily to a third country. University education is, therefore, one of the principal channels of emigration. Marrying abroad also contributes to emigration, but its influence is less than that of the prospective emigrant's career opportunities. A number of people have indeed married during their studies abroad and have returned to Jerusalem with their wives (I know of no case in which a woman brought her husband from abroad). The marriage age is generally high for both men and women (late twenties for men and mid-twenties for women) and education ends before marriage begins. The emigration of part of the young people, and others returning with wives from abroad, reduces some of the pressure of finding suitable mates within the community.[50] Marriages with non-Armenians are claimed to be rare, but they are a constant source of concern for the community. Sometimes marriages are arranged with Armenians living in other diaspora communities. Among those studying abroad there are more mixed marriages in Europe[51] and the United States but fewer in Lebanon where a very large and self-contained local Armenian community exists.

While the monastery cannot offer university education to the lay community, it is still instrumental in obtaining scholarships without which education abroad would be out of reach for all but a few of the wealthiest families. Most scholarships are obtained from international Armenian philanthropic organizations, such as the AGBU and the Gulbenkian Fund, or from the Soviet Armenian government for study in Erevan. While one may apply directly to these organizations, it certainly helps if the patriarchate sponsors the application and activates its connections with the Armenian establishment in both the diaspora and in Soviet Armenia.[52] The monastery thus can be of crucial help even when a service obviously cannot be procured within the monastery. This help is dispensed to laymen in the same manner that the more direct services are offered to the community.

Among the other community services of the monastery, three minor ones should be mentioned briefly, the library, the health clinic, and the museum. All are located inside the monastery and run by the patriarchate, but they were established by outside donations. The library, founded in 1929 with the donations of Calouste Gulbenkian, is nominally directed by one of the top-ranking clergymen though its daily operation is run by a lay librarian. Over the years, the library has accumulated one of the richest collections in the world of material on Armenian subjects in both Armenian and foreign languages. Relatively few people use it, however, except for occasional students checking out books for school assignments and a few people reading the daily newspapers. The health clinic was opened in 1951 with the donations of a rich pilgrim. Priests receive free medical services and laymen pay only a nominal fee. Though under the patriarchate's control, the clinic is run by an Armenian nurse and non-Armenian doctors replace each other at a high rate of turnover. This limits the usefulness of the clinic to caring for only the most elementary medical needs. For this reason, it has attracted limited attention from the community.[53] The museum, opened in 1978 in the old seminary building, displays part of the monastery's manuscripts, historical relics, and art treasury. Clearly, it does not serve the community but rather is a showcase for outside visitors. Its opening necessitated the use of the monastery's third side entrance, usually closed before. Leading directly into the courtyard where the museum is located, this entrance prevents visitors from strolling within the monastery until they reach the museum. As an added protection, signs in English were posted on the trees of the courtyard to remind visitors that they are in a private residential area and should not wander away from the museum.[54]

ENTERTAINMENT AND SOCIAL ACTIVITIES

The closing of monastery gates at night turns the Armenians inward to satisfy their entertainment needs. The clubs provide organized entertainment and social activities within the community. One of the clubs, founded by locals outside the monastery, is now inactive and has become a gathering place for a few elderly people during the day. By contrast, the two clubs formed by refugees inside the monastery, the

Hoyetchmen and Homenetmen, are very active and strongly competitive, each spurring the other to even greater activity. Even the locals prefer to go to one of these rather than to their own inactive club.[55]

The clubs are oriented above all toward young people. They provide meeting places for youngsters and enable them to engage in extracurricular activities within the community (such as sports, games, music, organizing dances). They have their own uniformed scouts who organize group activities and march in processions on holidays and other special occasions. Such processions of youth, all resplendent in their uniforms and preceded by drummers and flagbearers marching from the monastery to the Holy Sepulchre or to Mount Zion, add to the colorful events with which the Old City is so blessed. In the past activities for boys and girls were separated, but now they are mixed despite the frowns of some priests. One of the important functions performed by the clubs is, in fact, to provide a legitimate meeting place for boys and girls. While meeting and dating opportunities also exist in school and other areas of the monastery, youngsters do not feel as free in other places as they do in the clubs. Unlike youth in other urban communities reported in the literature, Armenian adolescents do not form street corner groups. This may be because the monastery is no place to "hang out" on corners but also because the clubhouse provides a viable alternative to such corners.[56]

The clubs have activities for adults too. Balls and bazaars held on festive occasions (New Year's Eve, Easter, end of school year, and others) are the high points of the year's entertainment for the community; these events also raise money for the clubs. Concerts by visiting Armenian singers, films on Armenian subjects, conferences, and art exhibitions are all held in the clubs. The adults also are involved in guiding and helping the young people in events that require long preparation, such as organizing plays and folk dances. Such performances by youngsters create a principal means of entertainment for the adults as well.[57] Most of the cultural activities held in the clubs have a rather narrow repertory of predominantly Armenian themes and, therefore, also serve as cultural transmitters; but these activities are secondary to the purely social ones. The clubs leave the primary function of cultural transmission to the school.

The patriarchate is not directly involved in club affairs. The clubs do occupy rent-free monastery property, like the general residential arrangements in the community, but only occasionally do the clubs receive direct financial help from the patriarchate. Most of the club income is derived from other sources (from fund-raising balls and bazaars, donations from abroad, and wealthy members). What distinguishes the clubs' activities from other services is their relative independence from the clergymen. The clubs, in a sense, form the "home territory" of the laymen vis-à-vis the monastic brotherhood. They are the foci of the laymen's distinctive activities, organized and run by themselves. To the extent that clergymen are invited to these activities, they become recipients of services offered by laymen.

Clergymen are forbidden to be members of the clubs or to take part in organizing any club activity, but they often are invited to club events. Indeed, the most important events, such as balls, bazaars, plays, and concerts, no matter how secular, do not start before the patriarch arrives in a solemn procession of priests and guards and "blesses" the event with a prayer and a brief speech. At purely entertainment activities the clergymen would then withdraw and the atmosphere would quickly turn from religious to secular. At more cultural activities, the priests remain throughout the event, seated in the front rows of honor.[58] Legitimization by the priests of important social events is deemed necessary out of respect and recognition for them as local authority and landlord. At more cultural events, their presence also supplies the necessary link between the event and Armenian culture and identity. The clergy, on its part, is eager to assert by its presence what could be easily forgotten, that the event takes place under its aegis and inside the monastery.

Music occupies a special place in the recreational and social activities of the Armenians in Jerusalem. In addition to bands and concerts organized in the clubs, a central role in this respect is played by the church choir. The choir is composed of both laity and clergy (mostly seminarians) and is one of the activities in which the two groups most closely mix. Because it includes laymen from different clubs, it is also an integrative factor within the laity. The choir accompanies religious service on Sunday and holiday masses and is joined by students at special religious services. Sometimes special singing groups are formed among choir members who sing on festive occasions, such as graduation ceremonies, holiday celebrations, or in special concerts taped for radio and television stations. The director of the choirs, and indeed the spark of all musical activity, is one of the central figures of the community. The choir is one of the central institutions of the community and a matter of great pride to all. Its activities attract great attention and its lay members include people from the community's most respectable families, especially wives. It is also an important showpiece to the outside, always happy to perform outside the community.[59]

Activities of a fourth Armenian club, the Armenian Catholics' Arax, should be briefly mentioned. Located in their headquarters on the Via Dolorosa's fourth station, quite far from the Armenian quarter, Arax is the platform for the organized activities of Catholic Armenians, especially their youth. It has its own sports team, band, and scout organization, but its activities are limited because of the small number of Armenian Catholics living in the city. Arax is often invited to take part in events organized in the Apostolic community, such as concerts in which its band plays. Armenian Catholics also are represented collectively by Arax in organized activities of a national Armenian character. Thus Arax participates in the Apostolic community's annual commemoration of the World War I holocaust. It even takes part in the Christmas procession of the Apostolic church in Bethlehem, which occurs at a different date than that of the Catholics. In 1975 Catholics also sent their own delegation to a reception committee set up for the visit to Jerusalem of the Catholicos of Echmiadzin.[60] These participatory events are intended to strengthen national solidarity and the ties of Armenian culture and identity centered on the Saint James Monastery.

DEPENDENCE OF LAYMEN ON THE MONASTERY: A SUMMARY

The preceding discussion has shown how much Armenian laymen depend on the Saint James Monastery for virtually all their economic needs. They live inside the monastery, or on the streets surrounding it, on property belonging to the monastery for which they pay little or no rent. Most of them either are employed by the monastery or have businesses on its property. Their shops and offices are minutes away from their homes. Their children go to the school operated by priests and located inside the monastery. A clinic established in the monastery provides simple medical services. Books and newspapers can be obtained in the monastery's Gulbenkian library, and the patriarchate's telephone can be used free of charge. Similarly, their social activities and entertainment take place within the monastery compound, mainly in the two clubs established by refugees. The patriarchate's help is sought even for services that cannot be procured within the monastery, such as scholarships for university education. If we add to all these extrareligious community activities those performed by religious institutions in any community, such as life-cycle ceremonies (baptism, marriage, and funerals) and religious services, we can see that almost all the community needs are supplied either by or within the monastery. Between 1948 and 1967 Armenians even were buried inside the monastery, because the Armenian cemetery on Mount Zion remained in the "no-man's land" between Israel and Jordan. Only after 1967 did the Armenians resume burying their dead in the cemetery on Mount Zion just outside the monastery walls.[61] The extent of community services supplied by the monastery to the laymen also can be seen by reference to the locality-relevant functions that, according to Roland Warren, have to be met in every community (though the community might depend on external organizations to procure these services). Warren has identified five such basic functions: (1) meeting the basic economic needs of the community, that is, production, distribution, and consumption of scarce commodities and services; (2) socialization of community members by which cultural legacies and social norms are transmitted to new members; (3) social control to ensure compliance with the community's norms; (4) social participation that provides opportunities for companionship and association among community members; and (5) mutual support, that is, help proffered when certain members of the community face crises or have needs not otherwise satisfied in the usual pattern of organized social behavior.[62] Looking at how these needs are met, one can see the striking self-containment of the Armenian community compared with other urban communities. Most people are either directly employed in the community or depend on community resources to set up their businesses. Even though they do not necessarily buy consumption items from fellow members or from stores located within the Armenian quarter, the symbolic aim of consumption is definitely oriented toward the community: Armenians want to impress one another with the consumption rather than show off to the outside. Similarly, socialization and social participation functions are almost exclusively performed within the community. Formal education is received in the monastery-operated school. The clubs provide additional socialization and are the formal instruments for social participation. More generally, inhabitants of the Armenian quarter have very few non-Armenian friends. Except for business, their ties with the outside are minimal and are certainly not encouraged by the physical closure of their residential area. Mutual support and social control also are provided internally by the community as a whole and more specifically by the religious organization. Thus, with the possible exception of certain consumption activities in which Armenians turn more to non-Armenian suppliers, all functions spelled out by Warren not only are performed within the residential community but also depend on services supplied to the community by the monastery. Most of these services originated as emergency welfare to homeless refugees; they then received permanence and helped crystallize a distinctive, very inward-oriented, and relatively self-contained residential community.

INTERNAL DIVISIONS WITHIN THE ARMENIAN COMMUNITY

Until now we have stressed the self-contained character of the Armenian community and the close ties binding its members to each other. To the outside observer, the community indeed gives the impression of a very closely knit unit. One is surprised, however, to find in it also some deep internal divisions. The basic division between laymen and clergymen, alluded to in this chapter, is the subject of more detailed examination later. Among laymen themselves, locals are differentiated from refugees (the latter term also includes the refugee's descendants born in Jerusalem). The locals were originally wealthier than the refugees and occupied a dominant position among laymen, but the more entrepreneurial refugees have gradually gained ascendance over the locals in both wealth and power. Locals, who at first welcomed and assisted the refugees, turned against them when they felt that they themselves were being pushed aside. They still look down on refugees, considering themselves more respectable because of their roots in the city than the "upstart" refugees. Rather than fight back, however, the locals retracted into their shells, in effect relinquishing to the refugees leadership positions within the lay community. The refugees, on their part, despised what they saw as passivity of the locals.[63]

Antagonism between the two groups was fed also by their cultural and political differences. Locals had stronger ties with the local Arabic culture compared with the more Turkish culture of the refugees. The locals had no part in the Armenian nationalist struggle in Anatolia and did not share the political sensitivity and activism of the refugees. They adopted a disdainful, neutral attitude toward political parties and such issues as the position toward Soviet Armenia. Refugees, on their part, saw in the locals' political neutrality another proof of apathy and lack of patriotic vigor.

The antagonism between them never reached great intensity and has been steadily diminishing since the 1930s, mainly because very few locals live in Jerusalem. The locals always formed a small minority compared to the refugees, but their numbers have further declined as a result of emigration. Today, there are only about two hundred locals left in Jerusalem, and their small numbers have prevented them from keeping up separate social and cultural activities. First their children, and then they themselves began attending activities organized in the refugees' clubs. At the same time, as an increasing number of refugees moved out to residences surrounding the monastery walls, the geographical differentiation between the two groups tended to disappear. Still, the locals are recognized as a distinctive group and close friendships between the two groups are rare.[64]

Another division of far greater importance affects the refugee population itself and is related to the worldwide split of Armenians into rival political factions, as discussed in chapter 2. In Jerusalem the split finds its expression in the deep-seated rivalry between the two social clubs, which are informally affiliated with opposing political parties. Hoyetchmen is affiliated with the Ramgavar and Homenetmen with the Dashnak party. Leaders of both clubs hotly deny any formal ties with political parties, claiming rightly that Armenian political parties have no legal existence in Jerusalem (they were forbidden under Jordanian rule). They admit, however, to having ties with Armenian philanthropic organizations, which are ostensibly nonpolitical but in fact are associated closely with rival political parties. The Hoyetchmen, for example, owes much of its financial strength to its close ties with the AGBU. In any case, whether they have formal ties or not, the clubs are identified openly with the two rival parties. They follow the respective party lines in taking opposing stands on the major issues that divide Armenian communities around the world.

By capturing center stage in the community's social life, the two clubs perpetuate the division within the community and make it more pervasive, affecting also the nonpolitical aspects of community life. Members of one club rarely set foot in the other. Their rivalry forces a duplication of all the important social events, such as balls, bazaars, concerts, and plays, each club trying to outshine the other. Membership in the club is by family tradition. Most friendship ties are created in the clubs and it is estimated even that 70 percent of all marriages occur with members of the same club.[65] Blum gives a vivid description of what could happen at a "cross-club" marriage:

> A daughter of a Hoyechmen Club member was given permission by her father to marry a Homentmen. At the wedding ceremony the young friends of the groom began chanting revolutionary Dashnak songs. The father of the bride, infuriated, proclaimed that he had not had a daughter so as to give her to a revolutionary. The singing of the Dashnak songs ended and the participants returned to the traditional wedding songs.[66]

A recurrent occasion for tension between the two clubs comes on May twenty-eighth each year when the Homenetmen celebrates the establishment of the Independent Armenian Republic and stages a procession around the monastery walls, while members of the other club look on and throw occasional disparaging remarks at the marchers. Despite their differences of allegiance to Echmiadzin or Antelias, however, both clubs were represented in the committee of reception organized to honor the Catholicos of Echmiadzin during his visit to Jerusalem in 1975. Both club members also received the Catholicos of Antelias on his previous visit to Jerusalem. The two clubs also take part together in certain national events such as religious feasts or the commemoration of the World War I events, but by and large, they try to keep as separate from each other as possible.[67]

The patriarchate tries to maintain a neutral attitude toward the two clubs. The patriarch and top clergymen are careful not to show any preference in attending the activities of or otherwise offering support to one club over the other. Even though individual priests are known to have political preferences, the ecclesiastical community as a whole tries to remain above the two factions and to provide an integrative counterpart to their divisive influence. Nevertheless, the Hoyetchmen, with a larger membership than its rival, is considered to have closer ties with the church hierarchy. Hoyetchmen is regarded as the more "establishment" club. It is bigger and richer but ideologically less articulate. Its clubhouse is more spacious and is situated more centrally within the monastery compound. Also, because its clubhouse is bigger, some events organized by the patriarchate and involving the entire community (such as kindergarten graduation ceremonies or an Armenian art exhibition) are held at the club.[68]

Homenetmen, by contrast, is smaller but more cohesive and more ideologically committed. It has more ambiguous relations with the community establishment, even though some top clergymen are among its sympathizers and one of its leading members is the owner of the tissue paper factory and the wealthiest person in the community.[69] Homenetmen's smaller but more tightly knit character is similar to that of pro-Dashnak groups everywhere in the diaspora. They form smaller but more cohesive and better-organized groups than the pro-Ramgavar groups, which are bigger but less organized, ideologically more lax and politically less active.

In the 1950s the Armenian community of Jerusalem was rocked by still another conflict, this one related to the election of a new patriarch. In contrast to the other divisions discussed above in which the clergy tried to keep above the conflicting laymen, this issue exploded within the monastic brotherhood itself and laymen offered support to rival factions of clergymen. The struggle started soon after the death

of Patriarch Israelian in 1949. At that time, the patriarchate
was faced with the particularly difficult task of taking care of
a new wave of refugees just when most of its property
remained on the Israeli side of the border. The election of a
new patriarch was postponed to tend first to the pressing
problem of the refugees and of the seizure of the patriarchate
property by the Israeli government. One of the top contend-
ers for the patriarch's position, Archbishop Derderian (the
present patriarch), was elected *Locum Tenens* (i.e., acting patriarch) until elections could be held.

In the years following his election as acting patriarch,
Derderian was sharply criticized in the community, accused
of misusing funds collected for refugees. In 1956, a fellow
member of the Saint James Brotherhood, Archbishop Tiran
Nersoyan, returned to Jerusalem from the United States to
lead the opposition to Derderian. Nersoyan's supporters
asked for an investigation of the patriarchate's finances and
put forward Nersoyan's candidature for the patriarch's position. It seems that the majority within the community and in
the monastic brotherhood sided with Nersoyan, but Derderian was still backed by a faction within the community and
also enjoyed the support of the Catholicos of Echmiadzin and
of the Jordanian government. Mounting local pressure
against Derderian forced him to leave Jerusalem (for Amman
and Echmiadzin). However the Jordanian government inter-
vened against his rival Nersoyan by expelling him from the
country in October 1956.[70]

Nersoyan's expulsion created great consternation in the
community. Armenian shops were closed in the Old City and
a procession headed by members of the Saint James Brotherhood proceeded from the patriarchate to the governor's
office demanding his return. Under strong pressure from the
community, the Jordanian government agreed to Nersoyan's
return in November 1956. He was given a hero's welcome
and immediately elected acting patriarch, while, at the urging
of the brotherhood, Derderian's apartment was searched by
the police for possible proof of misdeeds and he was expelled

from the brotherhood. Then, over Derderian's protests of illegal procedure, Nersoyan was elected patriarch in March 1957. But the Jordanian government interfered against him once more. His election was not ratified by King Hussein and in January 1958 he was expelled from the country for a second time. In order to appease the community, the Jordanian government declared that Derderian would also be prevented from returning to Jerusalem for a time.[71]

The decision to expel Nersoyan for the second time created a new wave of protests among the Armenians. People barricaded themselves behind the monastery gates to prevent the access of government troops to Nersoyan and the return of Derderian. Beyond these immediate purposes this was also a symbolic protest against Jordanian government interference in community affairs. It took the Jordanian army a few days to force the gates open.[72] However, in the next two years there was a change of attitude among the influential members of the brotherhood and of the lay community. Some kind of deal, its details unknown to me, was struck between Derderian and his former opponents, and as a result he returned to Jerusalem in March 1960. He finally was elected patriarch in June 1960; his election was ratified by the Jordanian king and he has served in that position since. Three clergymen most closely associated with Nersoyan were expelled from the Saint James Brotherhood and left the country.[73]

It is not clear whether or not the patriarchal succession crisis of the 1950s was related in any way to the split between Dashnak and Ramgavar supporters. It simply may have involved matters of personality unrelated to political divisions. It should be pointed out, however, that a similar succession crisis occurred in the Catholicosate of Cilicia in Lebanon almost simultaneously, and there Dashnakist partisans succeeded in getting one of their supporters elected against a preexisting anti-Dashnak church establishment (including the acting patriarch who was forced to resign).[74] The succession crisis in Jerusalem conceivably could be a continuation of the one in Lebanon, and strong opposition of

Dashnak supporters to the election of Derderian in the early stages of the crisis lends some credence to such an interpretation.[75] But opposition to Derderian was widespread among Ramgavar supporters, too. Indeed, Derderian's opponent Nersoyan was known to be even more openly pro-Ramgavar than his adversary.[76] Hence, the exact configuration of the opposing sides is not easy to make. There were also frequent shifts of support as the crisis unfolded. For example, in his efforts to recruit support Derderian changed his earlier stand and tried to get closer to the Dashnak supporters in Lebanon by recognizing the pro-Dashnak Catholicos and returning to him some relics of Saint Gregory taken away by the opposing faction. This caused the displeasure of the Catholicos of Echmiadzin to whom Derderian was subordinated. The Catholicos of Echmiadzin censured Derderian and recognized the election of his rival as patriarch of Jerusalem, but had to reverse himself when the election was not ratified by the Jordanian authorities.[77] The events of the 1950s clearly have left some deep scars in the community, as can be seen from the great reluctance of its members to talk about this subject.

The patriarchal succession crisis revealed the strong current of discontent that existed within both the clergy and the lay community. Although the struggle basically pitted one faction of clergymen against the other, this should not be seen simply as an internal conflict of the monastic brotherhood. The lay community was involved deeply in the crisis. From the outset the succession struggle was closely related to the long-standing frustrations of the laymen at their inability to take part formally in decision-making on the administration of their community. The issue of financial mismanagement that had precipitated the crisis was indeed a protest against their inability to participate formally in the allocation of the patriarchate's resources. Paradoxically, however, the succession crisis did increase the influence of laymen on the administration of the community. During the long years of stalemate, when the monastic brotherhood was deeply divided, the patriarchate was in effect run by a few top-ranking lay officials.[78] The succession crisis was also beneficial to the laymen in that the clergy, needing lay support, could not engage in policies that would have antagonized them and could not exert any pressure on them in matters such as rent, property rights, and other privileges. The laymen thus took advantage of the weakness of the monastic brotherhood caused by the dissension of the 1950s. Only toward the late 1960s did the patriarchate regain enough unity to reverse its power relations with the laymen.

5

The Life and Organization
of the Clergy

Discussion of the Armenian community of Jerusalem thus far has focused on the laymen who form the great majority of the population. Attention will now be given to the much smaller ecclesiastical sector to see how its life and social organization have been affected by proximity to the lay population. The monastery was originally built for clergymen and pilgrims and its official rules are still those set up to suit its ecclesiastical inhabitants. However, in practice the clergy has had to make great adjustments to accommodate itself to living so close to a large lay population. A discussion of the daily life and organization of the clergy in this chapter will enable us to examine, in the next chapter, the problems faced by clergymen with the influx of lay refugees into the monastery and the measures of adaptation that enable the coexistence and adequate role-performance of both sides.

The ecclesiastical sector of the Armenian community is composed of about twenty priests and bishops, ten deacons and subdeacons, four nuns, and about fifty seminarians, forming a total of about eighty to ninety people. As in other Eastern Christian monasteries, the priests of the Saint James monastery are organized as a religious brotherhood that is the sovereign body ruling the monastery. However, not all members of the brotherhood reside in Jerusalem. Of about one hundred ten living members of the brotherhood only about twenty actually live in the city. The others are posted in Armenian communities throughout the world. They still retain close ties with the monastery and whenever they return to Jerusalem they enjoy the same rights as all other members of the brotherhood.[1]

Only priests who make a vow of celibacy can become members of the Brotherhood of Saint James. The Armenian Apostolic church, like other Eastern churches, recognizes married priesthood, but sharply distinguishes between married and unmarried priests.[2] The married priests (called *derder*) are designed for pastoral functions. They concentrate on service to the community and are not expected to show high theological knowledge. For this reason, they cannot be promoted to high ranks in the church hierarchy and are not admitted to monastery membership. They are expected to live near lay members of the community, and like their congregation can marry, but marriage has to precede priestly ordination and widowers cannot remarry. In the past, married priests did not have to dress differently than the laity, but later a special ecclesiastical dress was adopted. Married priesthood has in many cases been sustained in the same families for a number of generations and was seen as an occupational specialization passed on from father to son. Married priests had deep roots in their respective communities. They could attend to their own domestic affairs and even engage in some other occupations within the limits of propriety.[3] The celibate priests (called *vartabed*), in contrast, are expected to serve the church first and the community second. They are trained to be scholars and form the church's elite. Higher ranks of the church are open only to them, as are monasteries where elite spiritual and educational activities are expected to take place.[4] This is different from the early years when bishops were often married and the headship of the Armenian church descended form father to son like any royal dynastic succession. The hereditary principle was stopped in the fifth century and soon afterward complete celibacy of bishops and monks became the rule.[5]

The married priesthood has a low status in church and community. These are low-paying jobs and since pastors' salaries are paid by lay members of the parish, married priests are economically dependent on the community and do not have secure incomes. Parishioners rarely turn to them as teachers and counselors, because they do not display much religious knowledge and wisdom beyond the technical conducting of religious services.[6] Nor do they form effective judges or mediators because they are embedded too closely in the social structure of the local community and too dependent on its powerful members. Celibate priests, if present, are preferred for such functions as counseling, teaching, and mediation, for their intellectual qualifications as well as their relative independence from the community. Until the First World War, however, celibate priests were a small minority of the Armenian clergy. At the outset of the war, the proportion of married to celibate priests was estimated at ten to one.[7] The holocaust changed this situation. Married priests perished in greater proportions than celibate priests, because they lived closer to lay communities and shared their fate. Today, there exists an acute shortage of married priests and the low prestige attached to the occupation prevents large-scale recruitment. Regular seminaries prepare only for the unmarried priesthood; married priests need little formal education and are usually ordained at a relatively late age. A special seminary for training married priests in Echmiadzin has attracted few students. The shortage has led to the use of celibate priests in pastoral functions. Still, the church has tried to keep the pastoral and monastic functions of the unmarried priests separate; pastoral functions are performed by priests posted near their communities outside monasteries. In Jerusalem this could not occur because the lay community developed within and around the monastery. There are no married priests in Jerusalem, and only two, both located in Bethlehem, are found in all the areas under the jurisdiction of the patriarchate of Jerusalem.[8]

The Monastery of Saint James is also the seat of a seminary where future priests are trained. This seminary is one of three presently functioning in the Armenian church; the other two are in Echmiadzin and Antelias. A fourth seminary, in Istanbul, ceased functioning in 1965 because of restrictions imposed on its curriculum by the Turkish government.[9] The great majority of members of the Saint James Brotherhood are graduates of the local seminary. One usually becomes a member of the brotherhood by being ordained a priest in Jerusalem, though there also have been cases of members of other brotherhoods who have renounced their original membership and have been admitted to the Saint James Brotherhood. Of those ordained in Jerusalem, almost all are graduates of the seminary and are ordained at a young age. A few are ordained at an older age, after they have served the church as deacons for many years (three such cases were known to me from 1975 to 1977). The practical knowledge acquired during the long period of service to the church exempts these people from a seminary graduation, though they have to pass examinations leading to the priesthood.

Not all graduates of the seminary are expected to elect the priesthood. For many, especially those from Turkey, the seminary simply supplies the best secondary education that they can obtain in the Armenian language and with a strong emphasis on Armenian culture and history. Nevertheless, more seminary graduates are ordained priests in Jerusalem than are required for the religious functions performed in the city. After a few years of service in Jerusalem, most are sent abroad to serve in various diaspora communities where they are more needed. Jerusalem, as a matter of fact, is becoming the main supplier of priests to the diaspora as most of the priests trained in Echmiadzin are used in Soviet Armenia and Antelias supplies priests only to the dioceses under its jurisdiction.[10]

The Administration of the Monastery

The patriarch is the spiritual and administrative head of the monastery. President of all the monastic assemblies and governor of church properties, he also represents his community (including laymen) before the state. A synod composed of seven members of the brotherhood assists the patriarch in the discharge of his functions. Patriarch and synod are elected by and accountable to the Central Assembly of the Brotherhood.[11] The patriarch's election also has to be ratified by the Catholicos of Echmiadzin to whom the see of Jerusalem is subordinated and by the chief of state ruling Jerusalem. Such ratification is not always granted automatically and can become part of the succession struggle, as seen above. The rules regulating the administration of the patriarchate of Jerusalem reflect the reforms introduced since the nineteenth century. These reforms granted greater powers to the brotherhood members at the expense of the patriarch, but they were not extended to laymen. Jerusalem is now the only Armenian community where laymen have no formal say on the selection of top church officials and on the government of their community. The Catholicos of Echmiadzin and Antelias are elected by assemblies in which special seats are reserved for lay representatives. The primates of each diocese, except Jerusalem, are elected similarly by votes of clerical and lay representatives of the parishes at the diocesan assembly.[12] This touch of democracy and lay participation in church affairs is a reflection of ancient Christianity of the apostolic times. It also further strengthens the links between nation and church, by considering the nation as the body politic of the church.[13] In these aspects, however, the monasteries form a different category, governed by autonomous clerical brotherhoods with no lay participation. The Monastery of Saint James in Jerusalem is no exception even though, unlike others, it is surrounded by a large lay congregation.

The General Assembly of the Brotherhood is the supreme decision-making body of the monastery and is occasionally convened for this purpose. Meetings of the General

Assembly are rare, however, as problems are usually solved informally among priests without involving formal meetings or before the issues are brought to formal approval. The system of informal decision-making is conducive to much greater manipulation of clientage ties; it favors those who control the scarce resources of the monastery and creates a large group of dependents around them. Personal influence rather than formal authority seems to be the principal basis for power in the monastery. This enables some laymen to wield informal power in monastery affairs and also permits some clergymen to hold more power than their official position provides.[14]

The patriarch and the synod also function as the religious court of the monastery, with jurisdiction over disciplinary problems regarding the clergy and civil status problems of the laymen. The monastery's authority on civil status affairs derives from the Ottoman millet system, which is still in force. Birth and death registration, marriage, divorce, and succession are all the patriarchate's responsibility. Divorce and inheritance cases are handled directly by the synod sitting as court; eligibility for marriage is investigated by a panel of three priests who report to the synod. In practice, the synod convenes very rarely as a religious court, because there have been only three divorces in the recent past and other litigations between parties preferably are solved by informal arbitration and mediation rather than by adjudication, which would intensify conflicts.[15] The patriarchate also has some law-and-order functions deriving partly from the millet system and partly from the government's respect for the sanctity and autonomy of the holy sites. The armed guards of the Ottoman period now have symbolic functions and have been transformed into doormen, but the city's security forces are still very reluctant to intervene within the monastery compound if unsolicited by church authorities. The patriarchate, on its part, makes every effort to solve problems within the community without requiring intervention of security forces from outside. Great uneasiness was felt when, on the occasion of two important thefts in the last years, Israeli police had to be invited to investigate. The intervention of Jordanian security forces during the patriarchal succession crisis of the 1950s was clearly exceptional and the extent of indignation that it aroused showed how serious a breach it was in the norm of nonintervention by government in the monastery's internal affairs.

The executive branch of the patriarchate is under overall control of the synod and is divided into different departments, each headed by a high-ranking clergyman. The grand sacristine is responsible for purely religious affairs, such as allocating priests to conduct religious services, upkeep of the churches, or matters related to conversion or eligibility for marriage. He is formally the second-highest officeholder in the monastery after the patriarch, and the only official besides the patriarch who must be a bishop and is elected by the general assembly of the brotherhood. Other department heads can be ordinary priests and are appointed by the patriarch and the synod. Their departments, while essential in any monastery, engage in more secular administrative matters. Among such departments are the department of estates, which manages the church property outside the monastery, and the closely related department of finance, which prepares the budget and is responsible for all financial affairs of the monastery. Another such department is the chief dragoman's office, which regulates secular aspects of life in the monastery and is responsible for maintaining order. The chief dragoman is in charge of closing the gates at night and issues special permission to those who have to return to the monastery after that time. He is responsible for the provision of food, cleaning, repairs, and other such facilities in the monastery. The chief dragoman is also the decision maker on the allocation of housing units within the monastery, but the crucial importance of this field also attracts intervention from other top clergymen.[16]

Recently a new executive position, that of chancellor, was created with overall responsibility for administration of

secular aspects of community life and contacts with government authorities. The chancellor's functions were not well-
defined and seemed to usurp some of the other officeholders'
functions.[17] The creation of the chancellor's office is probably
related to power balances within the monastic brotherhood.
The bishop who until April 1982 occupied the position of
chancellor was known to be the second most powerful person
in the patriarchate after the patriarch himself, even though,
officially, he was below the grand sacristine. Following a dispute with the patriarch, however, he recently was relieved of
all his functions in the brotherhood.[18]

There are also more specialized departments created to
direct a specific activity of the monastery. Such is the department in charge of relations with other churches and its main
task is to protect the Armenian church's rights in the Holy
Places. Other specialized departments were created to run
the seminary, the printing press, the library, and the lay
school. All these departments have clergymen as their titular
heads but some, such as the museum and the library, are run
by laymen. Delegating the actual work to laymen enables
clergymen to head many departments at the same time.
Indeed, the directorships of different executive departments
are distributed very unequally among clergymen. A few powerful priests control the most important departments and
have staffed them with their supporters. As I became
acquainted with the jobs held in the monastery, I was often
surprised to find the same laymen holding offices in different
areas and working for an even smaller number of clerical
titular heads.[19]

THE DAILY LIFE OF THE PRIESTS

Great differences exist in the everyday life of the priests,
depending on rank, age, and responsibilities. One important
difference is that between the bishops and other priests.
Bishopry is a basic line differentiating clergy in the Armenian
church.[20] Bishops are ordained by the Catholicos and in turn

can ordain ordinary priests. Bishops are regarded as the leaders of the church and are invested with positions of authority
in its administration. In contrast, their regular religious service obligations are very light. They do not officiate at or
even have to attend daily prayers or Sunday mass. Their
presence is required only at a few special holiday services.
Bishops are said to "descend" to church, honoring it by their
presence. Special songs are sung for them when they appear
and their robes are raised by attendants.[21] Regular services
are held by ordinary priests, assisted by deacons. In Jerusalem
ordinary priests take turns officiating in churches where regular services are held. One of these is the Armenian Chapel
within the Holy Sepulchre where midnight services are held
in addition to day services. As the gates of the Holy
Sepulchre have to be closed early in the evening, under the
status quo agreement, and because the Armenians (unlike
the Greek Orthodox) do not have an internal passage from
their chapel to living quarters in an adjacent building, service
in the Holy Sepulchre means being stranded in the chapel all
night. For this reason, the priests whose turn it is to serve in
the Holy Sepulchre are freed from all other duties.[22]

Another important difference in the activities of clergymen is the extent to which they are invested with administrative and educational tasks in the monastery. These tasks
are distributed very unequally in the Brotherhood of Saint
James. The younger members of the brotherhood, generally,
are busier than the older priests, because they are given
teaching functions in the seminary. A few top-ranking
bishops are busiest, because they control most of the extrareligious activities of the monastery.

Priests and some of the bishops live in rooms in a separate part of the monastery called the Priests' Courtyard. Even
though no physical barrier separates the Priests' Courtyard
from other areas of the monastery, laymen avoid entering
that area unless they have some specific business with a
priest (an unwritten rule that I unwittingly violated in my
first days in the field). In this way priests are provided with

some privacy, although exceptions exist to this separation. Some bishops live outside the Priests' Courtyard in much more spacious quarters, which are, however, adjacent to laymen's living quarters. Laymen are sometimes accommodated in the Priests' Courtyard when their apartments undergo some basic repairs or renovations. On the whole, there is great physical proximity between priests and laymen and one of the priests was only half-joking when he remarked that this is probably the only monastery in the world where a monk cannot have an afternoon rest because of children's noise.[23] The priests' rooms have their own kitchenettes, though most priests eat at the refectory. A few bishops sometimes join them, but most never appear in the common dining room.[24]

The life of the clergy is not very regimented. Ordinary priests have to get up at five A.M. for predawn services, which are followed immediately by morning services. In the past the predawn services were held in the middle of the night, but gradually they have been brought closer to daybreak. A third daily service is held at three P.M. Between services priests are free unless they have additional responsibilities, such as teaching in schools, administrative tasks, or officiating at weddings, baptisms, or funerals.[25] The number and identity of priests officiating at these ceremonies are determined by the grand sacristine, who also takes into consideration the priests' other duties and wishes of lay parties involved. The type of clerical attendance at these ceremonies is also an indication of the social status of the lay parties involved. Clergymen receive regular salaries from the patriarchate, according to their rank. They also receive additional sums for performing auxiliary functions, and often they receive unofficial gifts from laymen for officiating at life-cycle ceremonies. The clergy's salary is quite low and is often paid with months' delay, a matter for numerous complaints among my young clerical sources. Some clergymen, however, are known to have accumulated considerable personal wealth and in the past even invested it in small assets and real estate of their own, which reverted to the church upon their death. This personal wealth might be attributed to the clergymen's own funds held before they became priests or to gifts received from relatives rather than to income generated from religious services; nonetheless, it remains a curious phenomenon and leads to rumblings in the community about possible mismanagement of church finances.[26] The clergymen, generally, have plenty of leisure time to spend as they wish. They can be found visiting each other, tending the garden in the Priests' Courtyard, or going out of the monastery during the day. One young priest kept a pet dog in his room. They naturally form friendships on the basis of age, personal sympathy, views on political and social affairs, and leisure interests. Most priests spend much time alone in their rooms, reading and writing, as would be expected of a monastic life. Yet they are not fully detached from worldly affairs, because of the varied functions they perform, such as safeguarding the Holy Places, guiding pilgrims, training new priests, and taking care of refugees.[27]

THE MICROCOSM OF THE SEMINARY

Since the establishment of the seminary for priests in Jerusalem in 1845, its students have been added as a third component to the city's Armenian population, not quite part of the ecclesiastical sector but even more separated from the lay community. From the outset seminary students formed a separate group, leading a distinctive life characterized by a great degree of regimentation and segregation from the rest of the community.

There are about fifty students presently enrolled in the seminary, most of them from Turkey. Prior to the establishment of Israeli rule in 1967 most students came from Arab countries. Members of the local community are not allowed to enroll in the seminary and must go to Echmiadzin or Antelias if they want to become priests. Studies at the seminary start at the secondary school level. The first five years form the general section and its curriculum is similar to that of other secondary schools except for a stronger emphasis on armenological studies. Seminarians also have to participate in all daily religious services as part of their education. Religious service even takes precedence over classroom studies and classes are cancelled when they clash with religious service obligation, such as participation in a funeral. Still, less than half of the seminary teachers (eight out of twenty in 1975) are clergymen. Students graduate from the general section at the age of sixteen to seventeen and for most of them that marks the end of their studies. Those who want to continue their education toward the priesthood must study for another three or four years; during that time they also serve as tutors to the younger classes and as deacons in church. Ten of the forty students enrolled in the seminary in 1975 were in the higher studies section and three of them were subsequently ordained priests in 1977. Generally, less than one-fifth of the seminary students become priests.[28]

The monastery stresses the separation of seminarians from their original community and from local laymen. This is seen as an integral part of seminary education, accustoming them to detachment from family and community if they are to become priests. In the past seminary students were not sent home on vacation until their studies were completed. Now they usually are sent home in the summer every two or three years. Occasionally their families come from abroad to visit them in the monastery. The graduation ceremonies of 1977, for example, were attended by some of the graduates' families who had come from Turkey for the special occasion.[29]

The seminarians' contacts with the local community are also very strictly curtailed. The monastery is acutely aware of the difficulty of maintaining the seclusion considered necessary to the seminarians' training when local people of their own age live in their midst. The possibility of flirtation between seminarians and teenage girls of the community is feared as one of the great dangers of too much proximity between community and monastery. There was a notable case in which a seminary student fell in love with a girl of the community and they married after his graduation, putting an end to his ecclesiastical career.[30] The monastery makes great efforts to minimize contacts between seminary students and local youth. Seminarians never visit laymen's houses nor are they "adopted" by local families. They rarely are seen outside their group and they have to wear special uniforms at all times in public places. They have their own living quarters, out of bounds to the rest of the community, and they are absolutely forbidden to go to the clubs unless their supervisors take them there as a group to attend a cultural activity. Seminarians do meet with the local youth in the sports' field where the respective teams play against each other, but since this encounter is one of contest between opposing teams it maintains the segregative effect. On rare occasions seminarians do mix with local youth—in the church choir or in the special ceremonies held during the holidays—but the two groups are easily distinguishable by their attire. While local children are either dressed in a variety of clothes or wear their colorful school or club uniforms, seminarians invariably come in their dark gray suits. During church service, seminary students always arrive as a group and occupy a separate place under the supervision of their superiors.[31]

Daily life of the seminarians is rigidly structured, and they are left with little free time. They get up at five A.M. in order to participate in the predawn service, followed by the morning service. After breakfast their regular school program starts and continues until the afternoon with a lunch break. Following the afternoon service the seminarians have about two hours of free time, most of which they use to play soccer. After an early dinner the evenings are spent preparing homework for the next day under the supervision of tutors. Sunday mornings are devoted to church services and most afternoons are as piously devoted to playing soccer, unless some other collective entertainment (such as a picnic) is organized for them.[32] Seminarians rarely leave their group or vary their routine. They are constantly controlled by their tutors and have very few opportunities to meet other people. This regimentation and segregation imposed on the seminary stands in striking contrast to the relative laxity observed in the lives of clergymen and the lay community.

An important change has occurred in the lives of seminary students since 1975 with their passing to a new and bigger seminary building. Its construction was funded by an American Armenian, Alex Manoogian, who is president of the AGBU and one of the heaviest contributors to the patriarchate of Jerusalem. The inauguration of the new building was the occasion for one of the most important gatherings in many years, with the visit of the Catholicos of Echmiadzin, the Patriarch of Istanbul, the donor Manoogian himself, after whom the building is named, and many other church dignitaries and lay leaders of different communities in the diaspora. The main reason for the construction of the new seminary building was the wish to increase the number of students and make Jerusalem the principal supplier of priests to diaspora communities.[33]

From our point of view the most noteworthy fact about the new seminary building is its location *outside* the monastery walls. The old building was sited within the monastery and segregated from the rest of the monastery by internal walls. It was truly a separate cloister within the monastery. The new structure, by contrast, was built outside the monastery, across from the main gate, and has no enclosures separating it from outside. Surprising as the choice of location might seem (the reason was probably the lack of sufficient space within the monastery), quite inadvertently it creates an even greater separation between the seminary and the rest of the community as most of the community members live inside the monastery and conduct their social activities there. This is a small but telling example of the basic paradox of life in the Armenian quarter of Jerusalem.

"TOTALITY" IN THE ST. JAMES MONASTERY

Discussions of the Armenian community's daily life show that the lay and ecclesiastical sectors are not much differentiated in terms of "totality," with the notable exception of the seminary, which displays very totalistic features. Members of the Saint James Brotherhood lead a much less totalistic life than would be expected from a monastic order, while the lay community displays rather high levels of totality for a residential secular community, minimizing the difference between the two.[34] Segregation from outside is deemed very important but applies equally to clergy and to laymen who live within the monastery. Similarly, overcrowding and lack of privacy affect laymen as much as priests. Most laymen work either within or very near the monastery; they sleep, work, and play more or less in the same place and in the constant presence of the same others, quite like their ecclesiastical kinsmen and in great contrast to most contemporary urban communities, even those of rather homogeneous ethnicity, where places of work are clearly differentiated from residences.

The daily life of priests is, understandably, more regulated by formal rules and obligations than that of laymen. They are subject to many more religious restrictions, starting with celibacy and including many days of fasting or other dietary abstinence (e.g., Fridays and during Lent). As monks they are expected to achieve more control over themselves and their natural drives, but the difference is less than one would normally expect from a monastery versus a lay community. Neither laymen nor clergy have very strictly regulated daily routines. Priests have relatively ample free time between religious services and use it as they choose; in this respect the striking difference is that between priests and seminarians. Regarding uniformity, laymen work in a greater variety of occupations and dress in different ways, in contrast to the clergymen's more uniform work and dress patterns. In living accommodations and leisure activities both laymen and clergymen show great uniformity though not necessarily similarity. Within the monastic brotherhood there is a tendency to deformalize relations, handling them by informal persuasion and manipulation rather than on the basis of strict obedience to formal rules. Diffuse interactions prevail among both lay and clerical populations, and people relate to each other as whole persons rather than specific role-bearers. Across the clergy-laity barrier, however, relations are more role-specific, especially on the part of laymen toward clergymen.

The clergy-laity division of the Armenian quarter resembles the staff-inmate split of total institutions, but without the coercive relations that characterize the latter. The relations between priests and laymen have primarily normative and utilitarian bases. The utilitarian basis of compliance on the part of laymen may be said to derive from the many concrete economic advantages gained by laymen for living inside the monastery, in return for which they acquiesce to certain clergy-imposed restrictions on their daily life. Unlike the total institutions where inmates are paid symbolic wages for work performed while staff are salaried employees working to earn a living, here the staff gets a low salary not sufficient for, nor intended to earn a living; the laymen (or "inmates") are paid full salaries for work performed within the institution.

The various dimensions of totality are not, therefore, the main differentiating factors between the clergy and the laity. The two are more clearly differentiated in the nature of their goals and role-expectations; the monastic brotherhood's sense of religious mission is contrasted with the laity's more diffuse and more inward-oriented communal goals. The social implications of this difference and the role-tension created by their coexistence are the main issue of the next chapter.

6

Priests and Laymen: Problems of Coexistence and Dominance

The Armenian community of Jerusalem is a meeting place of contrasts. Closeness and separation, unity and division affect its daily life and organization simultaneously. Social roles are expanded and twisted to accommodate situations that nominally seem incompatible. These apparent contradictions may be explained by the fact that the Armenian quarter is the common territorial setting for two inherently different social organizations, a monastery and a secular residential community. This chapter will discuss the role-modification engendered within the clergy by the influx of a larger number of laymen into the monastery and then analyze the boundary-maintaining interactional mechanisms developed among the inhabitants of the monastery to emphasize separation and segmentation in a situation of too-close territorial proximity.

THE "VIRTUOSO" ROLE OF MONASTERIES

Monasteries usually have been established away from population centers; they have been places of recluse or retreat for people who wish to distance themselves from the

everyday interests and problems of the larger society. Turning away from worldly concerns and renouncing worldly ties
and pleasures are inherent to the basic asceticism necessary
in any monastic life, whether that of a solitary hermit or of a
group of ascetics living together in the same place and linked
by bonds of communion.

Closely related to this basic otherworldly orientation,
monastery members seek to reach levels of excellence that
are not expected of most people, whether in thinking, unfolding the secrets of the universe, or in piety, self-control,
renouncing mundane desires, or serving the supernatural
realm and complying with its values. While they might
merely try to find salvation, monks will readily concede that
their way to salvation is not the way for most people.[1] Max
Weber indicated the important difference (and inherent tension) between a relaxed mass religion in tune with the needs
and abilities of average persons and the ethical rigorism of
those few groups who reach a *virtuoso* religion.[2] In Bendix's
words:

> Since strict adherence to the Christian ideal cannot be
> expected of everyone, monastic asceticism is considered
> an accomplishment on behalf of the church by a select
> few who in this way accumulate a repository of bless-
> ings for the laity.[3]

Members of religious orders, whether monastic or not, strive
to be religious *virtuosi*. The aspiration toward "extraordinary"
levels of performance, surpassing those of average human
beings, motivates their action. If this performance is ascribed
to the group as a whole, then membership in this distinguished company is the personal reward of each.[4] As such,
"the religious virtuosi who work methodically at their salvation now become a distinctive religious 'status group' within
the community of the faithful."[5] In their closeness to spiritual perfection, the virtuosi represent larger human collectivities but are also clearly distinguished from them. In their
persons they represent others and thus inspire to that level

of excellence all those not strong or pure enough or lacking whatever other attributes necessary to reach it.

The monasteries' levels of excellence do not manifest themselves only in narrowly defined religious functions, such as prayers, meditation, liturgy, custody of holy shrines, and contact with the supernatural realm. Though these practices always have been considered the most important, monasteries also emerged in history as centers of virtuoso performance in activities less directly related to religion. For example, they became centers of general learning and research, even in such an "earthly" science as medicine. They developed linguistics, the recording of history, and different arts (music, architecture, manuscript illumination, etc.).[6] In all these spheres monasteries represented the peak of human performance at certain times and places.[7] As Weber pointed out, in the course of the development monastic orders generally underwent a process of "depersonalization" that transformed their asceticism from a means of escaping the world into one of extraordinary achievements in it.[8] In churches identified with certain ethnic or national groups, as in the Armenian case (also among the Maronites[9] and in a completely different place such as Ireland) monasteries were also the custodians of national culture and identity and were involved in political activities related to upholding nationalistic causes. These auxiliary functions of the monasteries did not contradict their virtuoso roles and did not interfere with their insulation from society. Unlike more individualized welfare and pastoral service, they did not require daily mixing with lay persons, oriented as they were toward human groups in their entirety rather than toward needy individuals. One should, therefore, differentiate between a more collectivistic this-worldliness that tried to affect social order as a whole and a more personalized this-worldliness that offered help to needy people. In monasteries, this-worldliness was manifested mainly in its collectivistic form, exerting influence on lay rulers and political movements or contributing to general knowledge, culture, and traditions, rather than offering welfare and community services. There were some exceptions of course, such as medical service in Medieval Europe,[10] but, generally, welfare and pastoral services did not impinge upon monasteries. They were the domain of pastors or else were handled by special nonmonastic religious orders.

To what extent is distancing oneself from the masses necessary for virtuoso performance? This question is far from settled, but it seems that some detachment from the environment is necessary in most virtuoso performances, at least in order to reach the concentration needed near the climax of performance. This is true even when, as in the case of most artists and authors, inspiration and material resources needed for the performance come from the surrounding society. The importance of such distancing is all the more easily recognized in monastic orders, because their principal goals are more clearly external to society. It is believed that to reach the virtuoso level members of monasteries ought not be bothered by daily problems that would distract them from their main tasks. Monks themselves might not be aware of the relationship between isolation and virtuoso performance. They might state that they distance themselves from other people not in order to reach higher levels of performance but simply to obtain the peace of mind needed for prayer.[11] Still, there is no reason why the prayer of a monk should require more peace of mind than that of average people unless his prayer is considered to be more profound and to reach levels untouched by ordinary people.

There are, however, other religious virtuosi who remain far closer to lay groups, and who seek in that closeness the fulfillment of religious excellence. This is the case of missionaries and religious orders expressly organized to spread the faith or offer help, charity, and guidance to the needy of the greater community. The Little Sisters of the Poor, the Jesuits, missionary organizations, and friars of the Mendicant Orders are among the best examples of such orders in Christianity.[12] Toward the end of the Middle Ages members of the Dominican and Franciscan orders broke away from traditional monasticism. They devoted themselves to public service "in the world," that is, in the growing cities. In the words of Pirenne:

> They asked no more of the burghers than their alms. In place of isolating themselves in the center of vast silent enclosures, they built their convents along the streets. They took part in all the agitations, all the miseries as well, and understood all the aspirations of the artisans, whose spiritual directors they well deserved to become.[13]

The degree of excellence in the performance of such people is measured by their behavior toward fellow human beings. Hence these orders should not be called monastic and Hillery is right in distinguishing between "1) the cloistered or contemplative monastery, i.e., the *monastic* convent, and 2) the *apostolic* convent, which is heavily concerned with work in the larger society."[14] It is unfortunate that Weber did not make this distinction explicit. On the contrary, he emphasized the process by which religious virtuosi moved from a contemplative to an apostolic (or missionary) role.[15] Members of religious orders dedicated to working with laymen are not, properly speaking, monks (or nuns). They do form a brotherhood (or sisterhood), abide by a special "rule" that governs them, and generally live in communal settings like members of monasteries, but resemblance between them stops there because the two groups chart themselves completely different paths to excellence.[16]

Even members of nonmonastic orders, for whom service to fellow human beings is so important, feel the need to separate themselves from the rest of the population and keep their distinct (and presumably superior) identity. In their daily contact with laymen this can be done by simple devices, such as wearing a special ring, or gown, or other kinds of personal apparel. It also can be achieved by more complex social obligations such as celibacy.[17] In an interesting study pointing out the important work of members of religious orders in American lay communities, Sister M. A. Neal quite perceptively indicated that this work "was accomplished in such a highly routinized way that it had become a work separated from 'life,' while life was increasingly secluded in a monastic withdrawal from the 'world' addressed within service systems defined as health, education and welfare works."[18] Thus members of religious orders, like other virtuosi, displayed an ambivalent attitude toward the larger society. They cannot reject the rest of the world totally, because they are usually inspired by, depend on, or at least represent it in higher realms.[19] Neither can they permit that imperfect world to compromise their own striving for perfection; hence they have to devise means to insulate themselves from normal social intercourse.[20]

The relationship between religious virtuosity and distancing oneself from the masses could also be discussed in terms of the separation between the sacred and the profane. Religious virtuosi strive to dwell in the sacred sphere and seek the sacred even in places and activities that are profane to others. As mentioned in the introduction, however, the sacred has to break the continuity of space and time as the very condition of its existence. To dwell in sacredness, religious virtuosi have to keep clear boundaries between the sacred and the profane. Most of them achieve this by spending longer times in prayers and religious rituals or by physically secluding themselves in places where such activities take prominence, as in monasteries and holy sites. To be sure, holy sites might contradict seclusion, as they are also places of attraction to multitudes who wish to enter into periodic contact with the sacred, but such visits in fact enhance the virtuoso nature of resident clergymen because they put the clergy in a position of mediation between the holy place and the profane background of the visitors. Residents receive the visitors into the sacred arena; they are the gate-keepers and guides to holiness. A more serious problem of boundary keeping between the sacred and the profane exists, however, when religious virtuosity is accomplished by reaching out to laymen in their profane everyday life and problems (as in missionary and charity organizations). Such nonmonastic religious virtuosi have to keep their link with the sacred while acting in a profane arena, in terms of space, time, and type of activity. Hence more subtle, but no less important symbolic means of separation are devised between these religious virtuosi and the laity whom they try to help.

The Mendicant Orders and other nonmonastic religious groups in which human welfare and spiritual roles converge did not develop in Eastern Christianity; they are Western phenomena. Monasticism in the East remained more faithful to its original tenets of renouncing worldly concerns, practicing penance, and Divine Worship.[21] Its auxiliary and more mundane functions were oriented toward general literacy and artistic work (mainly writing, copying, translating, and illuminating manuscripts) or the education of future priests, rather than providing individualized welfare services to laymen. The same was true of Armenian monasteries in which literacy and cultural excellence were also instrumental in preserving the Armenian national identity under alien rule.[22] As mentioned, the difference between the monastic and pastoral duties of the clergy was reflected in the creation of a separate category of married priests for specifically pastoral tasks.[23] When, for lack of married priests, celibate priests were given pastoral duties, they did not reside within monastery compounds. Monasteries were inherently differentiated from parishes and their elite performances required some kind of insulation from everyday problems of the laity. There are records of more than 250 Armenian monasteries that have flourished at different times between the Caspian and the Mediterranean seas. Most were established in rather inaccessible mountainous regions far from population centers, such as Datev, Gladzor, Sevan, Shooghr, Lim, Ktootz, and Armash. A few were formed near national political centers, such as Echmiadzin and Sis.[24] In the latter case, clergymen exerted strong influence on the secular elite, but through this influence they served and guided the national collectivity as a whole and not individual families or localities. The monastery of Jerusalem was the only one situated in a population center that was not at the same time an Armenian political center. It was, however, located on a holy site and it served the church, and the nation as a whole, by maintaining direct contact with the "core" of their faith.

ROLE-MODIFICATION IN THE MONASTERY OF SAINT JAMES

The diverse functions assumed by the Armenian clergy of Jerusalem until World War I were largely extensions of religious roles. Fighting with other Christian groups for control of holy shrines, building and embellishing churches, going on fund-raising tours for this purpose, guiding and serving pilgrims to the Holy Land were all part of the same religious mission for which the monastery was originally established. The only exception was the administrative role as head of the Armenian ethnic community according to the Ottoman millet system. Even though this was undoubtedly a communal function, it could still be conceived as one of national leadership oriented toward the entire collectivity.

After World War I the auxiliary functions of the clergy took the form of more individualized services to laymen. The establishment of lay refugees within the monastery compound forced new tasks upon clergymen that deviated from their traditional monastic role and brought them closer to a pastoral role. Serving the secular community, guiding and comforting it, helping it overcome the many difficulties it faced, became the most urgent matter. This indeed went beyond normal pastoral functions because of the special difficulties faced by laymen. The "Brothers of Saint James" were transformed not simply into pastors but rather into "welfare agents" or, borrowing Hillery's term, into a community "task force."[25] Laymen had to be fed, given shelter, and helped to find jobs. They had to be supplied facilities for education, entertainment, and cultural activities. Other Armenian communities had to be found for the relocation of the surplus population that could not be assimilated locally. The clergymen also had to advise the refugees, participate in their grief,

and offer them moral support. These tasks compounded regular administrative and financial responsibilities of the monastery. The refugees also had to be represented and their
interests protected before the government. Funds had to be
raised and distributed in a way that met the new needs of the
community. As we have seen, such services to laymen continued and even became more institutionalized after the
emergency passed. What was thought of as a temporary measure took on more permanent features. The Brotherhood of
Saint James found its monastery transformed into a parish, a
change compounded by the fact that, unlike other parishes,
here (a) the congregation lived inside the monastery and (b)
the church supported the congregation rather than being
supported by it.[26]

The influx of refugees also created a constant contact
between the sacred and the profane within the monastery.
As long as laymen were simply visitors (pilgrims) and resident clergy served them as guides to the sacred sphere, the
threshold between the sacred and the profane was preserved
and the clergy's ties with the sacred were enhanced. When
laymen were permanent inhabitants but lived outside the
monastery and/or performed specialized tasks for the monastery, the monastery walls and their specialized lay occupations (which were markedly nonreligious and freed the clergy
from direct involvement in them) maintained the boundaries.
But when laymen settled permanently *within* the monastery
compound, offered no specialized service to the monastery,
and formed the great majority of the inhabitants, the distinction between the sacred and the profane became blurred and
added further incongruence to the monastic brotherhood's
role expectations.

How did the clergy meet this challenge of role-modification? First, the changes discussed above did not necessarily
eliminate the role of the clergy as religious virtuosi; they
rather created a new dimension of religious excellence. By
reference to the distinction made earlier between monastic
and nonmonastic religious orders, virtuoso performance also

could manifest itself in works of charity and welfare to the needy in lay society. Members of the Saint James Brotherhood could conceive the attainment of spiritual excellence in the guidance and help offered to suffering fellow Armenians. This kind of excellence was uncommon in Eastern Christianity where pastoral and welfare functions did not carry high status, but in the given historical circumstances these welfare activities could be linked to a more general national leadership role. During World War I Armenians faced genocide and were threatened with extinction as a people; the church's help to refugees could be seen, therefore, in the context of attempts to save the whole nation. It was addressed not merely to the immediate needs of the local population but through them to the entire Armenian collectivity. Bishop Guregh Kapikian, principal of the lay school, expressed a similar thought eloquently when he said, "I am devoted to serve God but even more to serve my people, because God does not really need my help while my people do."[27]

The members of the Saint James Brotherhood thus could view themselves as continuing the traditional role of protecting the separate existence of Armenians as a nation. This basic aim, which always had been included in the definition of the clergy's virtuoso position, was reached by diverse means under different historical circumstances. In the past it was fulfilled mainly through the clergy's contribution to Armenian culture, literature, and art and through its direct contact with the sources of Christianity with which the separate Armenian national identity was closely interlinked. Now contributions to the same goal were manifest in caring for the remnants of a genocide in which nearly one-third of the total Armenian population lost their lives. The Monastery of Saint James adjusted to these circumstances; it undertook service to the nation in this new form, or at least this was how the clergy tried to explain its role-modification.[28]

Let us now ask the long-delayed question (which has lurked in the background ever since we discussed lay dependence on the monastery) of what the Brotherhood of Saint James received from laymen in return for its services. At first glance, it clearly obtained power and prestige. Laymen are respectful and submissive in the presence of clergymen. They bow to priests, sometimes kiss their hands, and move out of the way when they pass. Priests often are given presents by laymen. At social events the best food and places are reserved for them.[29] Clergymen are recognized as the supreme decision-makers in community affairs. All organized communal activities are held under the aegis of the brotherhood and need its approval. The laymen also accept certain church-imposed restrictive rules which regulate their lives (such as the closing of the gates at night). In view of the great dependence of laymen on the monastery, however, it is surprising that there are not many more such restrictive rules. Life in the shadow of the church is not oppressive. People do not feel pressured by the clergy. When lack of freedom is felt, this is caused more by overcrowding and lack of privacy than by the imposition of a certian life-style by the clergy. The patriarchate knows fairly well the limits of its power over laymen and realizes that were the use of this power pushed too far strong resistance and conflict would ensue.

Obtaining power and prestige is not a sufficient return for services the monastery supplies to its lay inhabitants and is certainly not the reason that it continued to provide these services. It seems that clergymen expect no direct reward for their services. In the past the very presence of laymen in Jerusalem was an advantage to the church, because a large lay community buttressed its claims to holy sites. However, since the status quo edict of the last century there is less danger of a church losing the Holy Places under its control, and having a large group of local followers has lost its immediate importance in this matter. At present Armenian priests would prefer to have fewer laymen living in their midst within the monastery and would like to reduce the dependence of laymen on patriarchal services. But they cannot force the laymen to reduce their dependence without the risk of cutting them off from the community altogether and perhaps pushing them toward assimilation in the non-Armenian environment. For example, moving people out of the monastery when there is not enough housing available in the immediate vicinity would disperse them all over the city and loosen their ties with the community. Similarly, if education is not subsidized, more families could be tempted to send their children to non-Armenian schools. In the absence of club activities inside the monastery, people would turn outside for entertainment and socializing. The clergy thus continues to offer many services to laymen, not because this confers added power and prestige or elicits important services in return or even because they think the laymen are in any great want, but simply because it helps strengthen the ties among community members and indirectly strengthens the entire Armenian nation. In a sense, whether laymen truly need this welfare system or merely take advantage of it is beside the point. The more relevant question is how best to preserve the whole nation's identity and culture and prevent assimilation into the non-Armenian environment.[30]

Offering their services to the important national survival mission is the explanation members of the Saint James Brotherhood give for their role-modification. Symbolic transference to the ideal of national survival helps bridge the difference between the clergy's monastic virtuoso role and the new pastoral functions. This is not to say, however, that real difficulties and tensions do not exist in trying to reconcile the monastic conception of the clergy's role and the new, more communal and nationalistic emphasis. While the clergymen of Jerusalem define their role-change in terms of nationalistic causes, they still rank teaching and welfare functions lower in importance than those for which the monastery was originally established, that is, guarding the Holy Places and glorifying the church by Divine Service in them. In the words of one of the more articulate priests:

Jerusalem is above all a holy place and the monastery is here to serve and keep the Holy Places. It is only secondarily and quite reluctantly a parish. Therefore priests' duties in Jerusalem, compared to other places, are more purely religious than pastoral or nationalistic.[31]

There is, however, no consensus among priests in this respect. For some, such as the principal of the lay school, nationalist functions are no less important than purely religious ones. However, the official policy of the brotherhood does seem to indicate a preference for the monastic-religious roles over others.

This ranking finds expression in various symbolic ways in the daily life of the clergy. I found, for example, that teacher priests whose duty to officiate in religious services conflicts with their classes in the lay school or the seminary invariably cancel the class and do not try to find a replacement. It is improper even to try to switch a service with another priest in order to avoid the clash, because that would acknowledge that Divine Service disturbs other obligations. Similarly, service in the Holy Sepulchre takes precedence over any other duty and those priests whose turn it is to serve there for a week are exempt from all other duties. Another example is provided by the occasional clash between Easter and the Day of Commemoration for the World War I events held on April 24. When the two coincide, the commemoration of the dead is invariably postponed for a week or so to give precedence to the religious holiday.[32]

The Brotherhood of Saint James deems it imperative to remind everyone that despite the influx of laymen, its compound is still a monastery and has not turned into just another residential community. The closing of the gates is scrupulously observed for this reason. The nonparticipation of laymen in the election of patriarchal officeholders also stresses that the Jerusalem community is above all a self-governing monastic collectivity from which laymen are excluded (even if some families have lived there for over a generation). The transfer of the patriarchate's dioceses in Syria and Lebanon to the jurisdiction of Antelias after World War I strengthened the monastic image and freed it from administrative functions as head of a millet covering a large area. The reasons for this transfer had no connection with the wish to stress the monastic character of Jerusalem; it resulted mainly from a wish to transfer some authority and possessions to the Catholicosate of Cilicia, which had incurred great losses after World War I and even had to abandon its headquarters in Sis. Nonetheless, the unintended effect was the same. Only the small communities of Palestine and Transjordan (in Jaffa, Haifa, Amman, and Bethlehem, together with Jerusalem itself) were left under the jurisdiction of Jerusalem, and they were never recognized as lay communities with a right to participate in the election of their religious leaders as was the general rule in the Armenian church.

The tension between the monastic and welfare roles of the clergymen and the blurring between monastery and residential community are strikingly reflected in the controversy over the use of the patriarchate's financial resources. Most laymen complain that the patriarchate does not allocate enough money for community needs, while the ecclesiastical sector claims that the funds should be used more for the church. When they first arrived in Jerusalem, doubtless, the refugees desperately needed the monastery's material support. Since then many have prospered but still continue to receive aid from the patriarchate. Some of my informants (not only clergymen) see this as an exploitative dependence and a "welfare recipient mentality." In contrast, most laymen consider this help their natural right as members of the ethnic community. In their view the material resources of the patriarchate belong to the community as a whole; the clergymen control them only in the name of the community and hence should use them largely for its needs. The patriarchate is seen as the corporate body that organizes and represents community life and hence controls the community's resources. For the same reason, all contributions coming from abroad are channeled through and controlled by the patriarchate, though this does not mean that they are not intended for the use of the community as a whole.[33] This view is symptomatic of the failure to distinguish between monastery and parish and is, understandably, hotly disputed by priests who claim that the patriarchate's financial resources are designed to serve the church and not the community. According to them the money should go first to such religious purposes as training priests and upkeep of the Holy Places. Employment of these funds for the lay community was a response to an erstwhile emergency, but now the funds should revert to their original more purely spiritual uses.[34] The patriarchate's policy of late indeed has been to reduce financial support to laymen and have them assume a larger share of the burden for services they receive. Examples of this trend already discussed are the monastery's determination to assert its property rights and its insistance on cutting its subvention to the lay school. As we have seen, however, the monastery has stopped short of using coercive measures against recalcitrant laymen to avoid causing rifts which might sever a part of the population from the community. Pressure is exerted more indirectly by manipulating the laymen's dependence on the monastery in other spheres of life.

SEPARATION AND SEGMENTATION IN TERRITORIAL PROXIMITY

The proximity in which laity and clergy live within the Saint James Monastery has led to the development of special boundary-maintaining mechanisms that stress the separation and distinction between them. This is especially important to the priests, because it is closely linked with their effort to sustain the monastic image of the brotherhood and their general virtuoso role. Just as discontinuity between the sacred and the profane is more necessary to the former than the latter, lack of separation creates more difficulties in the fulfillment of the monastic role than the lay one. That some detachment from the larger society is needed for any virtuoso performance is felt even by members of religious orders founded especially for providing charity and welfare. Hence, even in their new welfare functions, not just in their traditional monastic role, the clergy of Jerusalem have had to find means to keep their social distance from the lay community. Some of these were consciously devised. Others developed "naturally," sometimes resulting in invisible but clearly felt boundaries between the ecclesiastical and lay sectors of the population.

First of all, residents of Jerusalem as a rule are not allowed to enroll in the seminary or become members of the local monastic brotherhood. This rule existed prior to World War I and hence is not a special device created to cope with the problems generated by the influx of lay refugees into the monastery. But obviously it took on added importance after World War I.[35] Members of the local community who want to become priests have to study in Echmiadzin or Antelias and are posted outside Jerusalem.[36] The seminarians and priests of Jerusalem come from abroad and are not encouraged to develop local ties. Young graduates of the seminary are sent to serve elsewhere a few years after graduation. The church prefers to keep older priests in Jerusalem, while a higher turnover exists for younger priests. This is partly because the latter are in greater demand in diaspora communities and can adjust more quickly to a change of place, but it also serves to prevent the development of close ties with the local community by those clergymen who would be most attracted to it.

Great efforts also are made to minimize the priests' social ties with laymen while they serve in Jerusalem. Priests are strongly discouraged from socializing outside their own circle. Visits to lay families in their residences and long periods of leisure time spent together are not well regarded and might lead to gossip about illicit sexual relationships,[37] as discussed earlier. Such gossip, even if unfounded, is very effective in preventing close ties between the celibate clergy and lay persons. It also shows how the territorial proximity and its concomitant lack of privacy, by enabling a closer scrutiny of each group's behavior, prevents any deviation from the normative prescriptions attributed to different roles and thus, paradoxically, helps freeze the differences between the various sectors of the population.

Another means of separation is found in the priests' living quarters. As mentioned earlier, an invisible barrier exists between the Priests' Courtyard where almost all clergymen live and the rest of the monastery. Laymen never venture into the courtyard unless on some specific business with a clergyman, even though it is situated on the main thoroughfare of the monastery, linking the two chief inner courtyards where the public buildings (school, library, clubs, churches, patriarchate offices) are located. Rather than walk through the Priests' Courtyard, which is the easiest access route, laymen invariably use an alternative way through a low arch under which one has to bow deeply to pass. Similarly, the seminary's premises are closed to laymen, while priests never go to the clubs uninvited. Distancing and invisible territorial barriers are used in a manipulative way to help define the types of affiliations that groups want to keep toward each other.[38]

Priests are very careful about their appearances in public. They wear special black robes and conic hats at all times outside their rooms, which make them recognizable from great distances. The patriarch and some high-ranking priests also keep their distance from the community by rarely being seen in public. The patriarch appears only on special occasions, always accompanied by a procession of priests and guards, which adds solemnity to his appearances. In fact, an important function of the guards is to lead such processions, hitting their ceremonial sticks on the ground to announce the passage of the patriarch. These processions always cause some commotion and interrupt the regular flow of life in the community.[39] They break the continuity between the sacred and the profane by ceremonializing the appearance of the sacred in the midst of the profane.

Another symbolic expression of the separation between the clergy and the lay community is the use of various churches for different purposes. Religious services related to the laity's life-cycle ceremonies (marriages, baptisms, etc.) are not held in the principal church (Saint James Cathedral) but rather in the much smaller Church of the Archangels far from the public center of the monastery. The latter is considered the "parish church" in contrast to Saint James Cathedral, which is regarded as the domain of the monastic brotherhood. The symbolic differentiation between the two churches is further complicated by official nonrecognition of a lay congregation in Jerusalem. No daily services are held in the Church of the Archangels, because to do so would be to acknowledge that a parish does exist inside the monastery. The Church of the Archangels is, therefore, put to use only by special request of the laity, as in a life-cycle ceremony. In the Saint James Cathedral daily services are held even if no layman participates, because services there are held not for the community but to glorify God and the church. Saint James Cathedral also is recognized as the "national" center as opposed to the parish or community center. Holiday observances and other religious ceremonies related to national events (such as commemoration of the World War I massacres) are held in the Cathedral.[40]

Focus thus far has been on the clergy for whom boundary-maintenance was especially important because it came in response to the challenge of role-modification and the blurring of the sacred-profane distinction. Laymen did not have to worry about keeping the boundaries of the sacred sphere and did not face the same kind of role-modification, though they were undoubtedly affected by living inside a monastery and felt a strong urge to stress their distinction from monastic life and the patriarchate establishment. For example, the ascription of high status to those who achieve an independent position vis-à-vis the monastery (such as the industrialists from the northern suburbs) is probably related to the great overall dependence of the lay community on the monastery. In my talks with local residents I detected an ambivalent attitude in which most laymen find it profitable to continue to rely on the monastery's services and even object to the clergy's attempt to reduce that dependence, but at the same time they value independence from the monastery and are proud of those among them who have gained it.

Religiosity is another ambivalent subject in which closeness and separation meet in paradoxical ways. Most Armenian laymen claim to be religious but show very few external signs of it. Hardly any laymen attend daily church services and no more than forty to fifty do so on Sundays. Nor could I see other marks of religious observance such as frequent lighting of candles, or making the sign of the cross, or following dietary restrictions. By contrast they are very respectful toward priests in public encounters. Their explanation for abstaining from services is that, as many put it, "you do not have to attend church when you live in it."[41] By their absence from services and abstention from other external signs of religiosity (which is different from deference shown to priests) laymen wish to imply that despite their special habitat they are not bound by a monastic life-style. On national holidays, however, attendance is very high because it signifies participation in a national event which does not endanger their secular character and distinction from the monastic world. Life-cycle ceremonies also are well attended but are not whole-community affairs. Invitation and attendance are selective and reflect the status of the parties involved and differential association and distancing between subgroups within the larger community.[42]

Social clubs play an important part in fulfilling the laymen's need for differential attribution and association. Many urban community studies have pointed out the segmentation of neighborhoods into subcommunities, whether territorial block-units or subgroups based on lineage, ethnicity, or

regional origins.[43] This segmentation is reflected in differential friendship ties and in church or club memberships. Similar tendencies are also found in the Armenian quarter.
Rather than help create general social ties and integration
among all the inhabitants, the clubs reflect segmental ties
and keep the segments different from each other. While
above all the clubs provide areas where laymen are separated
from the clergy, they also provide an opportunity for segmentation among laymen themselves, distinguishing locals
from refugees, supporters of different political parties, and
more generally, varied cliques and friendship groups. They
create places and platforms of activity that these groups may
call their own and through which they can compare themselves with others. This need is made much more acute by
the centripetal effect of life within a monastery. At first I was
quite surprised by the degree of segmentation that existed in
such a small community with its members living so close
together. I shared some of my informants' rhetorical amaze-
ment at the divisiveness of the Armenian people just when
they had to be more united than ever.[44] Only later did I
understand that internal segmentation was in fact a response
to territorial proximity and social closure and that it did not
endanger their unity vis-à-vis the outside world.

The efforts of laymen to maintain boundaries and distinction between themselves and the clergymen are different
from similar efforts of the clergy in one crucial respect. While
both groups try to keep some separation from each other, the
clergy has to balance that with overall dominance. It cannot
let boundaries lead to loss of control over a portion of the
territory and the emergence of a *de facto* split between lay and
clerical sectors within the monastery. The unity (and special
characteristics) of the monastery cannot be put into question
and it should be absolutely clear that the laymen are the ones
incorporated into the clergy's territory and not the reverse.
Laymen understand and generally acquiesce in this fact,
which explains why clergymen are invited (and agree) to
honor with their presence every important club activity,

from fund-raising dinners to concerts, and usually legitimize them with some inaugural blessing. No matter how secular or remote from the clergy's interests, the event has to be sanctified, that is, proclaimed to be in accordance with the monastery's self-image. Members of the Brotherhood of Saint James thus have a delicate balancing act to perform. They must penetrate the other group's sphere and establish rules regulating it, yet at the same time keep themselves beyond its activities and concerns.

7

Monasteries and Urban Neighborhoods: Some Comparisons

This chapter will move beyond the Armenian case to a comparative discussion. As mentioned, the habitation patterns revealed in the Armenian quarter are by no means unique. There have been many urban neighborhoods similar to the Armenian quarter in terms of closure, inward orientation, and dependence on religious institutions. There are also numerous examples of collectivities in inherent tension with each other that share a common territory or in which one collectivity makes use of the other's territory. In history there have been many instances of monasteries and castles housing lay or civilian populations. In more modern settings, one can think of family quarters in military bases, workers' residences in big industrial plants, diplomatic enclaves, and frontier outpost communities in which similar hybrid situations exist, residential groups sharing the same place and being under the overall authority of an organization with inherently different goals and patterns of activity. The basic daily necessities, such as shelter, food, clothing, medical care, education, socializing, and entertainment are provided within and/or under the aegis of the organization and follow the standard norms and regulations set up by the organization. Relations among community members are also directly influenced by status distinctions deriving from formal rank or position in the organization. In all these hybrid cases we are bound to find some informal role-modification or reinterpretation to ease tension in adapting to coexistence with a different type of organization. In addition, various symbolic interactional mechanisms emerge, stressing differentiation and boundary-maintenance despite (or because of) spatial integration.

As noted in the introduction, however, the examples above differ from the Armenian case (and from preindustrial city wards, modern ethnic neighborhoods, and lay populations living in medieval monasteries) in at least two important respects. First, there is a much greater turnover of people living in those settings, as residence is generally limited to the tour of duty of one of the family members; hence, with the exception of company towns, it would be uncommon to find the same family living there for more than one generation. Second, at least one member of each family has to belong to both collectivities. As father, husband, and neighbor one would be part of the residential community, but at the same time, as soldier, diplomat, or industrial worker he would be part of the formal organization with which the residential community shares the same space. Indeed, the fact that the same person has to perform roles in both sectors is the reason for the spatial integration of the two different collectivities. This is not the case in the Armenian quarter. The head of the lay family is not at the same time a monk. The two collectivities live side by side, for more than a generation, and without the same person being part of both collectivities.

A detailed comparative study of such hybrid communities is a fascinating research topic in its own right but much beyond our scope.[1] Instead, three cases (only one of them a "hybrid" case) that seem to offer the greatest similarity to the Armenian example will be discussed here. First, focus will be placed on other Christian monasteries[2] that have housed lay populations at different places and times. Second, the Armenian quarter will be compared with other preindustrial urban quarters. Finally, the discussion will be extended to contemporary defended neighborhoods, placing the study in a broader frame of reference of modern community studies.

LAY COMMUNITIES WITHIN MONASTERIES

As a general rule monasteries seek separation from lay communities. The term monastery derives from the Greek root *mono*, which means single and has the connotation of being alone or isolated.[3] The tendency toward insulation from society is borne out clearly by the development of Christian monasticism in both East and West.[4] At first, following the way pioneered by Saint Anthony, monasticism took the form of solitary contemplation of God and mortification of the flesh by hermits who retreated to inaccessible places far from human communication. But quite early the movement also took a collective form, beginning with the cenobite communities organized by Saint Pachomius in the Egyptian desert in the fourth century and later emulating the organization set up by Saint Basil of Cappadocia. Groups of monks lived together and developed strong ties of communion. Submersion of the self in the collectivity became paramount, and one achieved perfection through membership in the group. In communal monasticism, far from being left in solitude, every detail of the monk's activity was prescribed by a rule: the brothers' dress, food, hours of sleep, travels, hours of work and worship were all regulated and a penal code was rigorously enforced against defaulters. These rules prevented monks from exaggerating in the torture of their bodies and provided the basic necessities required for subsistence in the wilderness. The monk had to be a useful human being for himself and his fellow brothers.[5] Palestine was prominent as an area where both types of monastic life developed. Saint Euthymius, Saint Sabas, and

Saint Theodosius, the first an Armenian, were the fore-
runners of solitary hermitage. Communal monasteries also
flourished in the Judean wilderness where turning away
from worldly affairs was strongly emphasized. However,
monasteries were also established in more populous parts of
Palestine where the major concern was protection of Christian Holy Places.[6] This task required more "earthly" activities, closer contacts with lay populations, and stronger ties
with political rulers.

Despite the underlying principle of separation between
monastery and laity, there is ample historical evidence of
close interaction between them, even without taking into
consideration the Mendicant Orders and other such religious
groups (called nonmonastic in the preceding chapter)
expressly located in population centers with the purpose of
extending welfare to laymen. Even in normal medieval monasteries there are several examples of close ties with lay populations. Monks offered education services to students who
lived there even when they were not training for the priesthood. They extended medical help to the sick, gave hospitality to travelers, and sheltered civilians in time of war or other
political disturbances.[7] In some monasteries lay workers who
performed menial jobs, usually maintenance, lived inside
the compound. The abbeys of the Cluniac order, in particular, employed such laborers to free the monks for more spiritual occupations. In Cistercian monasteries, by contrast,
there were fewer opportunities for the presence of lay communities within the monastery, because of their relative geographical isolation and their emphasis on manual labor. But
even in these monasteries a distinction was made between
monks who did relatively little physical work and the "lay-
brothers" on whom most of the menial tasks fell.[8]

Important lay communities also developed *around* monasteries. Monastery land was farmed by cultivators who settled
nearby. Under the system prevailing in Medieval Europe
most monastery lands, like those of feudal lords, were inhabited by serfs and tenant farmers; monasteries owned whole

villages and large manors.[9] As such, monasteries had administrative rights and duties over laymen. They levied taxes, kept law and order, administered alms, clothed and fed the poor, and protected the community from outside forces. A similar system prevailed in Armenia; the church and some of its monasteries were proprietors of large tracts of land and controlled a considerable population of lay farmers.[10] Some of the lay settlements established on monastery-owned estates became the nuclei of European towns.[11] The very building of monasteries often induced development of secular communities around them as the construction workers were almost always laymen. Products grown in the monastery were sold in neighboring markets and some monasteries engaged in specialized cultivation and stockraising for income purposes. The Cistercians, for example, were prominent in the production and trade of wool, grain, and wine.[12]

Monasteries attracted laymen above all as places of pilgrimage.[13] In Mumford's words:

> The presence of a saintly hermit walled up in his cell near its doors, or even the bones and relics of such a saint would be an attraction to the pious, all the more if he had a reputation for possessing miraculous powers.[14]

Even the solitary hermits often found themselves surrounded by a steady stream of visitors and disciples who sought their spiritual guidance or miraculous powers. Indeed, one of the most famous anchorites of the Syrian desert, Saint Simeon, was so disturbed by people touching him and taking pieces of his leather tunic as relics that he built himself a high pillar and lived on it, out of the visitors' reach. He was the first of a new type of hermit known as "the stylites," holy men who retired from the world to complete seclusion on top of ancient pillars, or pillars that they erected for themselves.[15] A whole settlement eventually arose around Saint Simeon's pillar and similar settlements or monasteries also were built around other caves, pillars, or mountain tops where hermits stayed.[16]

In the case of communal monasticism, pilgrims either were housed within the monastery compound or found accommodation around it and thus contributed to the growth of a lay settlement. The very existence of a famous monastery where saintly figures lived or were buried could be reason for pilgrimage, but the holiness of the site often preceded and caused the establishment of the monastery. Construction of the monastery facilitated and institutionalized pilgrimage to that site, and pilgrims were soon followed by merchants and others who hoped to profit from the development of the area. In this way secular towns developed around monasteries near holy places. The sites of the first Christian martyrs' tombs of the Roman empire became the embryos of many European medieval towns and countless more were formed near churches and monasteries.[17] Many scholars, in fact, consider aggregations around religious institutions to have been a key factor in explaining the origin of urban centers in widely different cultures.[18] On the whole Eastern Christian monasticism seems to have remained more insulated from lay communities than its Western counterpart, though in the East too one occasionally would find laymen living within the monastery compound or close by.[19] Jerusalem is of course a prime example of the causal effect of religious attraction on lay settlement near sacred sites. Lay communities were not only drawn to holy places in and around Jerusalem but were in fact *needed* there to bolster a religious institution's claim of control over those sites in its competition with rival churches and monasteries.

The more secluded monasteries, generally, were those which were *not* established on holy sites and they failed to draw many pilgrims or visitors. Even in places that attracted laymen, however, most lived outside the monastery compound. In this respect, evidence points toward two different possibilities. A few laymen would be accommodated in the monastery as temporary visitors or to perform some essential service, but their numbers would remain low and would not exceed that of the resident clergymen; or a larger lay community far exceeding the clerics would emerge *outside* the monastery walls. In the case of the Armenian quarter of Jerusalem, these two possibilities converged after World War I; laymen far outnumbered the clergy and also lived *inside* the monastery compound, making this a rather rare phenomenon of lay inhabitation connected with a monastery.[20]

PREINDUSTRIAL URBAN NEIGHBORHOODS

The Armenian quarter of Jerusalem shares many traits with residential areas in other historical, preindustrialized cities, and it is perhaps possible to refer to it simply as a typical example of a traditional urban quarter. The Armenians themselves are the first to refute such a claim, stressing the extent of the authority of clergymen over laymen and the extent of the latter's dependence on monastery services, which make it unusual even for a traditional urban neighborhood. There are, nonetheless, obvious similarities between the Armenian quarter and other traditional urban neighborhoods in terms of closure, internal organization, and community life-style. This does not invalidate the duality of the Armenian quarter. On the contrary, it might draw attention to the little-noticed fact that similar dual properties also might be found in other old city neighborhoods.

In most preindustrial cities, especially in the Muslim world, the population was segregated into wards that were self-contained social worlds in their own right. The inhabitants of each ward were connected by primordial ties, whether of religion, ethnicity, or common regional origin.[21] In most Middle Eastern cities under Muslim rule there were separate Jewish, Greek, Armenian, Latin, and other Christian quarters. Various Muslim sects and nationalities also were identified with separate sections of the city, Shi'ites being differentiated from Sunnites, Turks from Arabs, and most cities having discrete Persian, Turcoman, North African, and other districts.[22] The same pattern was found in Islamic cities of Spain and Mumford reports a similar division into different religious quarters in Mesopotamian towns of antiquity.[23] Medieval European towns also displayed the same form: they were a congeries of little wards, each with some autonomy and self-sufficiency, with its own churches and fountains. Each quarter was identified by its religious homogeneity and thus was interchangeable with "parish" boundaries.[24] It was not uncommon for these quarters to be surrounded by their own walls and gates sealing them off from other sections of the city and, in Sjoberg's words, "leaving little cells or sub-communities as worlds unto themselves."[25] Neighborhood walls were built in addition to the city's outer walls and gates girdling its perimeter, which were prominent features of most historical cities.[26] As were the city gates, the entrance to the walled quarters was closed at night, bringing communication among the city's different sections to a halt and providing added protection to the inhabitants. These walls reinforced the segmentation of social groups; minorities especially were shut up in wards of their own and had only tenuous relations with the rest of the population.[27]

The separate identity and segregation of quarters was somewhat impaired in Western towns by the fact that the town as a whole had an autonomous governing body and a collective civic spirit that encompassed all wards. Muslim cities, by contrast, generally did not have their own territorial autonomy and jurisdiction.[28] They were governed by larger polities which linked the quarters more directly with a governing body that stood above the city. Thus, the quarter and not the whole city was the relevant local administrative unit and the common organizing basis of urban life in pre-industrial Muslim cities.[29] The quarters were units of taxation and were responsible for law and order. They also acted in their own defense in time of trouble by organizing their own patrols.[30] Compared to quarters, other forms of popular associations were weak or inexistent. Independent professional associations apparently were little developed, though there is no consensus among scholars on this point.[31] Muslim

cities did have their urban elite, or "patrician" elements composed of leading clerics and merchants, but they did not pro-
duce city-wide formal civic institutions and did not break the
quarters' autonomy.[32] Consequently, different religious, ethnic, or other local groups could live side by side for centuries,
maintaining their separate customs and identities and avoid-
ing meaningful contacts with each other except for the most
basic economic activities.[33] Each quarter clustered around its
religious institutions and important social and administrative
responsibilities devolved upon its religious elite. They were
the managers, scribes, and accountants for community institutions and property held in trust; they ran the schools and
philanthropies.[34] These communal leadership functions of
clergymen were institutionalized further in the Ottoman
millet system, which also crystallized the ethnic and religious
fragmentation of non-Muslim populations under Muslim
rule. The existence of an elaborate administrative apparatus
in each community enabled the weaker, as well as the
stronger, of the minorities to maintain separate identities.[35]
It should be remembered that division along religious lines
was much more prominent in the Islamic city than in its
Western European counterpart where the only non-
Christian minority, the Jews, had less importance than the
considerable Christian and Jewish communities of the Islamic
cities.[36]

The autonomy of the quarters and their segregation
from each other were reflected also in their inward-oriented
territorial layout. In traditional Islamic cities, neighborhoods
were crossed by a maze of narrow alleys where strangers
could not find their way without local guidance. Houses were
very unassuming on their street sides but opened to elaborate interior courtyards where most of the socializing and
leisure-time activities took place. This design was conspicu-
ous in its lack of public space where a stranger could feel at
ease. It also concealed from public view areas where the most
important social activities occurred.[37] Buildings had absolute
precedence over streets and encroached upon them. Indeed,

public passages were simply residual areas left between buildings; streets developed around buildings rather than buildings along streets, which also explains the twisted form of many streets and the many blind alleys.[38]

This territorial layout obviously created a more defensible space, not only because it enlarged the private zones at the expense of public ones but also because it created a gradual transition from public to private territory, giving inhabitants advance knowledge and surveillance opportunities every time a person crossed from a public to a less public space.[39] The layout also facilitated the internal administration of the quarter. As Brown has judiciously noted, the narrow winding streets, blind alleys and internal courtyards were a built-in system of traffic control inhibiting movement of men and commodities and creating easily controllable "bridges" across which they had to pass. A sort of parochialism and intimate primary-group relations were established enabling the head of a ward to regulate the area as if it were his own household.[40] In consultation with other notables, the quarter-head served as chief spokesman and administrator of the community. His main duty was to mediate between the central government and the people, ensuring above all that taxes were duly paid by residents and the state's laws enforced. His responsibility extended to police functions, crime prevention, apprehending fugitives, restricting circulation at night, deciding opening and closing hours for shops, enforcing sanitary rules, and so forth. He also represented members of the community in requests from state authorities.[41]

In its territorial layout the traditional Middle Eastern (or Muslim) urban neighborhood differed somewhat from its counterparts in Europe and those of antiquity. While small alleys and gateways were common to all such neighborhoods, in European and ancient towns there were also major thoroughfares leading to a center where all the public edifices of the city were located and expressed its integration and collective identity. There have been discussions among scholars about the extent to which traditional Islamic cities differed from their Western or ancient counterparts in this regard.[42] Whatever the difference, there seems to be no doubt that Middle Eastern cities (perhaps more than other traditional cities) were designed not to ease mobility but rather to control and compartmentalize it.[43] According to Lapidus:

> . . . the protean encroachment of home and shopowners on the public way, the twisting narrow streets of the quarters and numerous blind alleys, cul-de-sacs and blank walls connote that withdrawal from public concerns and public life which ultimately is said to distinguish cities in the oriental tradition from those in the classical.[44]

Sauvaget has compared the regular plan of ancient cities of the Middle East with the tortuous streets of their Islamic successors and indicated how the straight streets of antiquity were gradually encroached upon by shops and houses in the Islamic period, resulting in a new townscape.[45] The difference between Muslim and West European urban layouts is well illustrated by changes reported by Gutkind in the Islamic cities of Spain after their conquest by Christian kingdoms:

> Introvert houses were opened to the streets and their plain facades were enriched by windows, balconies, portals and ornaments; blind alleys were turned into thoroughfares, and squares were cut out of the mass of houses and the maze of the streets.[46]

The discussion above shows that accounts of the traditional city apply very well to today's Old City of Jerusalem, with its internal courtyards, winding alleys, narrow gateways, and different quarters clustered around religious focal points, where closely knit communities live, led by their religious elite and with little intercommunity contact.[47] Ben Arieh claims that these features of the Old City do not reflect a typical "Muslim" pattern but rather a more general one of historical or religious towns. He also asserts that urban development in Jerusalem could be explained better by its sanctity than by any specific Islamic cultural influence.[48] Whether or not Jerusalem is typical of an Islamic model, there can be no doubt that its holiness had a strong impact on its growth and further reinforced the "traditional city" traits discussed above. The special sacred character of the Old City strengthened even more the prominence of religious institutions as communal focal points. The existence of holy shrines precluded significant alterations in use of land and structures by "urban development schemes"; any such development could occur only at the outskirts of the traditional Old City nucleus. Its sanctity for three major religions also contributed to the great pluralism of its population. People of different ethnic, religious, and regional backgrounds flocked into Jerusalem to live near the Holy Places. This increased the number of different communities that lived side by side in a small geographical area, stressing even further the lack of unity and integration of its inhabitants and making all the more striking the segregation maintained among them despite their great proximity.

The various communities living in Jerusalem were especially geared toward serving kinsmen who came from other places as pilgrims or travelers. Each community had hospices for housing and looking after visitors.[49] Ben Arieh claims that the number of Christian pilgrims in the nineteenth century sometimes surpassed that of resident Christians and in certain years even equalled the entire resident population of Jerusalem.[50] This flow of transients cared for by resident kinsmen was a typical feature of Jerusalem in all historical periods. We can see how similar to the present is Joachim Jeremias's description of pilgrims and communities in Jerusalem in the first century A.D. (i.e., before Christian Holy Places and Islam even existed):

> Having safely arrived in Jerusalem, our travellers' next concern was lodgings. . . . Fellow members of religious communities such as Essenes, Pharisees, Christians were lodged by their friends. Those who lived in

Cyrene, Alexandria and the provinces of Cilicia and Asia found shelter in the hospice connected with their synagogue on Ophel.[51]

and

The religious communities provided a social service somewhere between the private and public services. We have evidence that the Essenes had in each city and therefore in Jerusalem their own agents who provided their travellers with clothing and other necessities and similarly the Christian community in Jerusalem.[52]

At the same time, despite the commercial development that followed its religious attraction, the several resident communities of Jerusalem were far from being financially self-supporting. They could not depend on their own resources even for most of their daily necessities, let alone for building religious sanctuaries, serving incoming pilgrims, and engaging in other activities related to the holiness of the place. Throughout history inhabitants of Jerusalem depended on funds collected from kinsmen in other towns and countries to support both the religious organization and the surrounding lay community.[53]

In all the characteristics discussed above, the Armenian quarter of Jerusalem is similar to other ethnic communities and neighborhoods in the Old City or in other preindustrial Middle Eastern cities. The differences in closure, inward orientation, and reliance on church-sponsored community services are of degree rather than quality. The Armenian quarter is relatively more secluded and self-contained than other quarters, because most of it is sealed off from outside by monastery walls.[54] Yet neighborhood walls were not uncommon in traditional cities and existed, for example, in some Jewish communities of the Old City in the nineteenth century. The Armenian quarter also is distinguished from other quarters by the lay community's greater dependence on the authority, property, and services of religious institutions. This too is a difference of degree, since in traditional cities in general, and in the other sectors of the Old City of Jerusalem in particular, much property is owned and many community services dispensed by churches or by the Muslim Waqf.[55] Gutkind mentions cases of monasteries and feudal lords who owned whole urban districts in medieval European towns and governed them by their own private laws.[56] What has been special about the Armenian quarter is that the separate aspects of closure, inward-orientation, and reliance on church-sponsored community services found in previous traditional urban neighborhoods were combined and have persisted until now. Indeed, their crystallization was a fairly recent development related to political events of the early twentieth century; they were a response to a rather modern occurrence (the Armenian holocaust of the First World War) while similar traits of other urban neighborhoods were relics from a gradually vanishing heritage. Perhaps this has made the Armenian quarter unusual in the present, if not in the past.

Circumstances responsible for the peculiar ecological form of the Armenian community in Jerusalem thus are thoroughly modern and cannot be attributed to the preservation of traditional forms. Yet no matter how modern they might look otherwise (in education, occupations, life-style, etc.), the Armenians of Jerusalem are markedly "nonmodern" in one important aspect: they lack a sense of citizenship and civic consciousness that transcend primordial attachments.[57] In this respect they do resemble the populations of traditional Middle Eastern urban neighborhoods. As Weber pointed out, the concept of citizenship was basically an invention of the West that allowed people of diverse origin to claim common corporate membership. It rested, however, upon prior ability to transcend religion and primordial claims by means of a broader political solidarity.[58] Elements of citizenship existed in ancient Greece and the status was enlarged in "free towns" of Europe that received charters allowing them to make strangers into citizens. This accomplishment, however, was partial: among the Greeks citizenship was largely inherited while in the medieval period it occurred almost entirely among people of similar religion and primordial background. Only later, after the Reformation at the earliest, did the concept of citizenship transcend religious and other primordial identities. Such transcendence did not occur in the Middle East (at least not until the contemporary period). On the contrary, the Ottoman millet system, and similar patterns of Muslim polities that preceded it, tended to reinforce ethnoreligious primordialism. In Jerusalem, these tendencies were accentuated even further because of special political and cultural circumstances. The city's religious prominence and the centuries-old struggle of various national-ethnic groups for dominance over its holy places gave an "extraterritorial" nature to the city, belonging to all and none at the same time. The same international attraction and rivalry often made the political fate of the city a matter of international controversy and in modern history it has remained unsettled to the present.

On this point it might be useful to compare the sense of citizenship of Jerusalem Armenians with that of their kinsmen in other diasporas. Lack of local roots, the feeling of being a distant outpost away from one's cultural center, is a basic trait common to all Armenian communities outside Soviet Armenia.[59] The great sensitivity of the Armenians to their own nationalist distinctiveness and aspirations has led to rather tenuous ties with their host countries. This also explains the relative ease with which Armenians move from one country to another and adapt rather successfully to changing environments.[60] However, a crucial difference still exists between the civic consciousness of Jerusalem Armenians and that of their kinsmen in most other diasporas. While the latter, especially in the West, could develop a sense of citizenship and loyalty to their host countries, beyond their internal ethnic ties, in Jerusalem there was no clear political center with which to identify. In the interwar years Jerusalem was under British mandatory rule, which from the outset was declared to be temporary. Jordanian and Israeli rule, which succeeded the British at an interval of nineteen years, did not create any binding sense of political loyalty. On the contrary, by keeping the status of Jerusalem a burning international political issue, they contributed to a feeling of political vacuum above the multitude of ethnoreligious primordial local groups. Ethnoreligious pluralism was upheld as a positive value in Jerusalem, asserting the city's international and interfaith nature, at the same time reinforcing the primordialism and mutual closure of its inhabitants. After the capture of the Old City in 1967, the state of Israel did not impose its own citizenship on local inhabitants. The Armenians, like all other non-Jewish inhabitants of the Old City, have preserved their Jordanian citizenship. For Armenians, this was not political identification but convenience; it enabled them to travel freely to other Middle Eastern countries and was a measure of caution against possible future political developments. Having undergone no arabization, unlike most other local Christian groups, the Armenians of Jerusalem do not show any overt sympathy to Arab or Palestinian causes. They cautiously "sit on the fence," trying to keep their neutrality toward the Arab-Israeli conflict.

Defended Neighborhood

The Armenian quarter of Jerusalem raises interesting points of reference not only to traditional urban neighborhoods but also to modern urban communities inhabited by certain ethnic or cultural groups that stress their closure and distinction from their environment. These communities have been subject to intensive scrutiny by contemporary scholars[61] and have been referred to in preceding chapters. The concept of defended neighborhood that Suttles uses in his studies, rescucitating the term from earlier usages associated with the old Chicago School, seems especially appropriate to the Armenian quarter. The Armenian quarter displays some important differences from, as well as similarities to, other

contemporary urban neighborhoods discussed in the literature in terms of life-style and self-containment of the inhabitants and in the community's territorial layout, but beyond
these differences there is a common defensive attitude
toward the outside. The monastery walls that surround the
residential community only facilitate its defense and make it
an even more perfect example of the type.

Defended neighborhood, as used by Suttles, refers to an
urban residential community that seals itself off from its
environment in order to maintain better its separate identity
and culture.[62] The most persistent characteristics of the
defended neighborhood are its sharp boundaries and the
need for anyone who lives within them to assume a common
residential identity. In Suttles's view, this common identity
does not necessarily have to be founded on ethnic homogeneity and he criticizes Park and Burgess for overstressing
this aspect.[63] It is possible to claim that the neighborhood is
in itself a place to be defended, no matter how heterogeneous
ethnically, because an important segment of one's life is
spent there. Nonetheless, most sociological studies of
defended neighborhoods have been of homogeneous or at
least ethnically recognizable groups (i.e., groups in which
ethnicity is one of the most salient components of collective
identity). The residents of these neighborhoods are usually
immigrants from an outside culture, such as Italians, Serbi-
ans or Puerto Ricans in Boston or Chicago, Pakistanis in
London, or Chinese in Manila, whose collective identity is
closely interwoven with the cultural ties maintained with the
country of origin.[64] In the Armenian quarter, there is no
doubt that ethnic identity and homogeneity are the most
important features that the neighborhood wants to protect
against external encroachment.

Obviously one might also call such a neighborhood a
ghetto. I have refrained from doing so to avoid the ongoing
debate on the degree of voluntariness of ghetto residence.[65]
Originally ghetto had the connotation of a place where people of similar primordial traits lived together, because they

did not have the means or were not allowed to move to other areas. However, studies also have emphasized voluntary ghetto-formation, primordial groups preferring to live among their own kind. Robert Park observed in his foreword to Wirth's *The Ghetto*:

> Our greatest cities turn out, upon examination, to be a mosaic of segregated people—differing in face, in culture, or merely in cult—each seeking to preserve its peculiar cultural forms and to maintain its individual and unique conception of life. Everyone of these segregated groups inevitably seeks, in order to maintain the integrity of its own group life, to impose upon its members some kind of moral isolation; so far as segregation becomes for them a means to that end, every people and every cultural group may be said to create and maintain its own ghetto.[66]

In Park's sense the Armenian quarter is undoubtedly a ghetto. However, as Banfield rightly observed, "even if more segregation is voluntary than most people realize, the fact remains that a great deal is not voluntary."[67] Insofar as stigma is attached to living in the ghetto or any connotation of involuntary segregation remains, the Armenian quarter is not a ghetto and the use of the term would obscure rather than help the analysis. Hence, the concept of defended neighborhood is preferred.

In comparing the Armenian case with other modern ethnic communities, we should note that most contemporary studies of urban ethnic neighborhoods focus on inner-city slum areas in which residents display working-class or lower-class subcultural traits.[68] The Armenians of Jerusalem (as well as those in other diasporas), by contrast, display more middle-class features, as indicated by their occupational structure, the importance attached to education, and their use of leisure time (again showing greater resemblance to Jewish than to other ethnic communities). We have seen that most Jerusalem Armenians are self-employed shopkeepers and businessmen rather than unskilled or semiskilled workers that characterize the population of the above-mentioned community studies. Armenians stress educational achievements and many of their children go to college, unlike a small minority of "college boys" versus "corner boys" in the other examples.[69] Their adolescents do not hang out much on street corners and do not form gangs. Nor do adults spend much time in pubs and taverns as do most lower-class or working-class men.[70] The Armenians also display middle-class tendencies in their greater inclination to take part in voluntary associations and other organized activities for welfare and cultural purposes.

In the life-style of its inhabitants the Armenian community is even more different from black ghetto-type communities than from white ethnic neighborhoods, even though they might be more similar to the former in terms of closure and salience of external boundaries. Studies of black communities by Stack, Liebow, and Hannerz have emphasized the basic transience and instability of social life and the loose family relations that are closely related to poverty and to limited occupational opportunities.[71] Stack has especially stressed networks, centered on female kin, created to care for children and provide basic domestic needs, as an alternative to malfunctioning nuclear families.[72] In these respects the black ghetto is in great contrast to the Armenian community of Jerusalem that, like the Italian neighborhoods reported in the literature, emphasizes strong family ties as central to community life.[73]

The Armenian quarter is a much better defended neighborhood than its modern counterparts, in no small degree because of its location within a monastery. Gans's urban villagers could not prevent their relocation and dispersion by urban development schemes, and Suttles's defended neighborhoods needed to have recourse to various intricate boundary-maintaining devices, ranging from setting no-man's-lands (vacant lots, public buildings, parks, highways, and railroad tracks) to turf-defense activities of delinquent gangs and vigilante groups.[74] In the Armenian quarter, monastery walls and gates and ownership of land and structures by the religious organization fulfill the same aims more simply and fully. Symbolic boundary-maintaining mechanisms are needed more to keep the separation among different segments of the community than that of the entire community from its surroundings. The sanctity of the site further contributes to its defense, because it restrains governmental intervention in the use of land. While the holiness of the place attracts many foreign visitors, it also limits their behavior, protecting the home territory from encroachment by contamination.[75]

Residents of defended neighborhoods do not spend all their time inside the neighborhood. They go out to work on a daily basis, but entertainment and socializing are obtained within the neighborhood. Hence territorial boundaries are more porous in economic and occupational life but become more strict when leisure and recreation are concerned. This is true of the Armenian quarter, too, even though there is much less distance between place of employment and residence in this case and those people who work inside the monastery do not have to leave the neighborhood at all. As in other defended neighborhoods, territorial boundaries are more significant regarding children and women who do not go to work as much as men do and are considered more vulnerable outside the neighborhood.[76] The Armenian quarter, however, is less dependent on external agents than are other ethnic neighborhoods. Perhaps, as a corollary to the lower-class positions of their inhabitants, the latter depend to a large extent on external caretakers, school teachers, social workers, settlement-house directors, public librarians, outside-owned shops, and others.[77] In the Armenian quarter, by contrast, the caretakers are internal, most of them from the religious organization within which the community developed. It also should be stressed that in the Armenian quarter one does not feel the basic insecurity and vulnerability that characterize the inner-city slum areas reported in the literature.[78] The quarter is by no means a "problem area" on the urban scene. On the contrary, it is considered an attractive place, mysterious to outsiders but neither dangerous nor depressing, nor bland and uniform as are some new suburban settlements.

Defended neighborhoods are tightly structured socially. Their defensive measures generally call for some concerted action and solidarity among residents. Inhabitants of such neighborhoods are sentimentally attached to the locality, to their neighbors, and to local establishments and traditions.[79] This does not mean, of course, that internal unity and harmony always reign among residents. Defended neighborhoods can be riddled by deep-seated internal conflicts and by sharp differences in income, status, and political beliefs; but as Suttles pointed out:

> What needs emphasizing is that the defended neighborhood is primarily a response to fears of invasion from adjacent community areas. It exists then within a structure of parallel residential solidarities which stand in mutual opposition. And it is this mutual opposition rather than primordial solidarity alone which gives the defended neighborhood its unity and sense of homogeneity.[80]

In our case this feeling of opposition to adjacent residential groups is reinforced by the long Armenian history of defense against politically stronger neighbors who alternately tried to exterminate them or assimilate them culturally. It is fed further by the long history of confrontation among Christian groups in Jerusalem over the control of the Holy Places.

Residents of defended neighborhoods are drawn together and separated from outsiders by their exclusive familiarity with local affairs. Gossip plays a very important role in this respect. It also contributes to community norms, because it provides a way of measuring individual performance in terms of community standards.[81] Examples have been given of the use of gossip in the Armenian quarter to ensure compliance to local norms, including separation between ecclesiastical and lay segments of the population.[82] Defended neighborhoods are as much characterized by lack of privacy as by segregation from the outside. Both aspects of totality, congregative and segregative, are important in protecting the community's separate identity. The special salience of these aspects of totality in the Armenian quarter simply makes it a more successful, more accomplished defended neighborhood.

Studies of defended neighborhoods have shown that primary ties that characterize folk-villages also may be found in urban settings. Paraphrasing the title of Gans's book, "villagers" also can be found inhabiting modern city neighborhoods.[83] However, ties binding coresidents of defended neighborhoods are not necessarily of the gemeinschaft type that characterizes folk-villages; they also can have certain traits similar to the communion kind.[84] As the Armenian case illustrates so well, residents of a neighborhood may be well aware of the close, intimate, emotional ties that bind them to each other and distinguish them from the outside and they may make special efforts to safeguard these ties. Urban communities are not necessarily aggregations of people who find themselves living together and develop primary ties out of territorial closeness. They can also be composed of persons who consciously prefer to be neighbors and live at a given location in the hope of leading a more satisfactory life, whether that means safer streets, better education for their children, more entertainment, upward mobility, or the opportunity to live next to people who share their language, customs, and beliefs in a common past or future. The residential social organization thus remains the locus within which the life cycle is given a moral and symbolic meaning.[85]

The same considerations by which one decides where and with whom to reside also determine the importance of keeping away undesirables. The local community is the place where one exposes one's private, tender inner core and is more vulnerable to others.[86] This makes it all the more imperative that only really trustworthy people with whom one has bonds of communion be allowed to live in the same area and that the access of others be restricted and closely regulated. Communities thus are shielded from external encroachment; residents are conscious of shared feelings and life-style and deeply committed to their preservation. Defended neighborhoods basically are threatened neighborhoods and the subjective perception of threat on the part of inhabitants, whether it really exists or not, helps reaffirm their social ties and separate identity. In the Armenian case, the wish to preserve ethnic identity and live among those who share it has been further strengthened by the traumatic experiences of the turn of the century. Fellow Armenians not only want to live together but also to keep the memory of the holocaust alive, to transmit it to their children, and to keep the new generation aware of the nation's political grievances, of its attachment to the lost fatherland, and of the hope of regaining it in the future. This has created a very high level of consciousness and personal involvement in the meaning of collective life, reinforcing the communion-type bonds over the more taken-for-granted gemeinschaft ones. The exceptional chance to seal themselves off from the outside within the monastery has provided Armenians of Jerusalem an extreme but remarkably successful means to sustain those ties.

Characterization of the Armenian quarter of Jerusalem as a defended neighborhood, therefore, does more than supply a fairly accurate description of the lay community's properties. It also presents at least a partial explanation for the continued coexistence of monastic and lay segments of the population. Beyond the obvious economic advantages of living within the monastery, most laymen (including those who can afford more comfortable homes outside the Old City) are attracted to it by a conscious wish to maintain close ties, preferring to live next to people with whom they share a common culture and belief in a common fate. This corresponds to the monastic brotherhood's aim of protecting national identity and preventing assimilation by keeping local Armenians together, minimizing their dependence on non-Armenian sources for community services, and promoting knowledge of the national language, customs, and history. Two inherently opposed types of human collectivities are brought together by the common goal of preserving national and cultural identity. It should be remembered, however, that the rising importance of these community goals in the monastic order is a rather recent outcome of the role-expansion undergone by the Brothers of Saint James and that these goals still remain secondary to the more purely religious purposes for which the monastery was originally established. Furthermore, the monastery is interested in these subjects as a national mission that transcends the local community, while laymen are concerned with them simply as means to achieve a more satisfying local community life. Finally, both sides employ various interactional devices to stress their separate existence and the boundaries between them.

In his discussion of cities and monasteries Lopez eloquently refers to the hieroglyphic ideogram of the city as a cross enclosed in a circle. The cross represents the convergence of roads which bring in and redistribute men, merchandise, ideas. The circle indicates the wall surrounding the city, keeping citizens together, sheltered from the dangerous outside world. According to Lopez, a monastery, as opposed to a city, has the wall but not the crossroads, or at least "its roads have no terminus on earth."[87] The Monastery of Saint James in the Old City of Jerusalem, by contrast, has both the crossroads and the walls. It remains a monastery as well as a residential community and thus produces a remarkably well-defended neighborhood.

8

Conclusion: Community, Territory, and Solidarity

The main subject of this book has been the coexistence in the Armenian quarter of Jerusalem of two social organizations that are in inherent tension as analytical constructs (or prototypes) but share the same space and conduct symbiotic relations with each other. Several similar historical examples and a few contemporary ones have shown that this is not a unique social phenomenon. The special adaptation mechanisms enabling such coexistence have also been discussed, though the very need for them underlines the basic analytical contradiction of the Armenian quarter. People live so close and yet are so separate; they are so united but also deeply divided. There is a duality in most aspects of life; different, perhaps even contradictory goals and role-expectations exist simultaneously. The sacred and the profane are in constant touch and add a cultural-religious dimension to the contrast, beyond the ecological and organizational coexistence of incompatible entities.

In the spectrum of collectivities ranging from formal organizations to residential communities, the Armenian quarter occupies a middle ground. Even as a monastery it is qualitatively different from Goffman's total institution, because it is based on normative rather than coercive compliance and no staff-inmate split exists except for the teacher-pupil divide in the seminary for priests. Yet this is not even a conventional monastery, since the great majority of its inhabitants are laymen and perform no manifest religious functions. The difference between clergy and laity could be likened to that of staff and inmate; but, as it is not based on the coercive compliance that characterizes total institutions, this distinction loses much of the significance attributed to it by Goffman.[1] A dual world could be said to exist in the Monastery of Saint James; but in contradiction to the total institution where inmates have to live according to both their own world and that which the staff imposes on them, here most of the balancing act between the two worlds is done by the staff counterpart, that is, the clergy. Several examples have shown that they are the ones challenged by greater changes in role-performance and by loss of part of their territory as a result of laymen living in their midst. They have had to respond by taking all lay activities under their patronage, but trying at the same time to maintain a distinction from them.

The sharpest differentiation between the monastic brotherhood and the lay community is related to the clergy's sense of religious mission, that is, to the primacy of its outward-oriented goals. The primary goals of the Brotherhood of Saint James are Divine Office in and custody of places holy to Christianity. They preceded the formation of the brotherhood expressly created to ensure their fulfillment. The primacy of these external goals came under serious challenge with the influx of lay refugees into the monastery after World War I. The brotherhood turned its attention to the sufferings of fellow Armenians; it provided them with emergency welfare, housed them within the compound, found them jobs, supplied them education and entertainment facilities. These provisions were continued after the immediate emergency passed. Laymen remained within the walls of the monastery and continued to rely on the clergy's services. The new functions of the monastery were crucially different from the original ones in their relation to goals *internal* to the local collectivity. They provided services that contributed to a more secure, more comfortable, and more meaningful community life. Thus the monastery was faced with the prospect of assuming the role of a parish church, of meeting community needs as do other institutions, such as local government agencies, schools, supermarkets, and local voluntary associations. In the Armenian quarter, the church combined in itself most of these functions, but it was unlike other parish churches in that the parishioners were economically dependent on the church rather than vice versa.

The Monastery of Saint James has fought the above-mentioned trend and has not let itself be transformed entirely into a residential community or parish. By various structural and symbolic means, it has stressed that it is above all a monastery with a religious mission that transcends the local community. Pastoral and welfare functions have remained secondary to the original monastic obligations. The monastery's location on a Holy Place is of help in this respect. Priests' duties remained defined in a way that gave absolute priority to the custody of holy shrines and the conducting of Divine Service in them over any educational or community enterprise. The brotherhood also has kept its outward goal-orientation by reinterpreting its educational and welfare functions not as service to the local community but rather as contributions to the Armenian nation and culture as a whole. This transcendence of the community is reflected in the clergy's recruitment and emotional ties. Clergymen are recruited from outside the local community and most of them leave the city after a certain period of service. A high degree of turnover exists, especially among young priests. Priests ordained in Jerusalem remain members of the Saint James Brotherhood and are encouraged to keep strong ties with the monastery even when they do not reside in the city, that is, they are urged to keep symbolic but not ecological ties with the locality. Unlike laymen whose emotional attachment is to the locality per se, clerical attachment is to the specific religious significance of the locality and to membership in the given brotherhood. Locality thus serves merely as a means toward attaining a higher goal.

Focus on the lay sector of the population shows that it possesses the principal characteristics of a residential urban community, even though it is formed within and is greatly dependent on a very different type of organization that stresses its distinction from the community. The five basic social functions stipulated by Warren are performed by the community: the production, distribution, and consumption of basic economic goods and services, socialization, social control, social participation, and mutual support. In discharging these functions, the Armenian community is more self-contained and less reliant on external agencies than are most contemporary communities. Paradoxically, this relatively small dependence on input from the immediate environment is a result of the services received from the monastic organization whose territory coincides with the community although it does not consider itself part of the latter. This seems to be quite different from the vertical ties that, according to Warren, communities have to maintain with the outside in the performance of their functions.[2] The monastery is not, properly speaking, an external agency because its locality coincides with that of the residential community. Vertical ties to which Warren referred also exist in the Armenian quarter but most of them are maintained with fellow Armenians in the diaspora rather than with the immediate non-Armenian environment.

The lay community, in contrast to the ecclesiastical, is characterized by the primacy of inward-oriented goals and here the reasons for the formation of the lay community should be clearly distinguished from the reasons for its preservation. What created the Armenian lay community of Jerusalem in its present form was above all a search for sheer safety, an escape from physical annihilation. The immediate danger past, two principal factors have kept the community together in its distinctive form. One of these is the economic advantages of living within the walls of the monastery at little or no rent and with employment assistance and community services offered at very low cost. The second factor is the wish to live next to people who speak one's own language, understand and share one's customs, cherish the same ideals, and feeling a common fate can be trusted to extend help in times of need. This is the cultural and social counterpart to the economic and physical security sought by Armenians in their own quarter. All these aims are internal to the collectivity; they do not involve a more inclusive national mission or religious goal but simply indicate why a group of people want to live together to the exclusion of others. The collective memory of the holocaust adds a sense of urgency and heightened sensitivity to maintaining communal ties. However, it does not transform the community in the eyes of its lay inhabitants into an instrument for fulfilling national ideological goals (such as, for example, Jewish settlements set up by the Gush Emunim movement on the West Bank of Jordan). In this sense, the Armenian lay community of Jerusalem is still a truly residential community and not a social movement. No matter how important the national ideological issues are, they are not themselves the reason why people live together within the monastery. The importance attributed to national ties facilitates the acceptance of restrictions of life within a monastery, but basically this form of habitation is accepted not out of a sense of mission but simply because people want to live near their own folk, because life is easier, more secure, and more meaningful this way. Whatever the Armenian nation, culture, or religion as a whole gain from the existence of this community is a welcome side effect but not the primary goal of the inhabitants themselves. In this respect the present lay community is differentiated not only from the clergy but also from *past* lay communities, most of whose members had come to and decided to stay in Jerusalem out of some religious calling, to be near a locus of sanctity, and not in order to live with fellow Armenians. Thus the present lay population of the Armenian quarter, unlike its counterparts of the past, forms a residential community in its own right and is not simply an appendage to the monastic organization.

While the goals that keep the lay community together are primarily inward-oriented, they are nevertheless instrumental in creating particularly strong bonds among its members, more characteristic of communion than of gemeinschaft ties.[3] Fellow members of the community are very deeply conscious of the ties that bind them. They highly cherish these ties and the well-defined boundaries of the community that protect their distinctive identity. Their attachment to the community is very emotional and not taken for granted.[4] One can see here ties that may also characterize communes, but obviously the Armenian laity does not form a commune. It does have rather inclusive and self-contained features and most people could be seen as living under one roof (the monastery's), but the inhabitants do not engage in collective production and consumption. They stress sectoral affiliations rather than fuse within the collective whole. While the sense of collective purpose is more marked here than in other residential communities, the community was not created as an instrument of a predetermined goal. Nor is the community the outcome of a retreat from or rebellion against the conventional life of the larger society. On the contrary, people strive within their own culture to live as conventional a life as possible.

Characterizing the Armenian quarter as a defended neighborhood perhaps can solve some of its internal paradoxes by showing how and why traits attributed to collectivities situated at opposing poles could be found in the same entity. The Armenian quarter, however, clearly is more than a defended neighborhood and it would be too restrictive to view it only in reference to modern urban ethnic communities. After all, the Italians of Boston or of Chicago do not live within Franciscan monasteries. Nor do Armenians themselves live in monasteries elsewhere in the diaspora; indeed the ecological features of their communities show more resemblance to other modern ethnic communities than to that of their Jerusalem kinsmen. Discussing the Armenians in the general terms of ethnic minority communities, two major qualifications should be made: first, that the holocaust created stronger bonds of communion among Armenians (as it did among Jews) than among other ethnic minorities; and second, that the Armenians of Jerusalem whose communal ties are similar to those of their kinsmen in other diasporas (for the most part also World War I refugees) nevertheless live in an environment that is especially conducive to the maintenance of these ties. The communal ties of the Armenians of Jerusalem are further strengthened by special local circumstances, that is, living behind monastery walls, the unique religious features of the city, the extreme ethnocultural fragmentation of its population, and the lack of a political center to generate an overarching civic spirit. My informants were emphatic in stating that the ties binding the Jerusalem community are special and superior to those of all other Armenian communities of the diaspora. According to them, in Jerusalem more than in other places everyone knows that he is Armenian and what that means in terms of language, culture and history.[5] These ties are strengthened further during periodic religious ceremonies that the community, because of its special location, witnesses from close by. The ceremony renews the link with the sacred and reasserts the deeper meaning of community ties. Colorful processions and rituals attract great attention and provide the population with feelings of solidarity as well as greatly appreciated entertainment. Although the following quotation from Mumford deals with the importance of religion in historical cities as a whole, it seems especially appropriate to the Armenian quarter:

> Without the religious potencies of the city the wall alone could not have succeeded in molding the characters as well as controlling the activities of the city's inhabitants. But for religion and all the social rites and

economic advantages that accompanied it, the wall would have turned the city into a prison whose inmates would have had only one ambition: to destroy their keepers and break out.[6]

The Armenians of Jerusalem form more than an existential community whose members simply adapt to living together and arrange their interactions accordingly, but they are less than a social movement or ideological community— an instrument for attaining a higher goal. Ethnic minority communities generally tend to seek a broader meaning in their internal ties, beyond the mere consumption of locality-relevant facilities;[7] but because of historical circumstances the Armenians, like the Jews, are even more sensitive than other ethnic minorities to the normative-ideological aspect of community life. Furthermore, those of Jerusalem happen to live in a setting that is especially conducive to the symbolizing, conceptualizing, meaning-seeking aspects of human life. More than their kinsmen in other diasporas, the Armenians of Jerusalem attribute normative meaning to their community life, while at the same time they consider their quarter an ordinary place of residence. This is still another way in which the sacred and the profane meet in daily life.

From a slightly different view,[8] the Armenian community of Jerusalem delineates in extreme form the continuing connection between community and other social institutions. The main drift of history, especially in the West, has been the progressive differentiation between communities and other social institutions. In the modern Western world the point has been reached at which some communities are purely residential in character; their members are joined only by a common experience in consumption and often are organized to oppose any intrusion by the work place, the government, and for that matter, the church. Such "purified" communities, however, have their limits. They do not seem to apply to most ethnic neighborhoods, or to company towns, stockade communities, religious communes, and others, in which work, religion, and community continue to be mixed in the same territorial setting, not just tangentially but in a more inclusive sense. Such dedifferentiation is also seen in the prominent role played by churches in ethnic minority communities. Elements of home-culture become the focal points of collective consciousness to ethnic minorities in the new land and, as such, the ethnic church serves as a community center in a way that was perhaps unnecessary in the homeland (though not in the Armenian case). Around the church a whole array of institutions takes form: parochial schools, clubs, specialty grocery stores, foreign language newspapers, and others, all part of the effort to emphasize the distinctive culture and make people feel "at home."[9] Simirenko gives a very interesting example of a Catholic, Russian-immigrant community in Minneapolis, which, in order to keep its Slavic identity and gain access to church-related community activities, converted back to Russian Orthodoxy and triggered a similar reconversion to Eastern Orthodoxy among Slavic communities in other areas of the United States.[10] In our case, the special characteristics of Armenians and of Jerusalem, that is, high ethnicity in the aftermath of the holocaust and the controversy regarding Soviet Armenia, on the one hand, and the salience of religion and ethnocultural pluralism in their city of residence, on the other, stress even further the search for meaning and link church and community together.

The basic duality or hybrid nature of the Armenian quarter confounds analytical distinctions. But by being a meeting place for contrasts this case sheds light on theoretical distinctions between types of collectivities. It also enables the systematic examination of analytical themes common to all collectivities, such as integration versus division, consensus versus conflict, separation and unity of segments, the sacred versus the profane, dependence, totality, types of compliance, and scope and pervasiveness of influence on human life. The comingling of parts, however distinct and incompatible they seem in ideal-typical form, is something that people stubbornly accomplish. Ideal types still are useful, however, because they stimulate us to ask the right questions about how and why this is done. The Armenians in Jerusalem reveal to us both some of the conditions under which this mixing occurs and some of the principles by which a compromise is struck.

I hope to have raised in this book some critical questions on why people wish to live together and to what lengths they would go to attain this aim. Territorial contiguity was found to be a very important associational principle despite the rising challenge of nonterritorial bases of affiliation.[11] This is not to say that territorial proximity is a goal in itself or is necessarily the ultimate cause that explains affiliations; under given circumstances it also could create hostility and tension among coresidents.[12] Territoriality should rather be regarded as a tool, but one that has maintained a surprising degree of relevance in the modern world. People who, for various reasons, seek to develop communal ties or preserve them, still cling to it as a powerful means to achieve their goal. Almost any criterion that can be used to differentiate between groups of people may have a territorial expression and be a basis for physical separation.[13] Territorial groups maintain their importance despite general trends of expansion, internal differentiation, and loss of exclusivity.[14] Our case has shown how far members of a community are ready to go to remain a territorial group and what concessions they make on material comfort, free movement, and other conveniences of daily life to maintain a territorial closure, which in turn is expected to ensure a sense of belonging and distinctiveness from others. When this requires the coexistence of inherently incompatible social organizations, such as monastery and residential community, we have seen what devices are engendered to moderate the effects of such incongruency: how by redefinition of roles, by remodeling of structures, and by manipulating territories, distances, and symbols of interaction, separation between the two disparate social organizations is retained and each can pursue its own goals.

A basic question of communal ties was raised here in a paradoxical way. Most community studies are designed to discover what ties bind people together in a residential community or what should be done to create such ties. In our case the problem was reversed. The community was there, formed by historical circumstances over which the population had little control, and the nature of the links binding members of the community was quite clear. The more engrossing phenomenon was the peculiar spatial form the community took in order to keep those ties and how this affected the noncommunal goals and structure of an inherently different type of organization that provided the community with an indispensable territorial basis.

Notes

Preface

1. Gerald D. Suttles, *The Social Order of the Slum* (Chicago: University of Chicago Press, 1978); Herbert J. Gans, *The Urban Villagers* (New York: The Free Press, 1962); William F. Whyte, *Street Corner Society*, 2d ed. (Chicago: University of Chicago Press, 1955); William Kornblum, *Blue Collar Community* (Chicago: University of Chicago Press, 1974); Carole B. Stack, *All Our Kin: Strategies for Survival in a Black Community* (New York: Harper and Row, 1974); Elliot Liebow, *Tally's Corner: A Study of Negro Streetcorner Men* (Boston: Little, Brown, 1967).

2. Stack, *All Our Kin*, pp. 11-21.

3. Kornblum, *Blue Collar Community*, pp. 236-242.

4. Whyte, *Street Corner Society*, pp. 298-327; Liebow, *Tally's Corner*, pp. 232-256.

1: Introduction

1. In the Old City the Christian population alone is divided into more than ten different groups, including the Greek Orthodox, Roman Catholics, Armenian Apostolics, Copts, Greek Catholics, Jacobites, Syrian Catholics, Maronites, Nestorians, Ethiopians, and various Protestants. The Muslims and Jews living in Jerusalem are similarly divided into various subgroups, though fewer than the Christians. See Meron Benvenisti, *Jerusalem: The Torn City* (Minneapolis: University of Minnesota Press, 1976), p. 257; I. W. J. Hopkins, "The Four Quarters of Jerusalem," *Palestine Exploration Quarterly* 103d year (July-December 1971): 68-73; Yehoshua Ben-Arieh, "Patterns of Christian Activity and Dispersion in Nineteenth Century Jerusalem," *Journal of Historical Geography* 2, 1 (1976): 68.

2. I could not think of a common term to identify the persons who engage in religious occupation in Christianity, Judaism, and Islam. The term "clergy," meaning a group of people set apart by ordination to serve God and conduct worship, does not have a corresponding term in Islam and Judaism. Even the word "church," in the sense of ecclesiastical government of the body of believers, is special to Christianity. On this point see S. R. Shafaq, "The Clergy in Islam," in *Social Forces in the Middle East*, ed. S.N. Fisher (Ithaca: Cornell University Press, 1955), p. 184.

3. We have conflicting data on the number of Armenians living in the Old City. A figure of 2,000 people is given by the Armenians themselves and is accepted by some other sources. In contrast, the census carried out by the Israeli government in 1967 showed fewer than 1,000 Armenians living in the Armenian quarter. That census, however, was held immediately after the capture of the Old City, when the local population was deeply suspicious of Israeli intentions and hence its figures might not be very reliable though there is no special reason why they should be low. My own estimate, derived from personal acquaintance with a large number of residents in the Armenian quarter, is that about 1,500 Armenians currently live in the Old City, almost all of them in the Armenian quarter. On the total population of the Old City of Jerusalem in the 1960s and the number of its Armenian inhabitants, see Ori Stendel, "The Arabs in Jerusalem," in *Jerusalem*, ed. J.M. Oesterreicher and A. Sinai (New York: John Day, 1974), p. 159; Evan M. Wilson, *Jerusalem—Key to Peace* (Washington, D.C.: The Middle East Institute, 1970), p. 16; Assadour Antreassian, *Jerusalem and the Armenians* (Jerusalem: St. James Press, 1969), p. 52; Shlomo Gafni, *The Glory of Jerusalem* (Jerusalem: The Jerusalem Publishing House, 1978), p. 78; Zeev Vilnay, *Jerusalem, Capital of Israel: The Old City*, 2 vols. (Jerusalem: Archiever, 1972, in Hebrew), 2: 6; Arieh Sharon, *Planning Jerusalem* (New York: McGraw Hill, 1973), p. 84; *Census of Population and Housing 1967 — East Jerusalem* (Jerusalem: Central Bureau of Statistics, 1968), pp. 2, 6; Usiel O. Schmelz, "The Demography of Muslims and Christians in United Jerusalem" (Paper presented at the Seminar on Jerusalem and Occupied Territories, 1967-1977, The Van Leer Institution, Jerusalem, 1977). According to Schmelz's data 89.2 percent of the Armenian inhabitants of Jerusalem live in the Old City; the Armenians form 16.2 percent of the Christian population of the Old City and 10.1 percent of the total Christian population of Jerusalem ("Demography of Christians," p. 11).

4. Twenty-six acres according to Sharon, more than thirty acres according to Armenian sources. See Sharon, *Planning Jerusalem*, p. 84; Antreassian, *Jerusalem and the Armenians*, p. 53; Kevork Hintlian, *History of the Armenians in the Holy Land* (Jerusalem: St. James Press, 1976), p. 46; *Album of the Armenian Monastery of Jerusalem* (New York: The Delphic Press, 1950), p. 20.

5. Personal observations. See also Yehoshua Ben Arieh, *A City Reflected in its Times* (Jerusalem: Yad Izhak Ben Zvi, 1977, in Hebrew), p. 279. After 1967 some areas of the Armenian quarter inhabited by Arabs were expropriated and added to the renovated Jewish quarter. Although Armenians were not directly hurt by that move some fear lingers among them that the adjoining Jewish quarter might, in the future, expand at their expense. Interviews with informants (1975-1978); see also Benvenisti, *The Torn City*, p. 239.

6. There are about 6 to 7 million Armenians in the world. Less than 1,000 Armenians live in various towns of Israel and the West Bank outside Jerusalem. David M. Lang and Christopher J. Walker, *The Armenians* (London: Minority Rights Group, Report no. 32, 1977), p. 14; "The Tragic Armenians," *Jerusalem Post*, March 18, 1977; S. P. Colbi, *A Short History of Christianity in the Holy Land* (Jerusalem: Am Hasefer, 1965), p. 68; interviews with informants (1975-1978).

7. Hintlian, *Armenians in the Holy Land*, pp. 57-60; Bishop Shahe Ajamian, "Brief Notes on the Armenian People and the Armenian Patriarchate of Jerusalem," *Christian News From Israel* 18 (December 1967): 39-40.

8. Bishop Shahe Ajamian, in interview to the newspaper *Kol Ha Ir* (Jerusalem), 26 December 1980 (in Hebrew), p. 25.

9. On these churches see Aziz S. Atiya, *A History of Eastern Christianity* (London: Methuen, 1967), passim.

10. See Ben Arieh, *City Reflected*, p. 231; Ben Arieh, "Christian Activity," pp. 59-60; C. H. Malik, "The Orthodox Church," in *Religion in the Middle East*, ed. A. J. Arberry, 2 vols. (Cambridge: At the University Press, 1969) 1: 300, 327-328; K. Cragg, "The Anglican Church," in *Religion in the Middle East*, ed. Arberry, 1: 587.

11. The Armenian church is called by different names. Armenians strenuously object to the term Gregorian or Armenian Orthodox and prefer the terms Armenian Apostolic, Armenian National, or simply Armenian church. See "Arménie et Arméniens à Travers le Monde," *Revue Missi* (Belgium), no. 289 (April 1965): 135; *L'Eglise Arménienne* (Antelias, Liban: Catholicosat des Arméniens, 1936), p. 53. The latter three terms are used intermittently in this study, referring to the national church of the Armenians as differentiated from the much smaller Armenian Catholic church.

12. Hagop A. Chakmakjian, *Armenian Christology and Evangelization of Islam* (Leiden: Brill, 1965), p. 62. The Armenian church holds that salvation could be obtained through any Christian church; it does not attribute any superiority to itself in religious terms but rather sees itself better suited to the special national and cultural traits of the Armenian people just as some other church might be better suited to respond to the needs of other ethnic or national groups. See Malachia Ormanian, *The Church of Armenia*, 2d rev. ed. (London: Mowbray, 1955), pp. 99-100; K. A. Sarafian, *The Armenian Apostolic Church* (Fresno, Calif.: The Armenian Diocese of California, 1959), p. 31.

13. Interviews with informants (1975-1978). See also Benvenisti, *The Torn City,* pp. 258-259; Meron Benvenisti, *Facing the Closed Wall* (Jerusalem: Weidenfeld and Nicolson, 1973, in Hebrew), pp. 96-98; Lang and Walker, *The Armenians,* p. 14 and R.H. Dekmejian, "The Armenians: History, Consciousness and the Middle Eastern Dispersion," *Middle East Review* 9, 1 (1976): 27.

14. This is only one of many points of similarity between Jews and Armenians. Others include their propensity to economic entrepreneurial occupations, their wide geographic dispersion and establishment of closely knit communities, their ability to keep their separate ethnocultural identity despite the lack of political sovereignty for most of their history, and their long experience of persecutions, which reached genocidal proportions in the twentieth century.

15. George A. Hillery, Jr., "Definitions of Community: Areas of Agreement," *Rural Sociology* 20 (June 1955): 111-123.

16. *The Community,* rev. ed. (Alexandria, Va.: Time-Life Books, 1978), p. 8. On territorial and nonterritorial approaches to community see George A. Hillery, Jr., "Selected Issues in Community Theory," *Rural Sociology* 37 (December 1972): 534-541; Leo F. Schnore, "Community," in *Sociology: An Introduction,* ed. Neil J. Smelser (New York: Wiley, 1967), pp. 82-100; Roland L. Warren, *The Community in America,* 2d ed. (Chicago: Rand McNally, 1972), pp. 1-20.

17. Erving Goffman, "The Characteristics of Total Institutions," in *A Sociological Reader in Complex Organizations,* ed. Amitai Etzioni, 2d ed. (New York: Holt, Rinehart & Winston, 1969), p. 313. See also George A. Hillery Jr., *Communal Organizations* (Chicago: University of Chicago Press, 1969), pp. 130-131; Michael Hill, *The Religious Order* (London: Heinemann, 1973), p. 72. I share the unhappiness of many sociologists with the term total *institution* and would have preferred to call it total *organization* as it describes a pattern of organization of human collectivity rather than an institution which in sociological literature has a more cultural normative connotation (perhaps a Parsonian legacy). See E. Servais and F. Hambye, "Structure et Signification: Problème de Méthode en Sociologie des Organisations Claustrales," *Social Compass* 18, 1 (1971): 29; Etzioni, ed., *Reader in Complex Organizations,* p. vii. However the term "total institution" will not be changed here as it has gained widespread acceptance in the literature.

18. See Goffman, "Total Institutions," pp. 315-321; Hill, *The Religious Order,* pp. 54-55, 75; George A. Hillery, Jr., "The Convent: Community, Prison or Task Force?," *Journal for the Scientific Study of Religion* 7, 1 (1969): 140-146; Hillery, *Communal Organizations,* pp. 133, 138.

19. A third type of compliance, the utilitarian one, characterizes the ties of employees to an industrial organization. See Amitai Etzioni, *A Comparative Analysis of Complex Organizations* (New York: The Free Press, 1961), pp. xvi, 27, 31, 41-44, 66-67, 126; Hill, *The Religious Order,* pp. 7, 76-79; Servais and Hambye, "Organisations Claus-

trales," p. 33. It is interesting to note that Etzioni finds a strong relationship between coercive compliance and the staff-inmate split in organizations, thus bringing together two of the most characteristic features of total institutions. See Etzioni, *Complex Organizations*, pp. 125-126.

20. This is very similar to what Etzioni called the "pervasiveness" of organizations, which he defined as "the number of activities in or outside the organization for which the organization sets norms" (*Complex Organizations*, p. 163). His other criterion, the "scope" of organization, refers to the aggregate of characteristics that are included in Goffman's concept of "totality"; the more total the organization, the broader its scope.

21. For examples of such totality in villages, including striking photographic illustrations of their closure, see *The Community*, pp. 10-11, 44. On territorial closure in urban neighborhoods see Suttles, *The Social Order of the Slum*, passim.

22. On the importance of families as a differentiating factor between total institutions and residential communities see Goffman, "Total Institutions," p. 316; Hillery, "Community or Task Force," p. 147.

23. Mircea Eliade, *The Sacred and the Profane* (New York: Harcourt Brace and World, 1957), pp. 20-25.

24. Ibid., p. 25.

25. Clifford Geertz, *The Interpretation of Cultures* (New York: Basic Books, 1973), p. 119.

26. Goffman, "Total Institutions," p. 314.

27. See Peter M. Blau and W. R. Scott, *Formal Organizations* (London: Routledge and Kegan Paul, 1963), p. 5; Talcott Parsons, "Suggestions for a Sociological Approach to the Theory of Organizations," in *Reader in Complex Organizations*, ed. Etzioni, p. 33; Etzioni, *Complex Organizations*, p. xi; George A. Hillery, Jr., "Freedom and Social Organization: A Comparative Analysis," *American Sociological Review* 36 (February 1971): 53-54.

28. On this point I differ from Hillery who places monasteries in the category of communal organizations together with residential communities. (See Hillery, "Community or Task Force," pp. 148-151, and "Freedom and Social Organization," pp. 51-53.) One could reach different typologies by using different criteria for comparison, but if one refers to the nature of collective goals, monasteries should be differentiated from residential communities. Objecting to the use of the term "community" in reference to total institutions, Hillery rightly states that, "if vills [Hillery's own term for residential communities] are identified as community and if community is to have any distinctive meaning, then total institutions are not communities" (*Communal Organizations*, p. 142), but by the same token nor should monasteries be considered communities.

29. It is interesting to note that Hillery sensed the important ties between the goals of the collectivity and the presence or

absence of family units. He claimed that a collectivity would exclude families if it was oriented primarily toward the attainment of specific goals. He could not explain, however, why families are absent in monasteries, which according to him are not oriented toward specific goals. Had he directed his attention to the outward orientation of goals rather than their specificity, he could have solved the problem, claiming that the presence of families is incompatible with the outward-oriented goals of monasteries. See Hillery, "Freedom and Social Organization," pp. 51-63.

30. See Hillery, *Communal Organizations* and Shimon Gottschalk, *Communities and Alternatives* (Cambridge: Schenkman, 1975).

31. Hillery, *Communal Organizations*, p. 146.

32. Hillery, "Freedom and Social Organization," pp. 53-54.

33. George A. Hillery, Jr., "Families, Communes and Communities," in *Perspectives on the American Community*, ed. Roland L. Warren, 2d ed (Chicago: Rand McNally, 1973), p. 522. See also Gottschalk, *Communities and Alternatives*, p. 89.

34. For a fuller comparison of formal and communal organizations see Gottschalk, *Communities and Alternatives*, pp. 5-18.

35. Our discussion deals with collective goals and not with those of individuals forming the collectivity. For a discussion that takes into consideration different levels of community goals in addition to their specificity and their inward or outward orientation, see Gottschalk, *Communities and Alternatives*, pp. 18-33.

36. In a very interesting study Richard Brooks likens the first stage in the development of a planned town to total institution and shows how, in a specific case, the town gradually moves from the total institution phase to that of residential community. See Richard Brooks, "Social Planning in Columbia," in *Perspectives on the American Community*, ed. Warren, pp. 489-490.

37. For an interesting comparative discussion of such composite types, see Gottschalk, *Communities and Alternatives*, pp. 25-33, 44-93.

38. Ibid., p. 32.

39. For more details on communes, see Rosabeth M. Kanter, *Commitment and Community: Communes and Utopias in Sociological Perspective* (Cambridge: Harvard University Press, 1972); Rosabeth M. Kanter, ed., *Communes: Creating and Managing the Collective Life* (New York: Harper and Row, 1973); Laurence Veysey, *The Communal Experience* (New York: Harper and Row, 1973); Philip Abrams and Andrew Mc Culloch, *Communes, Sociology and Society* (London: Cambridge University Press, 1976); Andrew Rigby, *Alternative Realities* (London: Routledge and Kegan Paul, 1974).

40. On communion see Herman Schmalenbach, "The Sociological Category of Communion," in *Theories of Society*, ed. Talcott Parsons et al., 2 vols. (New York: The Free Press, 1961), 1:332-340. On gemeinschaft and gesellschaft see Ferdinand Toennis, "Gemeinschaft and Gesellschaft," in *The Sociology of Community*, ed. Colin Bell and

Howard Newby (London: Cass, 1974), p. 7. See also Kanter, *Commitment and Community*, p. 148. The gemeinschaft-gesellschaft dichotomy developed by Toennis is common knowledge among sociologists, but fewer people are familiar with Schmalenbach's important critique of that dichotomy, showing that it was not very helpful in accounting for human collectivities formed by people who had deep-seated religious or ideological bonds to each other and to their collective goals. I obviously disagree with Michael Hill who characterizes the religious order and the monastery as gemeinschaft-type groups (*The Religious Order*, pp. 43, 253).

41. Schmalenbach, "Communion," p. 334.

42. Ibid., pp. 332-335, 340; Veysey, *The Communal Experience*, pp. 3-7.

43. Hillery, "Families, Communes, and Communities," p. 512; Rigby, *Alternative Realities*, p. 4; David C. Thorns, *The Quest for Community* (London: Allen and Unwin, 1976), p. 137.

44. Kanter, *Commitment and Community*, p. 3. The same inward orientation also is apparent in Abrams and McCulloch's characterization of communes as a way of institutionalizing friendship within a chosen domestic place, though they admit that this does not apply to all types of communes (*Communes, Sociology and Society*, pp. 25-38). Hillery and Morrow, however, emphasize the similarities between commune and monastery by claiming that monasteries, too, might have inward-oriented communal goals ("The Monastery as a Commune," *International Review of Modern Sociology* 6 [Spring 1976]: 144). For different types of communes with inward and outward-oriented goals, see Rigby, *Alternative Realities*, chaps. 1, 5-6.

45. On this question, see Abrams and McCulloch, *Communes, Sociology and Society*, pp. 23-49; Rigby, *Alternative Realities*, chaps. 1, 5-6; Veysey, *The Communal Experience*, chaps. 4-5; Jay Ogilvy and Heather Ogilvy, "Communes and the Reconstruction of Reality," in *The Family, Communes and Utopian Societies*, ed. Sallie TeSelle (New York: Harper and Row, 1972), pp. 97-98. It would be very interesting to study possible tensions between outward-oriented goals of social movements and gradually emerging inward-oriented local goals of communal settlements belonging to the movement.

46. See among others, Gans, *The Urban Villagers*; Suttles, *The Social Order of the Slum*; Stack, *All Our Kin*; Ulf Hannerz, *Soulside* (New York: Columbia University Press, 1969).

47. Gerald D. Suttles, *The Social Construction of Communities* (Chicago: University of Chicago Press, 1972), pp. 264-268.

2: *The Armenians in History*

1. For details on the origins of the Armenians see Sirarpie Der Nersessian, *The Armenians* (London: Thames and Hudson, 1969), pp. 11-22; Leon Arpee, *A History of Armenian Christianity* (Princeton: Princeton University Press, 1946), p. 1; H. Pasdermadjian, *Histoire de*

l'Arménie (Paris: Samuelian, 1949), pp. 20-25; Lang and Walker, *The Armenians*, pp. 6-7.

2. David M. Lang, *Armenia: Cradle of Civilization*, 2d ed. (London: Allen and Unwin, 1978), p. 38.

3. For details on the traditional Armenian society and feudal structure see Der Nersessian, *The Armenians*, pp. 54-61; Pasdermadjian, *Histoire de l'Arménie*, pp. 45, 99, 123, 135-136, 159-160; F. Nansen, *L'Arménie et le Proche-Orient* (Paris: Massis, 1928), pp. 268-270; Sisag H. Varjabedian, *The Armenians* (Chicago: By the Author, 1977), pp. 32-39.

4. Nansen, *L'Arménie et le Proche Orient*, pp. 271-272; Der Nersessian, *The Armenians*, pp. 64-71; Pasdermadjian, *Histoire de l'Arménie*, pp. 98, 267, 282-285; Lang, *Armenia* pp. 172, 184, 191-193.

5. Der Nersessian, *The Armenians*, pp. 22-24; Pasdermadjian, *Histoire de l'Arménie*, pp. 27-38.

6. Der Nersessian, *The Armenians*, pp. 25-27; Antreassian, *Jerusalem and the Armenians*, pp. 9-10.

7. Der Nersessian, *The Armenians*, pp. 28-30. At the partition of Armenia the Byzantine and Roman empires still were formally united (the formal split occurred in A.D. 395), but historians generally identify the beginning of the Byzantine empire with the transfer of the center of administration from Rome to Constantinople in A.D. 334.

8. Antreassian, *Jerusalem and the Armenians*, pp. 22-23; Arpee, *Armenian Christianity*, p. 15; Sarafian, *The Armenian Apostolic Church*, pp. 29, 63-65; Pasdermadjian, *Histoire de l'Arménie*, pp. 113-117; Jean Mécérian, "Un Tableau de la Diaspora Arménienne," *Proche Orient Chrétien*, 6-12 (1956-1962), 12:22.

9. Atiya, *Eastern Christianity*, p. 307; Sarafian, *The Armenian Apostolic Church*, pp. 30-31.

10. Interview with Avedis K. Sanjian (Los Angeles, May 1979); Antreassian, *Jerusalem and the Armenians*, pp. 28-29; Ormanian, *The Church of Armenia*, pp. 37-44; Mécérian, "Diaspora Arménienne," 12: 23.

11. Lang, *Armenia*, pp. 264-268; Der Nersessian, *The Armenians*, pp. 84-86.

12. Nansen, *L'Arménie et le Proche Orient*, pp. 268-270; Der Nersessian, *The Armenians*, pp. 57-58; Pasdermadjian, *Histoire de l'Arménie*, pp. 99, 116, 159-160.

13. Interviews in the Armenian quarter of Jerusalem (1975-1978); Antreassian, *Jerusalem and the Armenians*, p. 28; Ormanian, *The Church of Armenia*, pp. 189-191; Atiya, *Eastern Christianity*, p. 342; Mary K. Matossian, *The Impact of Soviet Policies in Armenia* (Leiden: Brill, 1962), p.9.

14. Dekmejian, "Middle Eastern Dispersion," p. 27.

15. Der Nersessian, *The Armenians*, pp. 30-32; Pasdermadjian,

Histoire de l'Arménie, pp. 134-137; W. Wallis, *Fresno Armenians* (Lawrence, Kans.: Coronado Press, 1965), p. 69.

16. Antreassian, *Jerusalem and the Armenians,* pp. 11-12; Dekmejian, "Middle Eastern Dispersion," p. 27.

17. Avedis K. Sanjian, *The Armenian Communities in Syria under Ottoman Dominion* (Cambridge: Harvard University Press, 1965), p. 3; Lang and Walker, *The Armenians,* p. 7.

18. Atiya, *Eastern Christianity,* pp. 46-48, 56-58, 69-71, 176-179; Ormanian, *The Church of Armenia,* pp. 24-28; Der Nersessian, *The Armenians,* pp. 76-77; Antreassian, *Jerusalem and the Armenians,* pp. 27-28.

19. While the schism around the Council of Chalcedon accelerated the nascent nationalism of the Copts and the Armenians in the pale of their own church, the Syrian Jacobite church remained a much weaker focus of national identity. This was a result of the internal divisions within the Syriac-speaking people (the Eastern Syrians opted for Nestorianism, and a part of the Western Syrians broke away and formed the Maronite church, which accepted allegiance to Rome) and of the forced separation from their ancient center of Antioch, controlled by the Greek Orthodox. Throughout the Middle East, the Greek Orthodox used the imperial power of Byzantium to suppress the Monophysists as much as they could. For details on these questions see Atiya, *Eastern Christianity,* passim.

20. Dekmejian, "Middle Eastern Dispersion," p. 27. For a critical view of the Armenian church's monophysist stand and nationalistic spirit see Chakmakjian, *Armenian Christology,* passim. It is interesting to note that two events that shaped most strongly the development of Armenian ethnoreligious identity, the Council of Chalcedon and the Battle of Awarair, occurred in the same year, A.D. 451.

21. In the case of the Georgians, however, acceptance of the Greek Orthodox creed, rather than opposition to it, helped crystallize their national identity. The Georgians had followed the Armenians into the anti-Chalcedonian camp but later returned to the Orthodox fold. This prevented their cultural assimilation within the Armenian people and led to the emergence of a separate Georgian identity. Other local populations that accepted Armenian monophysitism were gradually assimilated within the Armenian group. Interview with Bishop Guregh Kapikian (Jerusalem, September 1975); Lang, *Armenia,* p. 171.

22. Sanjian, *Armenian Communities in Syria,* pp. 3, 8; Lang, *Armenia,* pp. 171-172, 185-186; Pasdermadjian, *Histoire de l'Arménie,* pp. 212-213.

23. Sanjian, *Armenian Communities in Syria,* p. 8; Pasdermadjian, *Histoire de l'Arménie,* p. 182.

24. For details on the Bagratid kingdom, see Pasdermadjian, *Histoire de l'Arménie,* pp. 148-149, 168-181; Der Nersessian, *The Armenians,* pp. 32-37.

25. Pasdermadjian, *Histoire de l'Arménie,* pp. 126, 199.

26. Der Nersessian, *The Armenians,* pp. 37-40; Pasdermadjian, *Histoire de l'Arménie,* pp. 181-188; Lang, *Armenia,* pp. 190-199.

27. Ormanian, *The Church of Armenia,* p. 47; Lang, *Armenia,* p. 193.

28. Richard G. Hovannisian, *Armenia on the Road to Independence* (Berkeley and Los Angeles: University of California Press, 1967), pp. 4-5; Pasdermadjian, *Histoire de l'Arménie,* pp. 280-283; interview with Sanjian (May 1979) and Richard G. Hovannisian, in a letter to the author (11 September 1980).

29. For details on the Armenian dominance in Cilicia, see Lang, *Armenia,* pp. 200-211; Antreassian, *Jerusalem and the Armenians,* p. 29; Sanjian, *Armenian Communities in Syria,* pp 8-17; Der Nersessian, *The Armenians,* pp. 44-53; Pasdermadjian, *Histoire de l'Arménie,* p. 235.

30. The Catholicosate did not move to Cilicia directly from Armenia but rather from Sebastea, because after the Byzantine conquest of Armenia the Catholicos was not permitted to reside in the historical homeland. This showed again the strong link between religious and political centers (Hovannisian, letter to the author, September 1980).

31. Sanjian, *Armenian Communities in Syria,* pp. 10-11, 16-17; Der Nersessian, *The Armenians,* pp. 47-52, 59; Pasdermadjian, *Histoire de l'Arménie,* pp. 243, 258; N. Iorga, *Brève Histoire de la Petite Arménie* (Paris: Gamber, 1930), pp. 60-62, 123.

32. Hintlian, *Armenians in the Holy Land,* p. 18; Iorga, *Petite Arménie,* p. 93; Arpee, *Armenian Christianity,* p. 160.

33. Pasdermadjian, *Histoire de l'Arménie,* pp. 242-244; Ormanian, *The Church of Armenia,* pp. 54-55.

34. Der Nersessian, *The Armenians,* pp. 68-69; Sanjian, *Armenian Communities in Syria,* pp. 17-18; Pasdermadjian, *Histoire de l'Arménie,* pp. 252-257.

35. *The Catholicosate of Cilicia: Her Place and Status in the Armenian Church* (Antelias, Lebanon: Catholicosate of Cilicia, n.d.), pp. 6-7; Antreassian, *Jerusalem and the Armenians,* p. 29; Mécérian, "Diaspora Arménienne" 12: 24; Ormanian, *The Church of Armenia,* pp. 56-57.

36. A similar split into rival churches occurred earlier but lasted only a few years; between 969 and 972 there were two heads of church seated at Ani and Aghtamar respectively and supported by different kings. See Lang, *Armenia,* p. 190.

37. *Catholicosate of Cilicia,* pp. 8-17; Ormanian, *The Church of Armenia,* pp. 115-118; Mécérian, "Diaspora Arménienne" 12:25-26.

38. Pasdermadjian, *Histoire de l'Arménie,* pp. 271-277; Hovannisian, *Road to Independence,* p. 5.

39. Pasdermadjian, *Histoire de l'Arménie,* pp. 281-283; James B. Gidney, *A Mandate for Armenia* (Kent, Ohio: Kent State University Press, 1967), p.16; Stanford J. Shaw and Ezel K. Shaw, *History of the Ottoman Empire and Modern Turkey,* 2 vols. (New York, Cambridge University Press, 1977), 2: 200; Marjorie Housepian, *Smyrna 1922*

(London: Faber and Faber, 1972), pp. 24-25; Vahakn N. Dadrian, "The Structural and Functional Components of Genocide: A Victimological Approach to the Armenian Case," in *Victimology*, ed. Israel Drapkin and Emilio Viano (Lexington, Mass.: Heath, 1974), pp. 126-127.

40. Sanjian, *Armenian Communities in Syria*, p. 34; Hovannisian, *Road to Independence*, p. 24.

41. H. Alojian, "Origins of the Armenian Colony in Constantinople," *The Armenian Review* 7, 2 (1954): 119-120; Sarkis Atamian, *The Armenian Community* (New York: Philosphical Library, 1955), pp. 29, 48-60; Varjabedian, *The Armenians*, p. 84; Sanjian, *Armenian Communities in Syria*, p. 36; Gidney, *A Mandate for Armenia*, pp. 14-16; Lang and Walker, *The Armenians*, p. 8; Dadrian, "Components of Genocide," pp. 126-127.

42. Alojian, "Armenian Colony," p. 119; Housepian, *Smyrna 1922*, p. 25; Mesrob K. Krikorian, *Armenians in the Service of the Ottoman Empire, 1860-1908* (London: Routledge and Kegan Paul, 1977), passim.

43. Leon Arpee, *A Century of Armenian Protestantism, 1846-1946* (New York: The American Missionary Association of America, 1946), p. 5.

44. Antreassian, *Jerusalem and the Armenians*, p. 29; Arpee, *Armenian Christianity*, p. 209; Hovannisian, *Road to Independence*, p. 25; Pasdermadjian, *Histoire de l'Arménie*, p. 271.

45. For more details on the millet system, see Sanjian, *Armenian Communities in Syria*, pp. 31-34; Atamian, *The Armenian Community*, p. 20; Hovannisian, *Road to Independence*, p. 25.

46. Alojian, "Armenian Colony," p. 120; Sanjian, *Armenian Communities in Syria*, pp. 36-37; Atamian, *The Armenian Community*, p. 29.

47. Sanjian, *Armenian Communities in Syria*, pp. 37-41; Shaw and Shaw, *Ottoman Empire* 2: 125-126.

48. For details on the development of Catholicism and Protestantism among the Armenians and the Apostolic church's struggle against them see Arpee, *Protestantism*, pp. 13-18, 40; Ormanian, *The Church of Armenia*, pp. 68-69, 72, 185; Atiya, *Eastern Christianity*, pp. 338-339. Varjabedian, *The Armenians*, pp. 52-56; *L'Eglise Arménienne*, pp. 35-36; Sanjian, *Armenian Communities in Syria*, p. 34; S.H. Stephan, "Three Firmans Granted to the Armenian Catholic Community, Jerusalem," *Journal of the Palestine Oriental Society* 13 (1933): 1; H.A. Chakmakjian, *The Armenian Evangelical Church and the Armenian People* (Yettem, Calif.: By the Author, 1961), p. 5.

49. Ormanian, *The Church of Armenia*, pp. 61-62; Atiya, *Eastern Christianity*, p. 336.

50. Atamian, *The Armenian Community*, pp. 48-49; H. Dasnabedian, *The Armenian Question* (Jerusalem: The Armenian Case Committee, 1977), p. 4.

51. Hovannisian, *Road to Independence*, pp. 25-26.

52. For details, see Pasdermadjian, *Histoire de l'Arménie*, pp. 353-421, 438-476; Hovannisian, *Road to Independence*, pp. 26-40, 48-57; Sanjian, *Armenian Communities in Syria*, pp. 283-285; Lang and Walker, *The Armenians*, pp. 8-11; Mécérian, "Diaspora Arménienne," 7: 119-138; Dasnabedian, *The Armenian Question*, pp. 7-14; Shaw and Shaw, *Ottoman Empire* 2: 200-204; Roderic H. Davison, "The Armenian Crisis, 1912-1914," *The American Historical Review* 53, 3 (1948): 481-506.

53. Lang and Walker, *The Armenians*, pp. 9, 11; Dasnabedian, *The Armenian Question*, p. 13; Ormanian, *The Chruch of Armenia*, p. 76. For a very different estimate, see Shaw and Shaw, *Ottoman Empire* 2: 316. It should be noted, however, that the Shaws' book is considered to have a strong pro-Turkish bias. Its data and analysis are at odds with most other scholarly work on the subject.

54. Hovannisian, *Road to Independence*, pp. 27-28; Lang and Walker, *The Armenians*, p. 9. For a different view of the events see Shaw and Shaw, *Ottoman Empire* 2: 203-204.

55. Hovannisian, *Road to Independence*, pp. 28-30; Lang and Walker, *The Armenians*, pp. 9-11; Sanjian, *Armenian Communities in Syria*, pp. 283-285; Dasnabedian, *The Armenian Question*, pp. 12-14; Robert Melson, "Provocation or Nationalism: A Theoretical Inquiry into the Armenian Genocide of 1915," (Paper, West Lafayette, Ind., n.d.). The divergent view comes again from Shaw and Shaw, *Ottoman Empire* 2: 315.

56. Housepian, *Smyrna, 1922*, pp. 120-151.

57. Davison, "The Armenian Crisis," pp. 483-485, 493; Melson, "Provocation or Nationalism," pp. 13-15.

58. Hovannisian, *Road to Independence*, pp. 35-37. See also Atamian, *The Armenian Community*, pp. 44, 52-53; Lang and Walker, *The Armenians*, p. 8; Shaw and Shaw, *Ottoman Empire*, 2: 200-201, 316.

59. For a different view see Dadrian, "Components of Genocide," pp. 126-131. See also Robert Melson, "A Theoretical Inquiry into the Armenian Massacres of 1894-1896," *Comparative Studies in Society and History* 24, 3 (July 1982): 481-509.

60. Melson, "Provocation or Nationalism," p. 10.

61. Interview with Archbishop Shahe Ajamian (Jerusalem, May 1976); "Chronique," *Proche Orient Chrétien* 15 (1965): 403; Housepian, *Smyrna, 1922*, p. 41.

62. Sanjian, *Armenian Communities in Syria*, pp. 284-285; Y. Chilingirian, *Description of Refugees and Monastics in Jerusalem, Aleppo and Damascus, 1914-1918* (Jerusalem: St. James Press, 1927, in Armenian), p. 55; Pierre Atamian, *Histoire de la Communauté Arménienne Catholique de Damas* (Beyrouth: Typo Press, 1964), p. 98.

63. Shaw and Shaw, *Ottoman Empire* 2: 203; Hovannisian, *Road to Independence*, p. 35.

64. Pasdermadjian, *Histoire de l'Arménie*, p. 277; Matossian, *Soviet Policies in Armenia*, p. 2; Mesrovb J. Seth, *Armenians and the East India*

Company (Calcutta: Government of India Press, 1926), pp. 3-6, 14-15; James R. Kirkland, "Armenian Migration, Settlement and Adjustment in Australia" (Ph.D. diss., Canberra: Australian National University, 1980), pp. 29-30.

65. Pasdermadjian, *Histoire de l'Arménie*, p. 276; Arpee, *Armenian Christianity*, p. 212.

66. K. Sarkissian, "The Armenian Church," in *Religion in the Middle East*, ed. Arberry, 1: 484-485; Hovannisian, *Road to Independence*, pp. 7-12; Dasnabedian, *The Armenian Question*, p. 3.

67. Hovannisian, *Road to Independence*, pp. 17-18; Sarkissian, "The Armenian Church," p. 496; Matossian, *Soviet Policies in Armenia*, pp. 19-20; Lang and Walker, *The Armenians*, p. 10; Pasdermadjian, *Histoire de l'Arménie*, pp. 346-347, 422-437, 444; Mécérian, "Diaspora Arménienne" 6: 343-344.

68. An earlier organization called Defenders of the Fatherland was formed in Erzurum in 1880, but this was simply a local self-defense organization without a general nationalist platform. See Atamian, *The Armenian Community*, p. 92.

69. For more details on these parties and other Armenian nationalist movements, see Louise Nalbandian, *The Armenian Revolutionary Movement* (Berkeley and Los Angeles: University of California Press, 1963), pp. 90-179; Atamian, *The Armenian Community*, pp. 70-74, 93-105, 165-169, 303-304; Davison, "The Armenian Crisis," p. 484; Mécérian, "Diaspora Arménienne" 12: 43-46; Varjabedian, *The Armenians*, pp. 88-90; M. Tololyan, *The Crusade Against the Armenian Revolutionary Federation* (Boston: Hairenik Press, 1962), pp. 30, 38.

70. Richard G. Hovannisian, "Caucasian Armenia Between Imperial and Soviet Rule: The Interlude of National Independence," (Paper, Los Angeles, n.d.), p. 5.

71. Lang and Walker, *The Armenians*, p. 12.

72. For details on the Armenian front in World War I and the postwar events that led to the establishment of the Soviet Republic of Armenia, see Hovannisian, *Road to Independence*, passim; Matossian, *Soviet Policies in Armenia*, pp. 24-31; Pasdermadjian, *Histoire de l'Arménie*, pp. 456-477; Mécérian, "Diaspora Arménienne" 7: 229-249, 311-322. For a different view of the events, see Shaw and Shaw, *Ottoman Empire* 2: 314-317, 322-327, 356-357.

73. Ormanian, *The Church of Armenia*, p. 83.

74. See Lang and Walker, *The Armenians*, p. 14; Aram Terzian, *An Armenian Miscellany* (Paris: Samuelian, 1969), p. 162. On the dispersion of Armenians to different countries after World War I, see Mécérian, "Diaspora Arménienne" 11: 152-168.

75. Ormanian, *The Church of Armenia*, pp. 80-81; *Catholicosate of Cilicia*, pp. 8-15.

76. See Dekmejian, "Middle Eastern Dispersion," p. 30; Kirkland, "Armenian Migration," pp. 248-253, 398.

77. For details on the AGBU, see Varjabedian, *The Armenians*, pp. 95-97; Atamian, *The Armenian Community*, p. 208; *Our Boys: Armenian American Veterans of World War II* (New York: Beechwood Press, 1951), pp. 475-481.

78. On the Armenian Relief Society, see Atamian, *The Armenian Community*, pp. 404-406: Lang and Walker, *The Armenians*, p. 17.

79. On the Gulbenkian Fund, see Nubar Gulbenkian, *Pantaraxia: The Autobiography of Nubar Gulbenkian* (London: Hutchinson, 1965), pp. 262-272. See also Mécérian, "Diaspora Arménienne" 12: 49-50.

80. Varjabedian, *The Armenians*, pp. 95-96; Mécérian, "Diaspora Arménienne" 12: 48; Chakmakjian, *The Armenian Evangelical Church*, p. 7; *Our Boys* (New York: The Delphic Press, 1942), p. 92.

81. Matossian, *Soviet Policies in Armenia*, pp. 28-30; Lang and Walker, *The Armenians*, p. 12; Mécérian, "Diaspora Arménienne" 7: 324-325.

82. Atamian, *The Armenian Community*, pp. 294-304, 388-401; Tololyan, *Armenian Revolutionary Federation*, p. 30; J.H. Tashjian, *The Armenians of the United States and Canada* (Boston: Hairenik Press, 1947), pp. 37-39; *Crisis in the Armenian Church* (Boston: Armenian Apostolic Church, Central Diocesan Board, 1958), pp. 68-69, 122-123.

83. Matossian, *Soviet Policies in Armenia*, pp. 91-95; Mesrob K. Krikorian, "The Armenian Church in the Soviet Union, 1917-1967," in *Aspects of Religion in the Soviet Union*, ed. Richard H. Marshall, Jr. (Chicago: University of Chicago Press, 1971), pp. 240-242.

84. Matossian, *Soviet Policies in Armenia*, pp. 92-93; Krikorian, "Soviet Union," pp. 242-243; Baljian, Vasken I, Catholicos of All Armenians, *Messages and Addresses Delivered During Visit to the United States* (New York: Diocese of The Armenian Church of America, 1969), p. 30.

85. Matossian, *Soviet Policies in Armenia*, pp. 162-169; Lang and Walker, *The Armenians*, p. 12; Sarkissian, "The Armenian Church," pp. 508-509; "Arménie et Arméniens," p. 136; Krikorian, "Soviet Union," pp. 244-256.

86. On the repatriation drive, see Atamian, *The Armenian Community*, pp. 405-413; Sarkissian, "The Armenian Church," p. 508; *Our Boys* (1951), pp. 480-481; Richard G. Hovannisian, "The Ebb and Flow of the Armenian Minority in the Arab Middle East," *The Middle East Journal* 28, 1 (1974): 23.

87. Interviews with informants in Jerusalem (1975-1976); R.B. Betts, *Christians in the Arab East* (Athens: Lycabettus Press, 1975) p. 99.

88. This point was brought to my attention by Richard G. Hovannisian in his letter of 11 September 1980. See also Aïda Boudjikanian-Keuroghlian, *Les Arméniens dans la Région Rhône-Alpes* (Lyon: Association de la Revue de Géographie, 1978), p. 56.

89. Interviews with informants (1976-1977); Boudjikanian, *Région Rhône-Alpes*, pp. 167, 178-179.

NOTES TO PAGES 53-57

90. Atamian, *The Armenian Community*, p. 357.

91. Tololyan, *Armenian Revolutionary Federation*, pp. 5-6; *Crisis in the Church*, pp. 45-46, 93; personal observation and interviews with informants (1975-1978).

92. Lang and Walker, *The Armenians*, p. 17; Jean Michel Hornus, "La Crise du Catholicosat Arménien de Cilicie," *Proche Orient Chrétien* 6-7 (1956-1957), 6:253.

93. Atamian, *The Armenian Community*, pp. 363-374, 425; *Crisis in the Church*, pp. 13, 45-46, 149-153; Tololyan, *Armenian Revolutionary Federation*, pp. 34-46.

94. Sarkissian, "The Armenian Church," p. 516; *Catholicosate of Cilicia*, pp. 20-35; Hornus, "Catholicosat de Cilicie," 6: 237-256; Mécérian, "Diaspora Arménienne" 12: 29-33; "Chronique," *Proche Orient Chrétien* 6 (1956): 92-93.

95. Atamian, *The Armenian Community*, pp. 372-374, 440-441; *Crisis in the Church,* pp. 149-151. For Echmiadzin's view on the rift with the Catholicosate of Cilicia, see Baljian, *Messages*, pp. 56, 68-69, 74. For Cilicia's view, see *Crisis in the Church*, p. 21; *L'Eglise Arménienne*, p. 45.

96. *Crisis in the Church*, p. 27; *Catholicosate of Cilicia*, p. 36; Sarkissian, "The Armenian Church," p. 514; Hovannisian, "Ebb and Flow," p. 27; Tololyan, *Armenian Revolutionary Federation*, pp. 23, 34; Mécérian, "Diaspora Arménienne" 12: 34; Hornus, "Catholicosat Arménien de Cilicie" 7 (1957): 173-179; "Chronique," *Proche Orient Chrétien* 6 (1956): 93; Kirkland, "Armenian Migration," pp. 81, 97-99, 297.

97. Conversation with Richard G. Hovannisian (Los Angeles, June 1979) and written communication to the author from George Bournoutian (6 December 1981). In 1963 there also occurred a beginning of reconciliation between the sees of Echmiadzin and Cilicia with the meeting in Jerusalem of the two Catholicoses, Vasken I of Echmiadzin and Khoren I of Cilicia. The latter succeeded the deceased Zareh I whose election in 1956 had precipitated the crisis with Echmiadzin. See "Chronique," *Proche Orient Chrétien* 13 (1963): 90-92, 190-191, 319.

98. On this point see Kirkland's very perceptive remarks in "Armenian Migration," p. 302.

3: *Armenians in Jerusalem: Historical Background*

1. Gafni, *Glory of Jerusalem*, p. 121; Sanjian, *Armenian Communities in Syria*, p. 4; Hintlian, *Armenians in the Holy Land*, p. 2. Armenian sources trace their presence in Jerusalem to even earlier dates; some even claim that people of Armenian stock lived in the city at the time of Jesus. See Antreassian, *Jerusalem and the Armenians*, pp. 21, 36-38; Hintlian, *Armenians in the Holy Land*, p. 1, Joachim Jeremias, *Jerusalem in the Time of Jesus* (London: SCM Press, 1969), p. 323.

2. Antreassian, *Jerusalem and the Armenians*, pp. 37-39; Hintlian, *Armenians in the Holy Land*, pp. 38, 54. Sanjian, on the other hand,

doubts the authenticity of Anastas Vardapet's list of Armenian monasteries, but this does not refute the general belief that Armenians had a strong presence in Jerusalem in the early Christian era. See Avedis K. Sanjian, "Anastas Vardapet's List of Armenian Monasteries in Seventh-Century Jerusalem: A Critical Examination," *Le Muséon-Revue d'Etudes Orientales* 82, 3-4 (1969): 265-268, 275-290.

3. Hintlian, *Armenians in the Holy Land*, p. 1.

4. Sanjian, "Armenian Monasteries," pp. 278-280; Ajamian, "Armenian Patriarchate," p.38.

5. Antreassian, *Jerusalem and the Armenians*, pp. 40-43; Hintlian, *Armenians in the Holy Land*, p. 2. The alleged original edict issued by the Caliph Umar has been preserved to the present in the treasury of the Armenian Patriarchate.

6. Sanjian, in conversation with the author in Los Angeles (May 1979) and also in *Armenian Communities in Syria*, pp. 5, 168-169.

7. Sanjian, "Armenian Monasteries," p. 282.

8. Antreassian, *Jerusalem and the Armenians*, pp. 43-44; Ajamian, "Armenian Patriarchate," p. 39; Sanjian, "Armenian Monasteries," pp. 290-291.

9. Antreassian, *Jerusalem and the Armenians*, p. 36.

10. Gafni, *Glory of Jerusalem*, pp. 79-80; Sanjian, *Armenian Communities in Syria*, pp. 12, 97; Eugene Hoade, *Jerusalem and its Environs* (Jerusalem: Franciscan Printing Press, 1964), p. 76; Christopher Hollis and Ronald Brownrigg, *Holy Places* (New York: Praeger, 1969), p. 187.

11. In Eastern churches there are no monastic orders as in the West, but monasteries are organized in autonomous brotherhoods. See Ormanian, *The Church of Armenia*, p. 126, and Stewart Perowne, *Jerusalem and Bethlehem* (London: Phoenix House, 1965), p. 19.

12. Hintlian, *Armenians in the Holy Land*, pp. 19-23; Sanjian, *Armenian Communities in Syria*, pp. 12, 17-18, 169.

13. Ajamian, "Armenian Patriarchate," p. 38; Mécérian, "Diaspora Arménienne," 12: 34; Sanjian, *Armenian Communities in Syria*, pp. 96-98 ; R. Janin, *Eglises Orientales et Rites Orientaux* (Paris: Letouzey & Ané, 1955), p. 351; H. Luke and E. Keith-Roach, *The Handbook of Palestine and Transjordan* (London: Macmillan, 1934), p. 51.

14. Sanjian, *Armenian Communities in Syria*, pp. 97, 170-171; Antreassian, *Jerusalem and the Armenians*, pp. 45-46; Hintlian, *Armenians in the Holy Land*, p. 39. Hintlian also claims that some of Salahaddin's closest associates were of Armenian origin.

15. Antreassian, *Jerusalem and the Armenians*, p. 47; Sanjian, *Armenian Communities in Syria*, pp. 172-173.

16. Personal observations and interviews with informants (1976-1978); Pasdermadjian, *Histoire de l'Arménie*, p. 271.

17. Sanjian, *Armenian Communities in Syria*, p. 174; Atiya, *Eastern Christianity*, p. 210.

18. Benvenisti, *The Torn City*, pp. 73-75.

19. Albert N. Williams, *The Holy City* (London: Parker, 1854), p. 435. See also Sanjian, "Armenian Monasteries," p. 291; Sanjian, *Armenian Communities in Syria*, pp. 174, 202, 224; Benvenisti, *The Torn City*, pp. 73-74; Uriel Heyd, "Jerusalem under the Mamlukes and the Turks," *Jerusalem Through the Ages* (Jerusalem: The Israel Exploration Society, 1968, in Hebrew), p. 200.

20. On religious institutions, mentioned by past travelers, which are no longer in Armenian hands see Hintlian, *Armenians in the Holy Land*, pp. 29-33. On the loss incurred by the Coptic church, for example, see O.F.A. Meinardus, "The Coptic Church in Egypt," in *Religion in the Middle East*, ed. Arberry, 1: 443-444.

21. For details see Sanjian, *Armenian Communities in Syria*, pp. 176-190, 202-203; Benvenisti, *The Torn City*, pp. 73-74.

22. Sanjian, *Armenian Communities in Syria*, pp. 190-199; Benvenisti, *The Torn City*, pp. 74-75; Eugene Hoade, *Guide to the Holy Land*, 7th ed. (Jerusalem: Franciscan Printing Press, 1973), pp. 129-130.

23. For details on Armenian possessions as recognized in the status quo agreement, see Sanjian, *Armenian Communities in Syria*, pp. 199-201; Hintlian, *Armenians in the Holy Land*, p. 57-60.

24. Sanjian, *Armenian Communities in Syria*, p. 203; Hoade, *Holy Land*, p. 130.

25. Benvenisti, *The Torn City*, p. 73. See also Williams, *The Holy City*, pp. 438-439.

26. Personal observations and interviews with informants (1977).

27. Interview with Father Haigazoun Melkonian (Jerusalem, April 1977).

28. Interviews with informants (1975-1978). For details on more secluded Armenian monasteries, see Hintlian, *Armenians in the Holy Land*, pp. 6-10; Der Nersessian, *The Armenians*, pp. 95-96; Arpee, *Armenian Christianity*, pp. 97-98; Lang, *Armenia*, pp. 160, 215, 275-276; Ormanian, *The Church of Armenia*, pp. 43, 57, 127.

29. Interviews with informants (1975-1978).

30. Personal observations (1975-1978).

31. Interviews with informants (1975-1978); Sanjian, *Armenian Communities in Syria*, pp. 68, 104; Hintlian, *Armenians in the Holy Land*, pp. 62-63.

32. Antreassian, *Jerusalem and the Armenians*, p. 48; Williams, *The Holy City*, p. 455; interviews with informants (1975-1978).

33. Interview with Kapikian (March 1976).

34. C. Wardi, "The Latin Patriarchate of Jerusalem," *Journal of the Middle East Society* 1 (Autumn 1947): 10. On the importance of Jerusalem for Eastern Christian churches see Atiya, *Eastern Christianity*, pp. 93, 157, 266.

35. See Eliade, *The Sacred and the Profane*, pp. 20-43, 59.

36. Sanjian, *Armenian Communities in Syria*, pp. 204-205; Terzian, *Armenian Miscellany*, pp. 202-203; interviews with informants (1976-1977).

37. Williams, *The Holy City*, p. 456.

38. Sanjian, *Armenian Communities in Syria*, pp. 143-146; Malachia Ormanian, *Armenian Jerusalem* (Jerusalem: St. James Press, 1931, in Armenian), p. 171; interview with Andranik Bakirjian (Jerusalem, June 1976).

39. Sanjian, *Armenian Communities in Syria*, p. 78.

40. Ibid., p. 78; Sion Manoogian, *Armenian Jerusalem* (Boston: Baikar Press, 1948, in Armenian), p. 122; Hintlian, *Armenians in the Holy Land*, p. 47; interviews with informants (1976-1977).

41. For more details on the seminary see Manoogian, *Armenian Jerusalem*, pp. 94, 119-127; Sanjian, *Armenian Communities in Syria*, pp. 79-82; Sarkissian, "The Armenian Church," p. 512; Ormanian, *Armenian Jerusalem*, p. 164; Atiya, *Eastern Christianity*, p. 336.

42. Sanjian, *Armenian Communities in Syria*, pp. 82-83; Hintlian, *Armenians in the Holy Land*, p. 47; Ormanian, *Armenian Jerusalem*, pp. 79, 85-86; Manoogian, *Armenian Jerusalem*, pp. 94-95.

43. Arpee, *Armenian Christianity*, p. 195; Hintlian, *Armenians in the Holy Land*, p. 50; Terzian, *Armenian Miscellany*, p. 203. See also N. Bogharian, *Grand Catalogue of the St. James Manuscripts*, 3 vols. (Jerusalem: St. James Press, 1966-1968) and Michael E. Stone, "The Manuscript Library of the Armenian Patriarchate in Jerusalem," *Israel Exploration Journal* 19 (1969): 20-43.

44. Sanjian, *Armenian Communities in Syria*, pp. 84-87; Sarkissian, "The Armenian Church," p. 512; Antreassian, *Jerusalem and the Armenians*, pp. 49-50.

45. Sanjian, *Armenian Communities in Syria*, pp. 141, 259; Hintlian, *Armenians in the Holy Land*, p. 4; Antreassian, *Jerusalem and the Armenians*, p. 32.

46. Personal observations and interviews with informants (1975-1978); Shahe Ajamian, "Le Sultan Abdulhamid et le Patriarcat Arménien de Jerusalem" (Paper presented at the International Seminar on the History of Palestine, Institute of Asian and African Studies, The Hebrew University, Jerusalem, 1970), p. 2; Moshe Sharon, "Palestine under the Mameluks and the Ottoman Empire," in *A History of Holy Land*, ed. Michael Avi-Yonah (Jerusalem: Jerusalem Publishing House, 1969), p. 280.

47. For details, see Sanjian, *Armenian Communities in Syria*, pp. 102-141. There were also unsuccessful attempts to unite the two patriarchates.

48. Ibid., pp. 116-141; Ajamian, "Abdulhamid," pp 3-5; Sarkissian, "The Armenian Church," p. 493; Atiya, *Eastern Christianity*, p. 336.

49. Sanjian, *Armenian Communities in Syria*, pp. 104, 112-113; Ormanian, *Armenian Jerusalem*, pp. 149-151.

50. Interview with Reverend Gamsarayan (Jerusalem, November 1975); Gafni, *Glory of Jerusalem*, p. 55; Stephan, "Armenian Catholic

Community," p. 1-2; Hoade, *Jerusalem and its Environs*, pp. 22-23. On Armenian Catholics in general see Mécérian, "Diaspora Arménienne" 12: 37-38 and Jean Louis Lingot, "L'Intronisation du Nouveau Patriarche Arménien Catholique; Sa Béatitude Hémayag Pierre XVII Guédigian A Bzommar (Liban) le 15 Août 1976," *Proche Orient Chrétien* 26 (1976): 230-232, 242-244.

51. "Liste des Arméniens Catholiques de Rite Arménien" (Mimeographed sheet, Armenian Catholic Church, Jerusalem, 1974). See also Erik Cohen and Hermona Grunau, *Survey of Minorities in Israel* (Jerusalem: The Institute for Asian and African Studies, The Hebrew University, 1972, in Hebrew), p. 54.

52. Interviews with Gamsarayan (November 1975) and other informants (1975-1977); Janin, *Eglises Orientales*, p. 362.

53. Interviews with informants (1975-1978); "Chronicle of Events," *Christian News From Israel* 11 (July 1960): 5; A. Wachtel, "The Church of the Nazarene in Israel," *Christian News From Israel* 11, 4 (1960): 23.

54. Interview with Gamsarayan (November 1975).

55. Interviews with informants (1975-1978).

56. Ben Arieh, "Christian Activity," p. 51. Vilnay's slightly different figures are 350 in 1844 and 515 in 1876 (*Jerusalem*, 2: 6).

57. Ben Arieh, "Christian Activity," p. 51.

58. Hovannisian, "Ebb and Flow," p. 20. However, there is some incongruence between this figure and the much lower British census figures of 1922. For more on this point, see note 61 in this chapter.

59. Ibid., pp. 19-20; Antreassian, *Jerusalem and the Armenians*, p. 50; Chilingirian, *Refugees and Monastics*, pp. 50, 55. For more details on Armenian refugees in Middle Eastern countries, see also Dekmejian, "Middle Eastern Dispersion," pp. 28-29; Mécérian, "Diaspora Arménienne," 11: 150-160; C.T. Bridgeman, *Armenian Reconstruction in Syria* (London: Jerusalem and the Near East Mission, 1926), pp. 15-22.

60. Interviews with informants (1975-1976).

61. This might provide a partial explanation for surprisingly low British census figures showing only 3,210 Armenian inhabitants in the whole of Palestine in 1922 and 3,000 Armenians in 1931. [Luke and Keith-Roach, *Handbook of Palestine*, pp. 50-51; Betts, *Christians, in the Arab East*, p. 66; Yehudit Blum, "The Armenian Community of Jerusalem" (Seminar paper, Jerusalem, n.d.), p. 1. See also Ben Arieh, *City Reflected*, p. 228.] These figures do not square well with the data of about 10,000 Armenian refugees arriving in Palestine after World War I as it is hard to imagine that, despite great efforts to relocate the refugees in other countries, 70 percent of them were sent from Palestine in a couple of years. However, the British census figures are also incompatible with sources indicating that about

8,000 Armenians lived in Palestine in 1948 [Ormanian, *The Church of Armenia*, p. 83; Hoade, *Holy Land*, p. 90; Y. Shimony, "Middle East Mosaic," *Palestine and the Middle East* 19, 9-10 (1947): 182]. Either the 1948 and World War I figures were inflated or British census figures missed a large part of the Armenian refugee population.

62. Hovannisian, "Ebb and Flow," p. 25; Chilingirian, *Refugees and Monastics*, p. 50; interviews with informants (1975-1978).

63. Antreassian, *Jerusalem and the Armenians*, p. 50; Gafni, *Glory of Jerusalem*, p. 79; interviews with informants (1975-1978).

64. Interviews with informants (1976-1980).

65. Hovannisian, "Ebb and Flow," p. 25; interviews with informants (1975-1978).

66. Hovannisian, "Ebb and Flow," p. 25; interviews with informants (1975-1980).

67. Joseph Mamour, "Au Patriarcat Arménien de Jerusalem" *Proche Orient Chrétien* 7 (1957): 64; *Album of the Monastery*, p. 56; "Armenian Church Representative," *Christian News From Israel* 1 (August 1949): 1-4; interviews with Garbis Hintlian (Jerusalem, October 1975), Hovannes Merguerian (Jerusalem, June 1976) and other informants (1975-1980).

68. Interviews with informants (1975-1980).

69. For the number of Armenians living in Israel between 1948 and 1967 see Colbi, *Christianity in the Holy Land*, p. 68; Cohen and Grunau, *Survey of Minorities*, p. 70; Blum, "Armenian Community," p. 2.

70. Interviews with informants (1976-1978); "Chronicle of Events," *Christian News From Israel* 2 (March 1951): 7, 9 (June 1958): 4, 11 (April 1960): 6.

71. Mamour, "Au Patriarcat Arménien," p. 65; interview with Kapikian (September 1975). On fund-raising tours by priests in history see Sanjian, *Armenian Communities in Syria*, pp. 126, 205-208, 224.

72. Interviews with informants (1975-1980); Gabriel Stern, "His Beatitude Elisha II: Armenian Patriarch and Poet," *Christian News From Israel* 21, 4 (1971): 41. It should be noted here, however, that my knowledge of the Armenian attitude toward Israeli rule is rather thin. I tried to avoid this subject in conversations with Armenians and deliberately refrained from asking them to compare life now with that under Arab rule. The subject was marginal to the main focus of the study and was not worth the risk of arousing uneasiness among them.

4: *The Life of the Lay Community in Jerusalem*

1. In this study "patriarchate," "monastery," and "monastic brotherhood" are used interchangeably even though they are not identical terms. Patriarchate denotes the church authority that has jurisdiction over an area in which Jerusalem is included (but comprises also Jordan and other towns in Israel and the West Bank). The

Monastery of St. James is the headquarters of the patriarchate and the monastic brotherhood is the collective body of clergymen that runs the monastery and whose supreme head is the patriarch. Thus, although they do not have identical definitions, the three terms do denote the same collectivity of clergymen, and it makes no difference whether we refer, for example, to the ownership rights of the patriarchate, of the monastery, or of the monastic brotherhood.

2. Interviews with informants (1975-1978).

3. Personal observation and interviews with informants (1975-1978).

4. According to Schmelz's figures from 1972, which unfortunately did not differentiate between structures located inside and outside the monastery, 62.3 percent of the households in the Armenian quarter had lavatories outside the building and 77.1 percent had no bathroom or shower facilities. In 30 percent of them four or more people lived in one room ("Demography of Christians," p.13). The Israeli government's census figures from 1967, which again did not differentiate between the dwellings inside the monastery compound and those outside, gave the following more detailed data on the housing situation in the Armenian quarter: 31.4 percent of the people had toilets inside their buildings and did not share them with other households, 24.3 percent had them inside the building but had to share them with other households, 44.3 percent had outside toilets. Regarding baths, 82.4 percent had no bath at all, 4.4 percent shared baths with other households, and 13.2 percent had their own baths. The situation regarding kitchens was much better: 73.7 percent did not share them with other households, 7.3 percent had shared kitchens, and 9 percent had no kitchen at all (*Census*, p. 57). Similarly the great majority of the population (82.1 percent) had electricity in their homes but many fewer (30.3 percent) had water taps inside their dwelling; 20.3 percent had taps in the yard, 4.1 percent obtained water from private wells, 25.4 obtained it from public wells, and 19.9 percent obtained it from unspecified sources (*Census*, p. 60). It should be pointed out, though, that these data reflect the situation at the beginning of Israeli rule in the Old City. Things have changed considerably in the last ten years. Household facilities improved in the Armenian quarter and in other places of the Old City (a fact which Israeli authorities are very proud to point out). My personal impression from visits to Armenian homes in 1976-1978 is that a much greater number of them have household facilities inside the building, but that on the whole housing still remains substandard especially within the monastery compound.

5. Personal observations and interviews with informants (1975-1978).

6. Interview with Kevork Hintlian (Jerusalem, October 1975).

7. Television is the one household commodity about which the most striking change has taken place since 1967. While only 6 percent of the population had television sets in their homes in 1967,

now almost every household has one (*Census*, p. 60; personal observations and interviews, 1975-1978).

8. Henry Kendall, *Jerusalem City Plan* (London: His Majesty's Stationery Office, 1948), p. 37. The quoted section from Kendall deals with the Old City as a whole but as Kendall himself indicated the best examples of this architectual layout are found in the Armenian quarter.

9. Personal observations and interviews (1975-1980).

10. Interview with Melkonian (April 1977).

11. The following quote from Gans about the Italians of the West End almost perfectly fits the Armenian picture:

Since everyone knows everyone else, life is an open book and deviant acts are hard to hide. This means that such acts are committed either outside the reaches of the group — as in the case of adolescents who do their misbehaving outside the West End — or that they are not committed at all (*The Urban Villagers*, pp. 85-86).

On the different situation in other slum neighborhoods, see Hannerz, *Soulside*, p. 66; Suttles, *The Social Order of the Slum*, p. 125.

12. Personal observations and interviews with informants (1975-1980). See also Blum, "Armenian Community," p. 24. Interestingly, local residents spoke to me rather freely about sexual gossip, and for once I was the one shying away from a subject of conversation.

13. Schmelz, "Demography of Christians," p. 13.

14. For similar segregation of leisure within the home in other ethnic communities see Gans, *The Urban Villagers*, p. 48, and Suttles, *The Social Order of the Slum*, pp. 77, 90-91.

15. Interviews with informants (1975-1978).

16. A few cases of eviction have been brought to my attention. People were moved from houses destroyed to make room for the building of the lay school in 1929 (Ormanian, *Armenian Jerusalem*, p. 87). In the 1970s a number of stores were destroyed in front of the monastery's main gate in order to build the new seminary building there. In both cases tenants were given alternative places for their home or store. Interviews with informants (1975-1978).

17. For example, I was told in the 1970s of the patriarchate's dilemma about whether to let an Armenian woman who had married a Muslim Arab live in the quarter (interviews with informants, 1975-1978).

18. In some eviction suits during the British mandate the patriarchate won its cases [interview with G. Hintlian (October 1975)], but in one famous lawsuit during Jordanian rule a local won his case against the patriarchate, which tried to evict him for refusing to pay rent and sign a lease [interview with Bakirjian (June 1976)].

19. Interviews with informants (1975-1978).

20. Ibid.

21. Interview with Varujan Diradurian (Jerusalem, March 1976).

22. Interview with Ara Kalaydjian (Jerusalem, September 1975). See also Benvenisti, *The Torn City*, p. 46.

23. Interviews with informants (1975-1978); Antreassian, *Jerusalem and the Armenians*, p. 52; C. Issawi, "The Entrepreneur Class," in *Social Forces in the Middle East*, ed. Fisher, p. 128.

24. Alfred E. Lieber, "An Economic History of Jerusalem," in *Jerusalem*, ed. Oesterreicher and Sinai, p. 39; interviews with informants (1975-1982).

25. See, for example, Kornblum, *Blue Collar Community*, p. 14 and Hannerz, *Soulside*, pp. 34-35.

26. Blum, "Armenian Community," p. 18; personal observations and interviews with informants (1975-1978). For similar bantering and socializing in shops without buying, see Suttles, *The Social Order of the Slum*, p. 84.

27. See, for example, Gans, *The Urban Villagers*, p. 14.

28. Interviews with informants (1975-1980).

29. S.P. Colbi, *Christian Churches in Israel* (Jerusalem: Israel Economist, 1969), p. 13; Ben Arieh, *City Reflected*, p. 148.

30. Daphna Tsimhoni, "The Christian Communities in Jerusalem and the West Bank, 1948-1967," *Middle East Review* 9, 1 (1976): 42-43; Benvenisti, *Facing the Closed Wall*, p. 95; Stendel, "Arabs in Jerusalem," p. 160.

31. Norman Gosenfeld, "Changes in the Business Community of East Jerusalem," *The New East* (Hebrew) 24, 4 (1974): 272-274 and English summary, p. iii; Vilnay, *Jerusalem*, 2: 16; Hovannisian, "Ebb and Flow," p. 24; *Album of the Monastery*, p. 20.

32. Interviews with informants (1975-1980).

33. Personal observation and interviews with informants (1975-1978); Blum, "Armenian Community," p. 8.

34. Interviews with informants (1975-1978); Ormanian, *Armenian Jerusalem*, pp. 160-170.

35. In this respect a great change occurred with the advent of Israeli rule. In 1967, for example, only 26.3 percent of households in the Armenian quarter had refrigerators (*Census*, p. 60), while today there is hardly a household without one [personal observations and interviews (1975-1980)].

36. Personal observations and interviews (1975-1978).

37. For a similar reluctance to do business with peer group members to avoid losing money by giving them preferential treatment, see Gans, *The Urban Villagers*, p. 93.

38. Personal observations and interviews (1975-1978).

39. Schmelz, "Demography of Christians," p. 13. My Armenian informants dispute these figures and claim that the level of education is even higher. Interviews with Kapikian and A. Kalaydjian (September 1975).

40. Saint Tarkmanchatz Armenian Secondary School, "Annual Report 1974-1975," Jerusalem (1975), p. 16. These figures seem to be too low for a community of about 1,500 people if almost all their children attend the same school, as my informants claimed. Assuming that school enrollment figures are correct and that 1974-75 was not an exceptional year, they show that either the community is much smaller than Armenian sources claim — providing indirect support to the much lower figures of the Israeli census (see note 3 in chapter 1) — or that not all the community's children attend the Armenian school. By the school principal's own admission, about 50 Armenian school-age children did not attend the Armenian school. Attendance at other schools increases at the high-school level. Some families prefer to send their children to other private schools, such as Collège des Frères, Schmidt's College, or Saint George's, which are considered to be better schools (interviews with informants, 1975-1978).

41. Saint Tarkmanchatz, "Annual Report," p. 16; Ajamian, interview to *Kol Ha Ir* (26 December 1980), p. 25; interviews with informants (1975-1980). Until 1978 the Turkish government did not stop the arrival of Armenian children from Turkey. Recently, however, it was alleged that an Armenian priest, a member of the Saint James brotherhood, was arrested in Turkey for trying to organize a new group of students for the seminary in Jerusalem.

42. Personal observations and interviews with informants (1975-1980).

43. See Tsimhoni, "Christian Communities," p. 44; Benvenisti, *Facing the Closed Wall*, pp. 94-95.

44. Personal observations and interviews with informants (1975-1980).

45. Ibid. Also see Gabriel Stern, "Chronicles of the Armenian Orthodox Patriarchate of Jerusalem," *Christian News From Israel* 21, 3 (1970): 6-8.

46. Saint Tarkmanchatz, "Annual Report," pp. 15-24; Stern, "Armenian Patriarchate," pp. 6-8; personal observations and interviews with informants (1975-1978).

47. Saint Tarkmanchatz, "Annual Report," p. 17; Stern, "Armenian Patriarchate," pp. 6-8; interviews with Kapikian (September 1975 and March 1976) and other informants (1975-1981).

48. The only other Armenian institution of higher learning outside Soviet Armenia known to me is the American Armenian International College in LaVerne, California, which grants a bachelor's degree in Armenian Studies. This information was brought to my attention by George Bournoutian in his written communication of December 1981.

49. Interviews with informants (1975-1978). See also Stern, "Armenian Patriarchate," pp. 6-8 and Hovannisian, "Ebb and Flow," pp. 29-30.

50. Personal observations and interviews with informants (1975-1978).

51. On the situation in France, see Boudjikanian, *Région Rhône-Alpes*, pp. 109-112.

52. Interviews with informants (1975-1978).

53. Personal observations and interviews with informants (1975-1978).

54. Personal observations (1978-1980).

55. Interviews with Apraham Surtukian (Jerusalem, March 1976) and other informants (1975-1978).

56. Personal observations and interviews with informants (1975-1978).

57. Ibid.

58. Ibid.

59. Ibid.

60. Interviews with Gamsarayan (November 1975) and other informants. Non-Apostolic Armenians are prominent in many areas of community life outside Jerusalem. The Haigazian College in Beirut, for instance, is run by Protestant Armenians. American chapters of the AGBU and the Armenian Relief Organization also have very prominent non-Apostolic members. See Betts, *Christians in the Arab East*, p. 56; Varjabedian, *The Armenians*, pp. 57-58; Chakmakjian, *The Armenian Evangelical Church*, p. 7.

61. Personal observations and interviews with informants (1975-1978).

62. Warren, *The Community in America*, pp. 161-208; *The Community*, pp. 27-36. Don Martindale proposes a similar approach when he states that three general types of problems must be solved for communities to maintain themselves: mastery of the material environment, socialization, and social control. See Don Martindale, "The Formation and Destruction of Communities," in *Explorations in Social Change*, ed. George K. Zollschan and Walter Hirsch (Boston: Houghton Mifflin, 1964), p. 72.

63. Interview with Bakirjian (June 1976).

64. Ibid and other interviews with informants (1975-1978).

65. Blum, "Armenian Community," p. 18; interviews with informants (1975-1978).

66. Blum, "Armenian Community," p. 18.

67. Personal observations and interviews with informants (1975-1980).

68. Ibid.

69. Despite his wealth and his influence on the community, however, the owner of the tissue factory is not as centrally located as some laymen who work for the patriarchate. Not even a resident of Jerusalem (he lives in Ramallah), he is neither in daily contact with the clergy nor directly involved in the daily life of the commun-

ity, as are some top lay officeholders in the monastery, most of whom lean toward Hoyetchmen.

70. Mamour, "Au Patriarcat Arménien," pp. 64-67; Blum, "Armenian Community," pp. 19-21.

71. Mamour, "Au Patriarcat Arménien," pp. 68-69; Blum, "Armenian Community," pp. 21-23; Hornus, "Catholicosat de Cilicie" 7: 360; "Chronique," *Proche Orient Chrétien* 7 (1957): 94, 348-350, 8 (1958): 80-81, 267-268.

72. Blum, "Armenian Community," pp. 24-25; "Chronique," *Proche Orient Chrétien* 8 (1958): 81.

73. Blum, "Armenian Community," p 23; "Chronique," *Proche Orient Chrétien* 10 (1960): 78, 165-166, 273; "Chronicle of Events," *Christian News From Israel* 11 (July 1960): 9; interviews with informants (1976-1979). One of them, Shenork Kalustian, who had arrived with Tiran Nersoyan from the United States to lead the struggle against Derderian was elected Patriarch of Istanbul in 1962 and even visited Jerusalem in his new capacity at the inauguration of the new seminary building in 1975. His visit indicated a reconciliation with the present Patriarch of Jerusalem. See "Chronique," *Proche Orient Chrétien* 10 (1960): 78, 12 (1962): 88.

74. On the succession crisis in the Catholicosate of Cilicia, see Hornus "Catholicosat de Cilicie" 6: 237-256 and 7: 173-179; "Chronique," *Proche Orient Chrétien* 6 (1956): 92-93; Mécérian, "Diaspora Arménienne," 12: 29-33.

75. Blum, "Armenian Community," p. 26. The anti-Dashnak attitude of the Jordanian government also might explain its support for Derderian. The Jordanian government distrusted the Dashnakists and saw in them potentially subversive elements (see Atamian, *The Armenian Community*, p. 443). Even though Nersoyan was not identified with Dashnak, both he and the Dashnak party were vocal proponents of reforms in the community and were opposed to Derderian. This might have made him suspicious in the eyes of the Jordanians, or at least Derderian's supporters in Amman could have successfully portrayed him as a radical and set the Jordanian government against him.

76. *Crisis in the Church,* p. 119.

77. Hornus, "Catholicosat de Cilicie" 7: 173-175, 360; Mécérian, "Diaspora Arménienne," 12: 35-36.

78. Interviews with informants (1975-1978).

5: *The Life and Organization of the Clergy*

1. Ajamian, "Armenian Patriarchate," p. 40; interviews with informants (1975-1978). In the Armenian church, as in most other Eastern Christian churches, nuns are unmarried women or widows who have retired to church service in their old age. In Jerusalem they are in charge of the Holy Archangels church and have their

own separate cloister within the monastery. Deacons are nominally part of the monastic brotherhood but cannot take part in its government. They are represented by two nonvoting members in the brotherhood's general assembly [interviews with informants (1975-1978). See also Ormanian, *The Church of Armenia*, pp. 147-148].

2. On married and celibate priests in other Eastern Christian churches see Atiya, *Eastern Christianity*, pp. 124-125, 221, 277, 392, 412-413.

3. Ibid., pp. 345-347; Ormanian, *The Church of Armenia*, p. 149.

4. Janin, *Eglises Orientales*, pp. 340-343; Antreassian, *Jerusalem and the Armenians*, p. 33; Ormanian, *The Church of Armenia*, pp. 104, 125-128, 150-151.

5. Lang, *Armenia*, pp. 159-160; Atiya, *Eastern Christianity*, pp. 322, 346.

6. Janin, *Eglises Orientales*, p. 342; Ormanian, *The Church of Armenia*, pp. 131-132.

7. Atiya, *Eastern Christianity*, p. 347.

8. Interviews with informants (1975-1978). It is not clear why married priests are posted in Bethlehem. The lay community there is small and married priests of Bethlehem offer no pastoral services to the Jerusalem community. They are occupied rather with upkeep of the Armenian portion of the Church of the Nativity, which theoretically should not be the task of married priests.

9. Interviews with informants in Jerusalem (1975) and Istanbul (August 1976).

10. Interviews with informants (1975-1980); Atiya, *Eastern Christianity*, p. 336.

11. Ajamian, "Armenian Patriarchate," p. 40; Ormanian, *Armenian Jerusalem*, pp. 149-151; interviews with Ajamian (May 1976), K. Hintlian (October 1975), and Kapikian (September 1975).

12. Antreassian, *Jerusalem and the Armenians*, pp. 31-32; Sarafian, *The Armenian Apostolic Church*, p. 24; Ormanian, *The Church of Armenia*, pp. 133-134; Hornus, "Catholicosat de Cilicie" 6: 240; interviews with Ajamian (May 1976) and Kapikian (September 1975). Since the 1940s the Catholicoses of Echmiadzin and Cilicia have the right to participate in each other's election (Ormanian, *The Church of Armenia*, pp. 81-82; Mécérian, "Diaspora Arménienne" 12: 28-29). This measure, thought to create a rapprochement between them, was instead a precipitating cause of the crisis during the election of the Catholicos of Cilicia in 1956.

13. Atiya, *Eastern Christianity*, pp. 303, 347.

14. Interviews with informants (1975-1978).

15. Ibid.

16. Ibid.

17. Personal observations and interviews with informants (1975-1978).

18. Interviews with informants (1982). The removal of the chancellor appears to be related to another problem that has severely strained the Israeli government's relations with the Armenian patriarchate in recent months, and has created consternation in other Christian communities of Jerusalem. In July 1982 the Israeli ministry of interior decided not to extend the residence permit of the present grand sacristine of the patriarchate, who is a foreign resident brought from Australia upon the death of the former grand sacristine. Israeli government circles refused to disclose the reason for their decision but newspaper reports indicated that this may have been related to efforts to help the former chancellor who is considered more sympathetic to Israeli interests than the present grand sacristine. If such reports are true, they would indicate an unprecedented intervention in the patriarchate's affairs on the part of the Israeli government, somewhat reminiscent of the Jordanian government's intervention in the patriarchal succession crisis in the 1950s. The affair was unfolding by the end of 1982 and no solution was yet in sight. The grand sacristine was still in the country despite the expiration of his residence permit. See Nadav Shragai, "The Armenian Affair," *Kol Ha Ir* (10 December 1982, in Hebrew), pp. 27-28 and Zvi Zinger "Intrigues in the Shadow of the Cross," *Yedioth Ahronoth Shiv'a Yamim* (24 December 1982, in Hebrew), pp. 12-13, 62.

19. Personal observations and interviews with informants (1975-1978).

20. For more details on different ranks in the Armenian church, see Ormanian, *The Church of Armenia*, pp. 103-104, 116-117, 147-152; Sarafian, *The Armenian Apostolic Church*, p. 23; Antreassian, *Jerusalem and the Armenians*, p. 33.

21. Interview with Melkonian (March 1977).

22. Interview with informants (1975-1978).

23. Interview with Father Joseph Mamour (Jerusalem, November 1975).

24. Personal observations and interviews with informants (1975-1978).

25. Ibid. For more details on the Armenian church's worship services and other clerical duties, see Janin, *Eglises Orientales*, pp. 323-328; Ormanian, *The Church of Armenia*, pp. 119-121.

26. Personal observations and interviews with informants (1975-1980); Ormanian, *Armenian Jerusalem*, p. 170; Sanjian, *Armenian Communities in Syria*, p. 206.

27. Personal observations and interviews with informants (1975-1980). On the daily life of the priests in the 1920s, see Ormanian, *Armenian Jerusalem*, pp. 56-59, 186-189.

28. Interviews with informants (1975-1978).

29. Observations during the seminary graduation ceremonies (June 1977) and interviews with informants (1975-1978).

30. Interviews with informants (1975-1978).

31. Personal observations and interviews with informants (1975-1978).

32. Ibid.

33. Personal observations (1975). Also see Jacques Nantet, *Les Mille et une Jerusalem* (Paris: Lattes, 1977), p. 57.

34. Residential communities sometimes take quite totalistic features, as in small isolated villages or ethnic ghettos. Some writers have found it useful to employ the concept of total institution as a metaphor for explaining such phenomena as ethnicity and urban slums, though in my view this overextends the use of the concept. [See David Lark, "The American Slum as a Total Institution," in *Exploring Total Institutions,* ed. Robert Gordon and Brett Williams (Champaign, Ill.: Stipes, 1977), pp. 129-151 and Richard Basham, "Ethnicity as a Total Institution," in *Exploring Total Institutions,* ed. Gordon and Williams, pp. 176-185.]

6: Priests and Laymen: Problems of Coexistence and Dominance

1. This point was brought to my attention by George A. Hillery, Jr. in his letter of 4 August 1980.

2. Hans H. Gerth and C. Wright Mills, eds., *From Max Weber: Essays in Sociology* (New York: Oxford University Press, 1958), pp. 287-291; Max Weber, *Economy and Society,* 3 vols. (New York: Bedminster Press, 1968) 3: 1170.

3. Reinhard Bendix, *Max Weber: An Intellectual Portrait* (Garden City, N.Y.: Doubleday, 1962), p. 317.

4. Hill, *The Religious Order,* pp. 2-3, 12, 45.

5. Weber, *Economy and Society* 2: 539.

6. See Lowrie J. Daly, *Benedictine Monasticism* (New York: Sheed and Ward, 1965), pp. 269, 277, 283-297, 325-327; Joan Evans, *Monastic Life at Cluny* (Hamden, Conn.: Archon Books, 1968), p. 116; E.A. Gutkind, *International History of City Development,* 8 vols. (New York: The Free Press, 1964-1972) 6: 206; David C. Lindberg, ed., *Science in the Middle Ages* (Chicago: University of Chicago Press, 1978), passim; Weber, *Economy and Society* 3: 1169; Bendix, *Max Weber,* p. 316.

7. This does not mean, however, that monasteries were necessarily elements of *progress* in those activities. They may well have been elements of conservation and stagnation; they may have represented the peak of performance at their time while also discouraging breakthroughs that could carry human knowledge and performance beyond that level. On this question, see Lindberg, ed., *Science in the Middle Ages,* passim.

8. Weber, *Economy and Society* 3: 1168-1169; Gerth and Mills, eds., *From Max Weber,* pp. 290-291; Bendix, *Max Weber,* p. 316.

9. On the nationalistic role of monasteries among the Maronites see Atiya, *Eastern Christianity*, pp. 393-425.

10. The nature of medicine was such that the advance of knowledge was difficult without its practice. Monasteries were not merely repositories of medical literature but also centers of medical practice. Still, the extension of medical help to the needy developed especially in the hospices of the nonmonastic Mendicant Orders, established much closer to lay population centers and on major axes of communication (particularly on major pilgrimage routes). See Charles H. Talbot, "Medicine," in *Science in the Middle Ages*, ed. Lindberg, pp. 395, 405.

11. Hillery, in letter to the author (August 1980).

12. On such religious orders, see Henri Pirenne, *Medieval Cities* (Garden City, N.Y.: Doubleday, 1956), pp. 118-119; P. Lavedan and J. Hugueney, *L'Urbanisme au Moyen Age* (Genève: Droz, 1974), p. 155; Hill, *The Religious Order*, pp. 292, 305; D. Attwatter, *The Christian Churches of the East* (Milwaukee: Bruce Publication, 1947), p. 220. For a systematic comparison of this-worldly orientations in religious orders, see A.L.T. Verdonk, "Réorientation ou Desintégration? Une Enquête Sociologique sur une Congrégation Religieuse Masculine aux Pays Bas," *Social Compass* 18, 1 (1971): 131-135.

13. Pirenne, *Medieval Cities*, pp. 118-119. See also Charles J. Erasmus, *In Search of the Common Good: Utopian Experiments Past and Future* (New York: The Free Press, 1977), p. 123.

14. Hillery, "Community or Task Force," p. 141.

15. Weber, *Economy and Society*, 3: 1166-1173; Bendix, *Max Weber*, pp. 316-317; Gerth and Mills, eds., *From Max Weber*, p. 290-291

16. Attwater, *Churches of the East*, p. 220.

17. Hill, *The Religious Order*, pp. 35-36, 51.

18. M.A. Neal, "A Theoretical Analysis of Renewal in Religious Orders in the USA," *Social Compass* 18, 1 (1971): 8.

19. Some religious orders depend as a matter of principle on alms received from laymen. As Delaney points out about the Buddhist example:

. . . the Buddhist temple, in contrast to its Benedictine counterpart never aimed at being self-sufficient and isolated from society. . . . Because the monks are not allowed to work but must rely on the laity for material and nutritional support, the Buddhist monkhood needs society. The laity provides the infrastructure, so to speak, for a higher spiritual culture to develop in their midst. (William P. Delaney, "The Uses of the Total Institution: A Buddhist Monastic Example," in *Exploring Total Institutions*, ed. Gordon and Williams, p. 19.)

20. Hill, *The Religious Order*, pp. 33-36; Servais and Hambye, "Organizations Claustrales," p. 44.

21. Attwatter, *Churches of the East*, pp. 222-223.

22. Der Nersessian, *The Armenians,* pp. 95-96; Sanjian, *Armenian Communities in Syria,* pp. 71, 76. In this context we should also mention the Mekhitarist monastic order that developed in the early eighteenth century among Armenian Catholics. It followed the Benedictine rule and established two monasteries, one in Vienna and, the other on the island of Saint Lazarus off Venice. In the late eighteenth century printing presses were established in those monasteries, the first among Armenians. Henceforth the two monasteries made substantial contributions to Armenian culture by publishing numerous monographs on Armenian subjects, as well as literary works, dictionaries, and grammars on the Armenian language. The Mekhitarist monasteries house some of the best collections of Armenian literature and are considered important centers of Armenian learning. See Sanjian, *Armenian Communities in Syria,* p. 72; Janin, *Eglises Orientales,* p. 362; "Arménie et Arméniens," pp. 132-133.

23. On the differentiation into celibate and married priesthood in Eastern Christianity see also Weber, *Economy and Society* 3: 1167-1173.

24. See Ormanian, *The Church of Armenia,* pp. 43, 57, 127, 205; Pasdermadjian, *Histoire de l'Arménie,* p. 285; Lang, *Armenia,* pp. 160, 275-276; Der Nersessian, *The Armenians,* pp. 95-96; Arpee, *Armenian Christianity,* pp. 97-98; Iorga, *Petite Arménie,* p. 89; Hintlian, *Armenians in the Holy Land,* pp. 6-10; Ara Baliozian, *The Armenians* (Toronto: Kar Publishing House, 1975), p. 63.

25. Hillery, "Community or Task Force," p. 140.

26. For an interesting example of another parish run by a religious order, see J. C. Falardeau, "The Parish as an Institutional Type," *The Canadian Journal of Economics and Political Science* 15 (August 1949): 359-365. Falardeau studies parishes in Quebec run by the Oblate Fathers. Functions performed by the Oblate Fathers are the familiar ones expected in any parish, that is, administration of the sacraments, preaching from the pulpit, teaching of religion to children in schools, and census of parishioners. The priests are community leaders and spiritual counselors. They also dispense nonreligious subsidiary services to the community, such as administration of a recreational center and library and publication of a weekly newspaper. Also, in surprising similarity to the Armenian quarter, Oblate Fathers do not depend on the congregation in performing these religious and community services. The parochial church and rectory belong to the Oblate who manage their property without any control from their parishioners. On the contrary, laymen depend more on the clergy for the services received. Unlike the Armenian laymen of Jerusalem, however, the Quebecois do not live surrounded by walls and gates that are closed at night and their residences do not belong to the Oblate Fathers. Their community is truly a parish, which happens to have as pastors members of a religious brotherhood.

27. Interview with Kapikian (September 1975).

28. Interviews with informants (1975-1978).

29. Personal observations (1975-1980).

30. The ultimate goal of preserving national identity might seem anticlimatic to many readers. It certainly is not a new thought and not very original as a source of explanation. What are new here are the special patterns of interaction and organization that helped attain this not-so-original goal, leading to a hybrid collectivity which combines traits of a monastery and ethnic ghetto and puts together different types of social organization that are in inherent tension with each other. We shall see below various mechanisms of adaptation to this unlikely coexistence.

31. Interview with Melkonian (March 1977).

32. Personal observations and interviews with informants (1975-1978).

33. Interviews with informants (1975-1978).

34. Ibid.

35. Ibid.; Sanjian, *Armenian Communities in Syria*, p. 117.

36. Bishop Kapikian who was born in Jerusalem of refugee parents is an exception to this rule. Not surprisingly, he is one of the priests most closely involved in the affairs of the community and one of the strongest advocates of the clergy's nationalist and communal functions over its more purely religious ones. Personal observations and interviews with informants (1975-1978).

37. Ibid.

38. Personal observations (1975-1980).

39. Ibid.

40. Ibid.

41. Interviews with informants (1975-1978).

42. Personal observations (1975-1980).

43. See Suttles, *The Social Order of the Slum*, pp. 20-25, 31-33; Kornblum, *Blue Collar Community*, pp. 26-33; Gans, *The Urban Villagers*, p. 11; Whyte, *Street Corner Society*, p. xvii.

44. Interviews with informants (1975-1978).

7: *Monasteries and Urban Neighborhoods: Some Comparisons*

1. On family quarters in military bases, see Hamilton McCubbin et al, eds., *Families in the Military System* (Beverly Hills: Sage, 1976) and C. H. Coates and R. J. Pellegrin, *Military Sociology* (University Park, Md.: Social Science Press, 1965), pp. 373-380. On the close relationship between urban ethnic community life and work in the steel mills of South Chicago, see Kornblum, *Blue Collar Community*. On the life of the American military community posted in Turkey, see Charlotte Wolf, *Garrison Community* (Westport, Conn.: Green-

wood, 1969). On the residential enclave of foreign workers in a Saudi Arabian oil field, see Solon T. Kimball, "American Culture in Saudi Arabia," *Transactions of the New York Academy of Sciences* 18 (1955-56): 469-484.

2. A fuller crosscultural comparison also would have to take into consideration monastic establishments outside Christianity with which I am not very familiar. Weber has some interesting comparative discussion of the relations between monastic institutions and lay populations and their effect on religious performance in different cultures. See Weber, *Economy and Society* 3: 1167-1173; Bendix, *Max Weber*, pp. 316-318; Gerth and Mills, eds., *From Max Weber*, pp. 289-297.

3. See Daly, *Benedictine Monasticism*, p. 34.

4. Christian monasticism first developed in the East, mainly in Egypt and Palestine. Only later did it spread to other areas of Christendom. See Atiya, *Eastern Christianity*, pp. 59-65, 184-189 and J. Leroy, *Moines et Monastères du Proche Orient* (Paris: Horizons de France, 1958), p. 27.

5. Atiya, *Eastern Christianity*, pp. 59-65; Daly, *Benedictine Monasticism*, pp. 34, 75-81, 158, 202-209; Erasmus, *Common Good*, p. 120; Hill, *The Religious Order*, pp. 45, 91; Eleanor S. Duckett, *Monasticism* (Ann Arbor: University of Michigan Press, 1961), pp. 29-30.

6. Leroy, *Moines et Monastères*, pp. 28-29; Hintlian, *Armenians in the Holy Land*, pp. 1-2, 6-10; Hoade, *Holy Land*, pp. 511-512.

7. Daly, *Benedictine Monasticism*, pp. 265, 268-269; Talbot, "Medicine," pp. 395, 405-406; Gutkind, *City Development* 6: 206; Henri Pirenne, "Commerce Creates Towns," in *Town Origins*, ed. John F. Benton (Lexington, Mass.: Heath, 1968), p. 2; Lewis Mumford, "Towns Create Commerce," in *Town Origins*, ed. Benton, p. 9.

8. Brian Stock, "Science, Technology and Economic Progress in the Early Middle Ages," in *Science in the Middle Ages*, ed. Lindberg, pp. 30-31; Daly, *Benedictine Monasticism*, pp. 80, 156, 177-178, 185-187, 222, 248; Gutkind, *City Development* 6: 200; Lavedan and Hugueney, *L'Urbanisme au Moyen Age*, p. 5; Erasmus, *Common Good*, p. 123; Bendix, *Max Weber*, p. 317.

9. Daly, *Benedictine Monasticism*, pp. 186-187; Y. Renouard, *Les Villes d'Italie de la Fin du Xe Siècle au Début du XIVe Siècle* (Paris: Société d'Edition d'Enseignement Supérieur, 1969), p. 19.

10. Pasdermadjian, *Histoire de l'Arménie*, pp. 116, 123, 159, 193.

11. Lavedan and Hugueney, *L'Urbanisme au Moyen Age*, p. 4; Gutkind, *City Development*, 2: 333, 6: 200-202, 7: 311.

12. Daly, *Benedictine Monasticism*, pp. 251-257; Stock, "Economic Progress," pp. 30-31; Gutkind, *City Development* 5: 221; M. Beresford, *New Towns of the Middle Ages* (New York: Praeger, 1967), p. 132.

13. Gutkind, *City Development* 3: 128; Beresford, *New Towns*, p. 130; Daly, *Benedictine Monasticism*, p. 266.

14. Lewis Mumford, *The City in History* (New York: Harcourt, Brace and World, 1961), p. 267.

15. Atiya, *Eastern Christianity*, pp. 185-187.

16. Ibid., pp. 61, 65, 189.

17. Edith Ennen, "The Variety of Urban Development," in *Town Origins*, ed. Benton, p. 13; Lavedan and Hugueney, *L'Urbanisme au Moyen Age*, pp. 4, 16, 33; Mumford, "Towns Create Commerce," p. 8.

18. See Mumford, *The City in History*, pp. 10, 277; Gideon Sjoberg, *The Pre-Industrial City* (New York: The Free Press, 1960), p. 35.

19. See Attwatter, *Churches of the East*, pp. 222-223; Leroy, *Moines et Monastères*, pp. 185, 232-233; Atiya, *Eastern Christianity*, 153, 189-192, 231, 292-293, 414-417; Robert Curzon, *Visits to Monasteries in the Levant* (London: Murray, 1849), p. 114.

20. For a similar example of a European village that grew up on the premises of a castle run by knights of the Order of the Templars, see Gutkind, *City Development* 5: 26-27. There also have been towns such as Saint Omer that apparently developed inside the monastery of the same name rather than around its walls. See Mumford, "Towns Create Commerce," p. 8.

21. Sjoberg, *The Pre-Industrial City*, pp. 91-92, 100; Ira M. Lapidus, *Muslim Cities in the Later Middle Ages* (Cambridge: Harvard University Press, 1967), p. 85.

22. L. C. Brown, ed., *From Madina to Metropolis* (Princeton: The Darwin Press, 1973), p. 54; P. English, "The Traditional City of Herat, Afghanistan," in *From Madina to Metropolis*, ed. Brown, p. 82; Lapidus, *Muslim Cities*, pp. 85-86. Housepian mentions the existence of such separate Armenian quarters in Izmir and Van. In Van the quarter was closed by walls, which helped Armenians to hold against a Turkish siege during World War I until they were saved by the arrival of the Russian army. See Housepian, *Smyrna, 1922*, pp. 41, 105.

23. Mumford, *The City in History*, p. 74; Gutkind, *City Development*, 3: 227.

24. Mumford, *The City in History*, p. 310.

25. Sjoberg, *The Pre-Industrial City*, p. 95.

26. Benton, ed., *Town Origins*, p. x; Renouard, *Villes d'Italie*, pp. 12-13; Mumford, *The City in History*, p. 304.

27. Sjoberg, *The Pre-Industrial City*, pp. 91-92; Gutkind, *City Development*, 3: 226; Brown, ed., *From Madina to Metropolis*, p. 32; Gabriel Baer, *Population and Society in the Arab East* (London: Routledge and Kegan Paul, 1964), pp. 191-192.

28. For this reason Weber claimed that a true urban community appeared only in the West. See Max Weber, *The City* (Glencoe, Ill.: The Free Press, 1958), pp. 80-89. See also Weber, *Economy and Society* 3: 1226-1233; A. H. Hourani, "Introduction: The Islamic City in the Light of Recent Research," in *The Islamic City: A Colloquium*, ed. A. H. Hourani and S. M. Stern (Oxford: Bruno Casirer, 1970), p. 13; S. M.

Stern, "The Constitution of the Islamic City" in *The Islamic City*, ed. Hourani and Stern, pp. 26, 32.

29. Hourani, "Islamic City in Research," pp. 15-16, 22; J. Aubin, "Elements Pour l'Etude des Agglomérations Urbaines dans l'Iran Médiéval," in *The Islamic City*, ed. Hourani and Stern, p. 72. For a similar description of Chinese cities, see J. Gernet, "Note sur les Villes Chinoises au Moment de l'Apogée Islamique," in *The Islamic City*, ed. Hourani and Stern, p. 80.

30. Ira M. Lapidus, "Muslim Urban Society in Mamluk Syria," in *The Islamic City*, ed. Hourani and Stern, p. 197.

31. Ibid., p. 199; Stern, "Constitution of the Islamic City," pp. 42-47; Hourani, "Islamic City in Research," pp. 14-15.

32. Lapidus, "Urban Society in Syria," p. 203; Stern, "Constitution of the Islamic City," pp. 31-33; Hourani, "Islamic City in Research," p. 19; Weber, *The City*, pp. 86-89.

33. English, "Herat," p. 82; Betts, *Christians in the Arab East*, p. 113, Renouard, *Villes d'Italie*, p. 17; N. Elisséef, "Damas à la Lumière des Théories de Jean Sauvaget," in *The Islamic City*, ed. Hourani and Stern, p. 174.

34. Lapidus, *Muslim Cities*, pp. 92-93, 108.

35. W. H. C. Frend, "Christianity in the Middle East: Survey Down to A.D. 1800," in *Religion in the Middle East*, ed. Arberry, 1: 255-256.

36. Stern, "Constitution of the Islamic City," p. 33.

37. Another welcome effect was to keep the temperature cool. In Fathy's words:

> In the desert nature at ground level is hostile to man, so he shuts his house entirely to the outside and opens it instead onto an internal courtyard or *sahn*. The temperature in the desert drops considerably during the nights . . . cool air deposits in the courtyard and flows into the surrounding rooms, keeping them cool to quite a late hour of the day. . . . The narrow and winding streets with closed vistas have the same function as the courtyard in a house, namely they act as a temperature regulator. Were the streets wide and straight, the cool night air would not be retained and they would heat up more readily during the day. (H. Fathy, "Constancy, Transposition and Change in the Arab City," in *From Madina to Metropolis*, ed. Brown, p. 322)

38. Ibid., p. 320; Brown, ed., *From Madina to Metropolis*, p. 63; R. Ettinghausen, "Muslim Cities Old and New," in *From Madina to Metropolis*, ed. Brown, p. 294; Lapidus, *Muslim Cities*, p. 2; Elisséef, "Damas," in *The Islamic City*, ed. Hourani and Stern, p. 173.

39. For a diagram showing how such a gradient from public to private zones reinforces the space's defense, see Oscar Newman, *Defensible Space* (New York: Macmillan, 1972), p. 9.

40. Brown, ed., *From Madina to Metropolis*, pp. 32-34, 56.

41. Lapidus, *Muslim Cities*, pp. 92-93.

42. Ibid., pp. 2-5; Stern, "Constitution of the Islamic City," p. 26.

43. Brown, ed., *From Madina to Metropolis*, p. 34.

44. Lapidus, *Muslim Cities*, p. 2.

45. Referred to in Stern, "Constitution of the Islamic City," p. 25.

46. Gutkind, *City Development* 3: 234. See also Stern, "Constitution of the Islamic City," p. 25.

47. See Hopkins, "The Four Quarters of Jerusalem," pp. 68-84; Kendall, *Jerusalem City Plan*, pp. 34, 37. During most of the nineteenth century, the gates of the Old City of Jerusalem were closed at sundown and opened at sunrise. Toward the end of the century gradually they were left open at night too. See Ben Arieh, *City Reflected*, p. 36.

48. Ben Arieh, *City Reflected*, pp. 239-242.

49. Ben Arieh, "Christian Activity," pp. 52-53; Bertha S. Vester, *Our Jerusalem* (Garden City, N.Y.: Doubleday, 1950), pp. 78, 82.

50. Ben Arieh, "Christian Activity," p. 51.

51. Jeremias, *Jerusalem*, p. 60.

52. Ibid., p. 130. For similar descriptions in Crusader and Islamic periods see Yehoshua Praver, "Jerusalem in the Period of the Crusaders," *Kadmoniut* 1, 1-2 (1967-68): 39-41 (in Hebrew) and Heyd, "Mamlukes and Turks," p. 196.

53. Yehoshua Ben Arieh, et al., "The Jewish Quarter in the Old City: Site, Growth and Expansion in the Nineteenth Century," in *Chapters in the History of the Jewish Community in Jerusalem*, ed. Menachem Friedman et al., 2 vols. (Jerusalem: Yad Izhak Ben Zvi, 1973, 1976, in Hebrew), 2: 24-27; Ben Arieh, *City Reflected*, pp. 321-333, 336, 443; Heyd, "Mamlukes and Turks," pp. 195-197; Jeremias, *Jerusalem*, p. 132; Vester, *Our Jerusalem*, p. 82.

54. Yehoshua Ben Arieh, "The Growth of Jerusalem in the Nineteenth Century," *Annals of the Association of American Geographers* 65 (June 1975): 255; Perowne, *Jerusalem and Bethlehem*, p. 61.

55. See for example Ben Arieh, *City Reflected*, p. 148; Lapidus, *Muslim Cities*, p. 195.

56. Gutkind, *City Development* 4: 90. See also F. Rörig, *The Medieval Town* (London: Batsford, 1967), p. 174.

57. This point was brought to my attention by Gerald Suttles in his letter of 4 December 1980.

58. Weber, *The City*, passim (especially pp. 83, 96, 103, 194).

59. Ajamian, interview to *Kol Ha Ir* (26 December 1980), p. 25.

60. In his study of Sydney Armenians, Kirkland characterizes the Armenian adjustment to Australian society as merely "accommodation." He also thinks that their relatively successful adaptation to Australian life is caused by the very fact that the host country did

not require a deeper cultural assimilation. The study found that Armenians generally are satisfied with their new life in Australia; they have made those changes in habits and values that they feel are required by their new environment or that they see as "advantageous" for their acceptance there but have made little "optional" change beyond that. Possibly more binding attachments were forged to the host country in other disaporas, such as the Untied States or France, but the general picture should not be very different. See Kirkland, "Armenian Migration," passim, especially pp. v, 193, 389, 398.

61. Gans, *The Urban Villagers;* Suttles, *The Social Order of the Slum;* Suttles, *The Social Construction of Communities;* Kornblum, *Blue Collar Community;* Stack, *All Our Kin;* Hannerz, *Soulside,* and others. See also *The Community,* pp. 79-95.

62. Suttles, *The Social Construction of Communities,* p. 21. Suttles distinguishes the defended neighborhood from other types of urban communities such as the community of limited liability, the contrived community, and the defeated neighborhood which is a former defended neighborhood that lost its fight against external encroachment. For a discussion of these different urban community types, see Suttles, *The Social Construction of Communities,* pp. 47-107, 266.

63. Ibid., pp. 27-28. See also Andrew Greeley, *Neighborhood* (New York: Seabury Press, 1977), p. 24.

64. *The Community,* p. 82. See also Kornblum, *Blue Collar Community,* pp. 24, 34-35.

65. On this question see Edward C. Banfield, *The Unheavenly City* (Boston: Little, Brown, 1968), pp. 80-83.

66. Louis Wirth, *The Ghetto* (Chicago: University of Chicago Press, 1956), p. ix.

67. Banfield, *The Unheavenly City,* p. 82. See also Hannerz, *Soulside,* p. 11.

68. See Gans, *The Urban Villagers,* pp. 242-249; Suttles, *The Social Order of the Slum,* pp. 3, 46; Suttles, *The Social Construction of Communities,* pp. 28-34; Kornblum, *Blue Collar Community,* p. 17; Stack, *All Our Kin,* pp. 1-5.

69. See Whyte, *Street Corner Society,* p. xviii; Kornblum, *Blue Collar Community,* p. 209; Gans, *The Urban Villagers,* pp. 131-132, 240-241.

70. See Liebow, *Tally's Corner,* pp. 20-21; Suttles, *The Social Order of the Slum,* pp. 47-50; Kornblum, *Blue Collar Community,* pp. 75-81.

71. See Liebow, *Tally's Corner,* passim; Stack, *All Our Kin,* pp. 1-5, 28-31, 44-45; 112-113; Hannerz, *Soulside,* pp. 46-54, 70-78, 204-205, 218-219.

72. Stack, *All Our Kin,* pp. 90-91, 112-119.

73. See Gans, *The Urban Villagers,* pp. 37-39, 240-241; Whyte, *Street Corner Society,* p. xvii.

74. Gans, *The Urban Villagers,* pp. 281-304; Suttles, *The Social*

Construction of Communities, pp. 235-241. See also Kornblum, *Blue Collar Community,* pp. 26-32.

75. For different types of encroachment on home territory, see S. Lyman and M.B. Scott, *A Sociology of the Absurd* (New York: Meredith, 1970), pp. 98-105.

76. Interviews with informants (1975-1978). See also Suttles, *The Social Order of the Slum,* pp. 265-266.

77. See Hannerz, *Soulside,* pp. 12, 34-35; Whyte, *Street Corner Society,* pp. 102-103; Gans, *The Urban Villagers,* pp. 145-147.

78. See for example Suttles, *The Social Order of the Slum,* pp. 122-125.

79. Suttles, *The Social Construction of Communities,* pp. 34-35.

80. Ibid., p. 58. See also ibid., p. 13.

81. *The Community,* pp. 46-47. See also Suttles, *The Social Order of the Slum,* p. 77.

82. There is also some interesting evidence on the role of gossip in other Armenian communities. In a doctoral dissertation on Armenians in California, for instance, the author shows how the fear of being gossiped about by their kinsmen led Armenian immigrants to maintain old values and avoid change. See H. Nelson, "The Armenian Family: Changing Patterns of Family Life in a California Community," (Ph.D. diss., University of California, Berkeley, 1954), pp. 138-139.

83. Gans, *The Urban Villagers; The Community,* p. 82. See also Colin Bell and Howard Newby, *Community Studies* (London: Allen and Unwin, 1971), p. 51 and Charles Tilly, ed., *An Urban World* (Boston: Little, Brown, 1974), p. 8.

84. See Suttles, *The Social Construction of Communities,* p. 265.

85. Morris Janowitz, *The Last Half-Century: Societal Change and Politics in America* (Chicago: University of Chicago Press, 1978), p. 268; Duncan Timms, *The Urban Mosaic* (Cambridge: At the University Press, 1971), p. 251.

86. Suttles, *The Social Construction of Communities,* p. 265.

87. Robert S. Lopez, "The Crossroads within the Wall," in *The Historian and the City,* ed. O. Handlin and J. Burchard (Cambridge: MIT and Harvard University Press, 1963), p. 27-28.

8: Conclusion: Community, Territory, and Solidarity

1. Goffman, "Total Institutions," pp. 315-325, 330-337; Etzioni, *Complex Organizations,* pp. 27-44, 66-67, 125-126.

2. Warren, *The Community in America,* pp. 161-162, 208.

3. Schmalenbach, "Communion," pp. 332-340; Toennies, "Gemeinschaft and Gesellschaft," pp. 7-9.

4. Kirkland, "Armenian Migration," pp. 248, 252-253; Boudji-kanian, *Région Rhône-Alpes,* p. 181; Dekmejian, "Middle Eastern Dispersion," p. 30.

5. Interviews with informants (1975-1980).

6. Mumford, *The City in History,* p. 49.

7. On this point, see Suttles, *The Social Order of the Slum,* pp. 5-6, 26-27, 59, 234; Hannerz, *Soulside,* pp. 144, 157-158, 197-200 and Yona Ginsberg, *Jews in a Changing Neighborhood* (New York: The Free Press, 1975), pp. 196-198.

8. This point was suggested to me by Gerald D. Suttles in his letter of 4 December 1980.

9. See Alex Simirenko, *Pilgrims, Colonists and Frontiersmen: An Ethnic Community in Transition* (New York: The Free Press, 1954), pp. x, 5-6.

10. Ibid., pp. 42-43.

11. On this point, see Janowitz, *The Last Half Century,* pp. 264-269 and Morris Janowitz and Gerald D. Suttles, "The Social Ecology of Citizenship," in *The Management of Human Services,* ed. Rosemary C. Sarri and Yeheskel Hasenfeld (New York: Columbia University Press, 1978), pp. 80-104.

12. See Timms, *The Urban Mosaic,* pp. 12, 251; *The Community,* p. 161; Leo Kuper, ed., *Living in Towns* (London: The Cresset Press, 1953), p. 27.

13. Timms, *The Urban Mosaic,* p.1; Tilly, ed. *An Urban World,* pp. 181-188; Janowitz and Suttles, "The Social Ecology of Citizenship," pp. 85-90, 101.

14. See Suttles, *The Social Construction of Communities,* passim.

Works Cited

Books

Abrams, Philip, and McCulloch, Andrew. *Communes, Sociology, and Society.* New York: Cambridge University Press, 1976.

Album of the Armenian Monastery of Jerusalem. New York: The Delphic Press, 1950.

Antreassian, Assadour. *Jerusalem and the Armenians.* Jerusalem: St. James Press, 1969.

Arberry, A.J., ed. *Religion in the Middle East.* 2 vols. Cambridge: At the University Press, 1969.

Arpee, Leon. *A Century of Armenian Protestantism.* New York: The Armenian Missionary Association of America, 1946.

————. *A History of Armenian Christianity.* Princeton: Princeton University Press, 1946.

Atamian, Pierre. *Histoire de la Communauté Arménienne Catholique de Damas.* Beyrouth: Typo Press, 1964.

Atamian, Sarkis. *The Armenian Community.* New York: Philosophical Library, 1955.

Atiya, Aziz S. *A History of Eastern Christianity.* London: Methuen, 1967.

Attwater, D. *The Christian Churches of the East.* Milwaukee: Bruce Publications, 1947.

Avi-Yonah, Michael, ed. *A History of the Holy Land.* London: Weidenfeld and Nicolson, 1969.

Baer, Gabriel. *Population and Society in the Arab East.* London: Routledge and Kegan Paul, 1964.

Baliozian, Ara. *The Armenians.* Toronto: Kar Publishing House, 1975.

Baljian, Vasken I, Catholicos of All Armenians. *Messages and Addresses Delivered During Visit to the United States in 1968.* New York: Diocese of Armenian Church of America, 1969.

Banfield, Edward C. *The Unheavenly City.* Boston: Little, Brown, 1968.

Bell, Colin, and Newby, Howard. *Community Studies.* London: Allen and Unwin, 1971.

————, eds. *The Sociology of Community.* London; Cass, 1974.

Ben Arieh, Yehoshua. *A City Reflected in its Times.* Jerusalem: Yad Izhak Ben Zvi, 1977 (in Hebrew).

Bendix, Reinhard. *Max Weber: An Intellectual Portrait.* Garden City, N.Y.: Doubleday, 1962.

Benton, John F., ed. *Town Origins.* Lexington, Mass.: Heath, 1968.

Benvenisti, Meron. *Facing the Closed Wall.* Jerusalem: Weidenfeld and Nicolson, 1973 (in Hebrew).

————. *Jerusalem: The Torn City.* Minneapolis: University of Minnesota Press, 1976.

Beresford, M.W. *New Towns of the Middle Ages.* New York: Praeger, 1967.

Betts, R.B. *Christians in the Arab East.* Athens: Lycabettus Press, 1975.

Blau, Peter, and Scott, W.R. *Formal Organizations.* San Francisco: Chandler, 1962.

Bogharian, N. *Grand Catalogue of the St. James Manuscripts.* 3 vols. Jerusalem: St. James Press, 1966-1968.

Boudjikanian-Keuroghlian, Aïda. *Les Arméniens dans la Région Rhône-Alpes.* Lyon: Association de la Revue de Géographie, 1978.

Bridgeman, C.T. *Armenian Reconstruction in Syria.* London: Jerusalem and the East Mission, 1926.

Brown, L.C., ed. *From Madina to Metropolis.* Princeton: The Darwin Press, 1973.

Census of Population and Housing, 1967 — East Jerusalem. Jerusalem: Central Bureau of Statistics, 1968.

Chakmakjian, Hagop A. *Armenian Christology and Evangelization of Islam.* Leiden: Brill, 1965.

————. *The Armenian Evangelical Church and the Armenian People.* Yettem, Calif.: By the Author, 1961.

Chilingirian, Y. *Descriptions of Refugees and Monastics: Jerusalem, Aleppo, Damascus, 1914-18.* Jerusalem: St. James Press, 1927 (in Armenian).

Coates, C.H., and Pellegrin, R.J. *Military Sociology.* University Park, Md.: Social Science Press, 1965.

Cohen, Erik, and Grunau, Hermona. *Survey of Minorities in Israel.* Jerusalem: The Institute of Asian and African Studies, The Hebrew University, 1972 (in Hebrew).

Colbi, S.P. *A Short History of Christianity in the Holy Land.* Jerusalem, Am Hasefer, 1965.

————. *Christian Churches in Israel.* Jerusalem: Israel Economist, 1969.

Crisis in the Armenian Church. Boston: Apostolic Church, Central Diocesan Board, 1958.

Curzon, Robert. *Visits to Monasteries of the Levant.* London: Murray, 1840.

Daly, Lowrie, J. *Benedictine Monasticism.* New York: Sheed and Ward, 1965.

Dasnabedian, H. *The Armenian Question.* Jerusalem: The Armenian Case Committee, 1977.

Der Nersessian, Sirarpie. *The Armenians.* London: Thomas and Hudson, 1969.

Drapkin, Israel, and Viano, Emilio, eds. *Victimology.* Lexington, Mass.: Heath, 1974.

Duckett, Eleanor S. *Monasticism.* Ann Arbor: University of Michigan Press, 1961.

Eliade, Mircea. *The Sacred and the Profane.* New York: Harcourt Brace and World, 1957.

Erasmus, Charles J. *In Search of the Common Good: Utopian Experiments Past and Future.* New York: The Free Press, 1977.

Etzioni, Amitai. *A Comparative Analysis of Complex Organizations.* New York: The Free Press, 1961.

————, ed. *A Sociological Reader in Complex Organizations.* 2d ed. New York: Holt, Rinehart and Winston, 1969.

Evans, Joan. *Monastic Life at Cluny.* Hamden, Conn.: Archon Books, 1968.

Fisher, S.N., ed. *Social Forces in the Middle East.* Ithaca: Cornell University Press, 1955.

Friedman, Menachem, et al., eds. *Chapters in the History of the Jewish Community in Jerusalem.* 2 vols. Jerusalem: Yad Izhak Ben Zvi, 1976 (in Hebrew).

Gafni, Shlomo. *The Glory of Jerusalem.* Jerusalem: The Jerusalem Publishing House, 1978.

Gans, Herbert J. *The Urban Villagers.* New York: The Free Press, 1962.

Geertz, Clifford. *The Interpretation of Cultures.* New York: Basic Books, 1973.

Gerth, Hans H., and Mills, C. Wright, eds. *From Max Weber: Essays in Sociology.* New York: Oxford University Press, 1958.

Gidney, James B. *A Mandate for Armenia.* Kent, Ohio: Kent University Press, 1967.

Ginsberg, Yona. *Jews in a Changing Neighborhood.* New York: The Free Press, 1975.

Gordon, Robert, and Williams, Bret, eds. *Exploring Total Institutions.* Champaign, Ill.: Stipes, 1977.

Gottschalk, Shimon. *Communities and Alternatives.* Cambridge: Schenkman, 1975.

Greeley, Andrew M. *Neighborhood.* New York: Seabury Press, 1977.

Gulbenkian, Nubar. *Pantaraxia: The Autobiography of Nubar Gulbenkian.* London: Hutchinson, 1965.

Gutkind, E.A., ed. *International History of City Development.* 8 vols. New York: The Free Press, 1964-1972.

Handlin, Oscar, and Burchard, John, eds. *The Historian and the City.* Cambridge: MIT Press and Harvard University Press, 1963.

Hannerz, Ulf. *Soulside.* New York: Columbia University Press, 1969.

Hill, Michael. *The Religious Order.* London: Heinemann, 1973.

Hillery, George A., Jr. *Communal Organizations.* Chicago: University of Chicago Press, 1969.

Hintlian, Kevork. *History of the Armenians in the Holy Land.* Jerusalem: St. James Press, 1976.

Hoade, Eugene. *Guide to the Holy Land.* 7th ed. Jerusalem: The Franciscan Press, 1973.

————. *Jerusalem and its Environs.* Jerusalem: The Franciscan Press, 1964.

Hollis, Christopher, and Brownrigg, Ronald. *Holy Places.* New York: Praeger, 1969.

Hourani, A.H. and Stern, S.M., eds. *The Islamic City: A Colloquium.* Oxford: Bruno Casirer, 1970.

Housepian, Marjorie. *Smyrna, 1922.* London: Faber and Faber, 1972.

Hovannisian, Richard G. *Armenia on the Road to Independence.* Berkeley and Los Angeles: University of California Press, 1967.

Iorga, N. *Brève Histoire de la Petite Arménie.* Paris: Gamber, 1930.

Janin, Raymond. *Eglises Orientales et Rites Orientaux.* Paris: Letouzey & Ané, 1955.

Janowitz, Morris. *The Last Half Century: Societal Change and Politics in America*. Chicago: University of Chicago Press, 1978.

Jeremias, Joachim. *Jerusalem in the Time of Jesus*. London: SCM Press, 1969.

Jerusalem Through the Ages. Jerusalem: The Israel Exploration Society, 1968 (in Hebrew).

Kanter, Rosabeth M. *Commitment and Community: Communes and Utopias in Sociological Perspective*. Cambridge: Harvard University Press, 1972.

————, ed. *Communes: Creating and Managing the Collective Life*. New York: Harper and Row, 1973.

Kendall, Henry. *Jerusalem City Plan*. London: His Majesty's Stationery Office, 1948.

Kornblum, William. *Blue Collar Community*. Chicago: University of Chicago Press, 1974.

Krikorian, Mesrob K. *Armenians in the Service of the Ottoman Empire, 1860-1908*. London: Routledge and Kegan Paul, 1977.

Kuper, Leo, ed. *Living in Towns*. London: The Cresset Press, 1953.

Lang, David M. *Armenia: Cradle of Civilization*. 2d ed. London: Allen and Unwin, 1978.

Lang, David M., and Walker, Christopher J. *The Armenians*. London: Minority Rights Group, 1977.

Lapidus, Ira M. *Middle Eastern Cities*. Berkeley and Los Angeles: University of California Press, 1969.

Lavedan, P., and Hugueney, J. *L'Urbanisme au Moyen Age*. Genève: Droz, 1974.

L'Eglise Arménienne. Antelias, Liban: Catholicosat des Arméniens, 1936.

Leroy, J. *Moines et Monastères du Proche Orient*. Paris: Horizons de France, 1958.

Liebow, Elliott. *Tally's Corner: A Study of Negro Streetcorner Men*. Boston: Little, Brown, 1967.

Lindberg, David C., ed. *Science in the Middle Ages*. Chicago: University of Chicago Press, 1978.

Luke, H.C., and Keith-Roach, E., eds. *The Handbook of Palestine and Transjordan*. London: Macmillan, 1934.

Lyman, S., and Scott, M.B. *A Sociology of the Absurd*. New York: Meredith, 1970.

McCubbin, Hamilton et al., eds. *Families in the Military System*. Beverly Hills: Sage, 1976.

Manoogian, Sion. *Armenian Jerusalem*. Boston: Baikar Press, 1948 (in Armenian).

Marshall, Jr., Richard H., ed. *Aspects of Religion in the Soviet Union*. Chicago: University of Chicago Press, 1971.

Matossian, Mary A.K. *The Impact of Soviet Policies in Armenia*. Leiden: Brill, 1962.

Mumford, Lewis. *The City in History*. New York: Harcourt, Brace and World, 1961.

Nalbandian, Louis. *The Armenian Revolutionary Movement*. Berkeley and Los Angeles: University of California Press, 1963.

Nansen, F. *L'Arménie et le Proche Orient*. Paris: Massis, 1928.

Nantet, Jacques. *Les Mille et Une Jerusalem*. Paris: Lattès, 1977.

Newman, Oscar. *Defensible Space*. New York: Macmillan, 1972.

Oesterreicher, J.M., and Sinai, A., eds. *Jerusalem*. New York: John Day, 1974.

Ormanian, Malachia. *Armenian Jerusalem*. Jerusalem: St. James Press, 1931 (in Armenian).

————. *The Church of Armenia*. 2d. rev. ed. London: Mowbray, 1955.

Our Boys. New York: The Delphic Press, 1942.

Our Boys: Armenian-American Veterans of World War II. New York: Beechwood Press, 1951.

Parsons, Talcott, et al., eds. *Theories of Society*. 2 vols. New York: The Free Press, 1961.

Pasdermadjian, H. *Histoire de l'Arménie*. Paris: Samuelian, 1949.

Perowne, Stewart. *Jerusalem and Bethlehem*. London: Phoenix House, 1965.

Pirenne, Henri. *Medieval Cities*. Garden City, N.Y.: Doubleday, 1956.

Renouard, Y. *Les Villes d'Italie de la Fin du Xe Siècle au Début du XIVe Siècle*. Paris: Société d'Edition d'Enseignement Supérieur, 1969.

Rigby, Andrew. *Alternative Realities*. London: Routledge and Kegan Paul, 1974.

Rörig, F. *The Medieval Town*. London: Batsford, 1967.

Sanjian, Avedis K. *The Armenian Community in Syria under Ottoman Dominion*. Cambridge: Harvard University Press, 1965.

Sarafian, K.A. *The Armenian Apostolic Church*. Fresno, Calif.: The Armenian Diocese of California, 1959.

Sarri, Rosemary C., and Hasenfeld, Yeheskel, eds. *The Management of Human Services*. New York: Columbia University Press, 1978.

Seth, Mesrovb. *Armenians and the East India Company*. Calcutta: Government of India Press, 1926.

Sharon, Arieh. *Planning Jerusalem*. New York: McGraw Hill, 1973.

Shaw, Stanford J., and Shaw, Ezel K. *History of the Ottoman Empire and Modern Turkey.* 2 vols. New York: Cambridge University Press, 1977.

Simirenko, Alex. *Pilgrims, Colonists, and Frontiersmen: An Ethnic Community in Transition.* New York: The Free Press, 1954.

Sjoberg, Gideon. *The Pre-Industrial City.* New York: The Free Press, 1960.

Smelser, Neil J., ed. *Sociology: An Introduction.* New York: Wiley, 1967.

Stack, Carole B. *All Our Kin: Strategies for Survival in a Black Community.* New York: Harper and Row, 1974.

Suttles, Gerald D. *The Social Construction of Communities.* Chicago: University of Chicago Press, 1972.

_____. *The Social Order of the Slum.* Chicago: University of Chicago Press, 1968.

Tashjian, J.H. *The Armenians of the United States and Canada.* Boston: Hairenik Press, 1947.

Terzian, Aram. *An Armenian Miscellany.* Paris: Samuelian, 1969.

TeSelle, Sallie, ed. *The Family, Communes, and Utopian Societies.* New York: Harper and Row, 1972.

The Catholicosate of Cilicia. Antelias, Lebanon: Catholicosate of Cilicia, n.d.

The Community. Rev. ed. Alexandria, Va.: Time-Life Books, 1978.

Thorns, David C. *The Quest for Community.* London: Allen and Unwin, 1976.

Tilly, Charles, ed. *An Urban World.* Boston: Little, Brown, 1974.

Timms, Duncan. *The Urban Mosaic.* Cambridge: At the University Press, 1971.

Tololyan, M. *The Crusade Against the Armenian Revolutionary Federation.* Boston: Hairenik Press, 1962.

Varjabedian, Sisag H. *The Armenians.* Chicago: By the Author, 1977.

Vester, Bertha. *Our Jerusalem.* Garden City, N.Y.: Doubleday, 1950.

Veysey, Laurence. *The Communal Experience.* New York: Harper and Row, 1973.

Vilnay, Zeev. *Jerusalem, Capital of Israel: The Old City.* 2 vols. Jerusalem: Achiever, 1972 (in Hebrew).

Wallis, W. *Fresno Armenians.* Lawrence, Kans.: Coronado Press, 1965.

Warren, Roland L., ed. *Perspectives on the Armenian Community.* 2d ed. Chicago: Rand McNally, 1973.

————. *The Community in America.* 2d ed. Chicago: Rand McNally, 1972.

Weber, Max. *Economy and Society.* 3 vols. New York: Bedminster Press, 1968.

————. *The City.* Glencoe, Ill.: The Free Press, 1958.

Whyte, William F. *Street Corner Society.* Chicago: University of Chicago Press, 1961.

Williams, Albert N. *The Holy City.* London: Parker, 1854.

Wilson, Evan M. *Jerusalem, Key to Peace.* Washington, D.C.: The Middle East Institute, 1970.

Wirth, Louis. *The Ghetto.* Chicago: University of Chicago Press, 1956.

Wolf, Charlotte. *Garrison Community.* Westport, Conn.: Greenwood, 1969.

Zollschan, George K., and Hirsch, Walter, eds. *Explorations in Social Change.* Boston: Houghton Mifflin, 1964.

Articles and Unpublished Works

Ajamian, Shahe. "Brief Notes on the Armenian People and the Armenian Patriarchate of Jerusalem." *Christian News From Israel* 18 (December 1962): 37-41.

————. Interview in *Kol Ha Ir.* Jerusalem (26 December 1980).

————. "Le Sultan Abdulhamid et le Patriarcat Arménien de Jerusalem." Paper presented at the International Seminar on the History of Palestine. Institute of Asian and African Affairs, The Hebrew University, Jerusalem, 1970.

Alojian, H. "Origins of the Armenian Colony in Constantinople." *The Armenian Review* 7, 2 (1954): 119-121.

"Armenian Church Representative." *Christian News From Israel* 1 (August 1949): 1-4.

"Arménie et Arméniens à Travers le Monde." *Revue Missi* (Belgium), 289 (April 1965): 115-146.

Aubin, J. "Elements Pour l'Etude des Agglomérations Urbaines dans l'Iran Médieval." *The Islamic City: A Colloquium.* Edited by A.H. Hourani and S.M. Stern. Oxford: Bruno Casirer, 1970.

Basham, Richard. "Ethnicity as a Total Institution." *Exploring Total Institutions.* Edited by Robert Gordon and Brett Williams. Champaign, Ill.: Stipes, 1977.

Ben Arieh, Yehoshua. "Patterns of Christian Activity and Dispersion in Nineteenth Century Jerusalem." *Journal of Historical Geography* 2, 1 (1976): 49-69.

————. "The Growth of Jerusalem in the Nineteenth Century." *Annals of the Association of American Geographers* 65 (June 1975): 252-269.

————, et al. "The Jewish Quarter in the Old City: Site, Growth and Expansion in the Nineteenth Century." *Chapters in the History of the Jewish Community in Jerusalem*. Edited by Menachem Friedman et al., vol. 2. Jerusalem: Yad Izhak Ben Zvi, 1976 (in Hebrew).

Blum, Yehudit. "The Armenian Community of Jerusalem." Seminar paper. The Hebrew University, Jerusalem, n.d.

Brooks, Richard. "Social Planning in Columbia." *Perspectives on the American Community*. 2d. ed. Edited by Roland L. Warren. Chicago: Rand McNally, 1973.

"Chronicle of Events." *Christian News From Israel* 2, 8-9, 11 (1951, 1957-1958, 1960).

"Chronique." *Proche Orient Chrétien* 6-8, 10, 12-13, 15 (1956-1958, 1960, 1962-1963, 1965).

Cragg, K. "The Anglican Church." *Religion in the Middle East*. Edited by A. J. Arberry, vol. 1. Cambridge: At the University Press, 1969.

Dadrian, Vahakn N. "The Structural and Functional Components of Genocide: A Victimological Approach to the Armenian Case." *Victimology*. Edited by Israel Drapkin and Emilio Viano. Lexington, Mass.: Heath, 1974.

Davison, Roderic. "The Armenian Crisis, 1912-1914." *The American Historical Review* 53, 3 (1948): 481-506.

Dekmejian, H. "The Armenians: History, Consciousness and the Middle Eastern Dispersion." *Middle East Review* 9 (Fall 1976): 26-32.

Delaney, William P. "The Uses of the Total Institution: A Buddhist Monastic Example." *Exploring Total Institutions*. Edited by Robert Gordon and Brett Williams. Champaign, Ill.: Stipes, 1977.

Elisséef, N. "Damas à la Lumière des Théories de Jean Sauvaget." *The Islamic City: A Colloquium*. Edited by A.H. Hourani and S.M. Stern. Oxford: Bruno Casirer, 1970.

English, P. "The Traditional City of Herat, Afghanistan." *From Madina to Metropolis*. Edited by L.C. Brown. Princeton: The Darwin Press, 1973.

Ennen, Edith. "The Variety of Urban Development." *Town Origins*. Edited by John F. Benton. Lexington, Mass.: Heath, 1968.

Ettinghausen, R. "Muslim Cities: Old and New." *From Madina to Metropolis.* Edited by L.C. Brown. Princeton: The Darwin Press, 1973.

Falardeau, J.C. "The Parish as an Institutional Type." *Canadian Journal of Economic and Political Science* 15 (August 1949): 353-367.

Fathy, H. "Constancy, Transposition, and Change in the Arab City." *From Madina to Metropolis.* Edited by L.C. Brown. Princeton: The Darwin Press, 1973.

Frend, W.H.C. "Christianity in the Middle East: Survey Down to A.D. 1800." *Religion in the Middle East.* Edited by A.J. Arberry, vol. 1. Cambridge: At the University Press, 1969.

Gernet, J. "Note sur les Villes Chinoises au Moment de l'Apogée Islamique." *The Islamic City: A Colloquium.* Edited by A.H. Hourani and S.M. Stern. Oxford: Bruno Casirer, 1970.

Goffman, Erving. "The Characteristics of Total Institutions." *A Sociological Reader in Complex Organizations.* 2d ed. Edited by Amitai Etzioni. New York: Holt, Rinehart and Winston, 1969.

Gosenfeld, Norman. "Changes in the Business Community of East Jerusalem." *The New East* 24, 4 (1974): 261-279 (in Hebrew).

Heyd, Uriel. "Jerusalem Under the Mamlukes and the Turks." *Jerusalem Through the Ages.* Jerusalem: The Israel Exploration Society, 1968 (in Hebrew).

Hillery, George A. Jr. "The Convent: Community, Prison or Task Force?" *Journal for the Scientific Study of Religion* 8, 1 (1969): 140-151.

_____. "Definitions of Community: Areas of Agreement." *Rural Sociology* 20 (June 1955): 111-123.

_____. "Families, Communes and Communities." *Perspectives on the American Community.* 2d ed. Edited by Roland L. Warren. Chicago: Rand McNally, 1973.

_____. "Freedom and Social Organization: A Comparative Analysis." *American Sociological Review* 36 (February 1971): 51-65.

_____. "Selected Issues in Community Theory." *Rural Sociology* 37 (December 1972): 534-552.

_____, and Morrow, Paula C. "The Monastery as a Commune." *International Review of Modern Sociology* 6 (Spring 1976): 139-154.

Hopkins, I.W.J. "The Four Quarters of Jerusalem." *Palestine Exploration Quarterly* 103d year (July-December 1971): 68-85.

Hornus, Jean Michel. "La Crise au Catholicosat Arménien de Cilicie." *Proche Orient Chrétien* 6 (1956): 237-256 and 7 (1957): 173-179, 359-363.

Hourani, A.H. "Introduction: The Islamic City in the Light of Recent Research." *The Islamic City: A Colloquium.* Edited by A.H. Hourani and S.M. Stern. Oxford: Bruno Casirer, 1970.

Hovannisian, Richard G. "Caucasian Armenia Between Imperial and Soviet Rule: The Interlude of National Independence." Paper, Los Angeles, n.d.

———. "The Ebb and Flow of the Armenian Minority in the Arab Middle East." *Middle East Journal* 28, 1 (1974): 19-32.

Issawi, C. "The Entrepreneur Class." *Social Forces in the Middle East.* Edited by S.N. Fisher. Ithaca: Cornell University Press, 1955.

Janowitz, Morris, and Suttles, Gerald D. "The Social Ecology of Citizenship." *The Management of Human Services.* Edited by Rosemary C. Sarri and Yeheskel Hasenfeld. New York: Columbia University Press, 1978.

Kimball, Solon T. "American Culture in Saudi Arabia." *Transactions of the New York Academy of Sciences* 18 (1955-1956): 469-484.

Kirkland, James R. "Armenian Migration, Settlement, and Adjustment in Australia," Ph.D. dissertation, Australian National University, Canberra, 1980.

Krikorian, Mesrob K. "The Armenian Church in the Soviet Union." *Aspects of Religion in the Soviet Union.* Edited by Richard H. Marshall, Jr. Chicago: University of Chicago Press, 1971.

Lapidus, Ira M. "Muslim Urban Society in Mamluk Syria." *The Islamic City: A Colloquium.* Edited by A.H. Hourani and S.M. Stern. Oxford: Bruno Casirer, 1970.

Lark, David. "The American Slum as a Total Institution." *Exploring Total Institutions.* Edited by Robert Gordon and Brett Williams. Champaign, Ill.: Stipes, 1977.

Lieber, Alfred E. "An Economic History of Jerusalem." *Jerusalem.* Edited by J.M. Oesterreicher and A. Sinai, New York: John Day, 1974.

Lingot, Jean Louis. "L'Intronisation du Nouveau Patriarche Arménien Catholique: Sa Béatitude Hémayag Pierre XVII Guédiguian A Bzommar (Liban) le 15 Août 1976." *Proche*

242 THE ARMENIAN QUARTER OF JERUSALEM

Orient Chrétien 26 (1976) 230-244.
"Liste des Arméniens Catholiques du Rite Arménien." Mimeographed sheet. Armenian Catholic Church, Jerusalem, 1974.
Lopez, Robert S. "The Crossroads Within the Wall." *The Historian and the City.* Edited by Oscar Handlin and John Burchard. Cambridge: MIT Press and Harvard University Press, 1963.
Malik, C.H. "The Orthodox Church." *Religion in the Middle East.* Edited by A.J. Arberry, vol. 1. Cambridge: At the University Press, 1969.
Mamour, Joseph, "Au Patriarcat Arménien de Jerusalem." *Proche Orient Chrétien* 7 (1957): 65-69.
Martindale, Don. "The Formation and Destruction of Communities." *Explorations in Social Change.* Edited by George K. Zollschan and Walter Hirsch. Boston: Houghton Mifflin, 1964.
Mécérian, Jean. "Un Tableau de la Diaspora Arménienne." *Proche Orient Chrétien* 6-12 (1956-1962).
Meinardus, O.F.A. "The Coptic Church in Egypt." *Religion in the Middle East.* Edited by A.J. Arberry, vol. 1. Cambridge: At the University Press, 1969.
Melson, Robert. "Provocation or Nationalism: A Theoretical Inquiry into the Armenian Genocide of 1915." Paper, West Lafayette, Ind., n.d.
_____. "A Theoretical Inquiry into the Armenian Massacres of 1894-1896," *Comparative Studies in Society and History* 24, 3 (July 1982): 481-509.
Mumford, Lewis. "Towns Create Commerce." *Town Origins.* Edited by John F. Benton. Lexington, Mass.: Heath, 1968.
Neal, M.A. "A Theoretical Analysis of Renewal in Religious Orders in the USA." *Social Compass* 18, 1 (1971): 7-27.
Nelson, H. "The Armenian Family: Changing Patterns of Family Life in a California Community." Ph.D. dissertation, University of California, Berkeley, 1954.
Ogilvy, Jay, and Ogilvy, Heather. "Communes and the Reconstruction of Reality." *The Family, Communes and Utopian Societies.* Edited by Sallie TeSelle. New York: Harper and Row, 1972.
Parsons, Talcott. "Suggestions for a Sociological Approach to the Theory of Organizations." *A Sociological Reader in Complex Organizations.* 2d ed. Edited by Amitai Etzioni. New York: Holt, Rinehart and Winston, 1969.
Pirenne, Henri. "Commerce Creates Towns." *Town Origins.* Edited by John F. Benton. Lexington, Mass.: Heath, 1968.

Praver, Yehoshua, "Jerusalem in the Period of the Crusaders." *Kadmoniut* 1, 1-2 (1967-1968): 39-46 (in Hebrew).

Saint Tarkmanchatz, Armenian Secondary School. "Annual Report 1974-75." Jerusalem, 1975.

Sanjian, Avedis K. "Anastas Vardapet's List of Armenian Monasteries in Seventh Century Jerusalem: A Critical Examination." *Le Muséon: Revue d'Etudes Orientales* 82, 3-4 (1969): 265-292.

Sarkissian, Karekin. "The Armenian Church." *Religion in the Middle East.* Edited by A.J. Arberry, vol. 1. Cambridge: At the University Press, 1969.

Schmalenbach, Herman. "The Sociological Category of Communion." *Theories of Society.* Edited by Talcott Parsons et. al. vol. 1. New York: The Free Press, 1961.

Schmelz, Usiel O. "The Demography of Muslims and Christians in United Jerusalem." Paper presented at the Seminar on Jerusalem and Occupied Territories, 1967-1977, The Van Leer Institution, Jerusalem, 1977.

Schnore, Leo F. "Community." *Sociology: An Introduction.* Edited by Neil J. Smelser. New York: Wiley, 1967.

Servais, E., and Hambye, F. "Structure et Signification: Problème de Méthode en Sociologie des Organisations Claustrales." *Social Compass* 18, 1 (1971): 27-44.

Shafaq, S.R. "The Clergy in Islam." *Social Forces in the Middle East.* Edited by S.N. Fisher. Ithaca: Cornell University Press, 1955.

Sharon, Moshe. "Palestine Under the Mameluks and the Ottoman Empire." *A History of the Holy Land.* Edited by Michael Avi-Yonah. London: Wiedenfeld and Nicolson, 1969.

Shimony, Y. "Middle East Mosaic." *Palestine and the Middle East* 19, 9-10 (1947): 181-183.

Shragai, Nadav. "The Armenian Affair." *Kol Ha Ir* 10 December 1982 (in Hebrew), pp. 27-28.

Stendel, Ori. "The Arabs in Jerusalem." *Jerusalem.* Edited by J.M. Oesterreicher and A. Sinai. New York: John Day, 1974.

Stephan, S.H. "Three Firmans Granted to the Armenian Catholic Community, Jerusalem." *The Journal of the Palestine Oriental Society* 13 (1933): 1-9.

Stern, Gabriel. "Chronicles of the Armenian Orthodox Patriarchate of Jerusalem." *Christian News From Israel* 21, 3 (1970): 6-8.

_____. "His Beatitude Elisha II: Armenian Patriarchate and Poet." *Christian News From Israel* 21, 4 (1971): 40-42.

Stern, S.M. "The Constitution of the Islamic City." *The Islamic City: A Colloquium.* Edited by A.H. Hourani and S.M. Stern. Oxford: Bruno Casirer, 1970.

Stock, Brian, "Science, Technology, and Economic Progress in the Early Middle Ages." *Science in the Middle Ages.* Edited by David C. Lindberg. Chicago: University of Chicago Press, 1978.

Stone, Michael E. "The Manuscript Library of the Armenian Patriarchate in Jerusalem." *Israel Exploration Journal* 19 (1969) 20-43.

Talbot, Charles H. "Medicine." *Science in the Middle Ages.* Edited by David C. Lindberg. Chicago: University of Chicago Press, 1978.

"The Tragic Armenians." *The Jerusalem Post.* 18 March 1977.

Toennis, Ferdinand. "Gemeinschaft and Gesellschaft." *The Sociology of Community.* Edited by Colin Bell and Howard Newby. London: Cass, 1974.

Tsimhoni, Daphna. "The Christian Communities in Jerusalem and the West Bank, 1948-1967." *Middle East Review* 9 (Fall 1976): 41-46.

Verdonk, A.L.T. "Réorientation ou Désintegration? Une Enquête Sociologique sur une Congrégation Religieuse Masculine aux Pays Bas." *Social Compass* 18, 1 (1971): 123-141.

Wachtel, A. "The Church of the Nazarene in Israel." *Christian News From Israel* 11, 4 (1960): 23.

Wardi C. "The Latin Patriarchate of Jerusalem." *Journal of the Middle East Society* 11, 3-4 (1947): 5-12.

Zinger, Zvi, "Intrigues in the Shadow of the Cross." *Yedioth Ahronoth, Shiv'a Yamim* 24 December 1982 (in Hebrew), pp 12-13, 62.

Index

Designer: UC Press Staff
Compositor: Etc. Graphics
Printer: Thomson-Shore
Binder: John H. Dekker & Sons
Text: Andover Medium
Display: Andover